The Cult of the Ego

Eugene Goodheart

The Cult of the Ego

The Self in Modern Literature

The University of Chicago Press

Chicago & London

International Standard Book Number: 0-226-30286-5
Library of Congress Catalog Card Number: 68-9847

The University of Chicago Press, *Chicago 60637*
The University of Chicago Press, Ltd., *London*

To my son Eric

Acknowledgments

Chapter 2, "The Aesthetic Morality of Stendhal," first appeared in a different version in *Symposium*, Summer, 1966 as "Energy and Style in the Charterhouse of Parma." Chapter 7, "Lawrence and Christ," is a somewhat altered version of an essay that appeared under the same title in *Partisan Review*, Winter, 1964. Passages from the Introduction appeared in an essay, "The New Apocalypse," first in the Centennial Issue of *The Nation* and subsequently in *The State of the Nation*, edited by David Boroff, published by Prentice-Hall in 1966. The translations of Baudelaire's poems are taken from Angel Flores' *Anthology of French Poetry from Nerval to Valéry*, published by Doubleday.

Prefatory Note

The essays that follow the Introduction are in roughly chronological order. However, since I have no obligation to strict historical order, I have made an exception in chapters 2 and 3. Stendhal follows immediately upon Rousseau and immediately precedes Goethe, who antedates him, because I wanted Rousseau and Stendhal together for purposes of comparison and contrast.

The bibliography at the end is necessarily limited to books quoted. It would be impossible in so extensive a study to make a list of all debts incurred. With few exceptions, all references are to English texts. I have translated passages from certain French books unavailable in English translation.

The title is a translation of *"le culte du moi,"* a phrase of Maurice Barrès, which characterizes an important aspect of his work. Barrès has affinities with the writers I discuss, but I have not felt restricted by his use of the phrase. I have understood "the cult of the ego" in my own way.

For Goethe's *Die Leiden des jungen Werthers*, discussed in chapter 3, I have used the shortened English title, *The Sorrows of Werther*.

It is difficult to recollect all the help one gets from friends and colleagues in preparing such a book. Certain obligations, however, stand out. I am especially grateful to Baruch Hochman, B. L. Reid, and Paul Zweig for constructively critical readings of the manuscript. I have also benefited from the suggestions of Jacques Barzun, Saul Bellow, Michael Hamburger, Alvin C. Kibel, and Richard Stern.

The financial assistance generously provided by a fellowship from the American Council of Learned Societies and by a Willett Faculty Scholarship from the University of Chicago gave me the time to pursue my work and an opportunity to sit in the libraries of Paris and London. I also want to thank the Faculty Grants Committee of Mount Holyoke College for funds to cover typing and related expenses.

And finally to my wife, Patricia Somer Goodheart, an acknowledgment deeper than gratitude for all and sundry.

Contents

I have watched the soul, Ferdinand, give way bit by bit,
lose its balance and dissolve in the vast welter of apocalyptic
ambitions. It began in 1900. That's the date! From that
time onwards the world in general and psychiatry in
particular frantically raced to see who could be perverse,
salacious, original; more disgusting, more creative, as they
say, than his little next-door neighbor. A first-class
scramble. Each strove to see who could immolate himself
the soonest to the monster of no heart and no restraint.
. . . The monster will scrunch us all, Ferdinand, that's how
it is, and rightly so. . . . What is this monster? A great brute
tumbling along wherever it listeth. Its wars and its
droolings flood in towards us already from all sides. We
shall be swept away on this tide—yes swept away. The
conscious mind was a bore, apparently. . . . We shan't be
bored any longer! We've begun to give Sodom a chance
and from that moment on we've started having
"impressions" and "intuition."

Louis Ferdinand Celine, Journey to the End of Night

Introduction

The Contemporary Situation

Samuel Beckett's Mulloy listens, "and the voice is of a world endlessly collapsing."[1] It is the voice of modern literature. Beckett takes us into the vertiginous heart of the wasteland. His heroes (Malone, for instance) seek "the rapture of vertigo, the letting go, the fall, the gulf, the relapse to darkness, to nothingness."[2] The source of the apocalyptic vision in Beckett is the peculiar nature of the self, the *I* which is "streaming and emptying away as through a sluice."[3] Malone at one point speaks of "a blind and tired hand delving feebly in my particles and letting them trickle between its fingers."[4] This hand ransacks and ravages Malone out of the sheer frustration of not being able to "scatter" him with one sweep. The tired hand will ultimately kill Malone, but not immediately, as it would like: meanwhile, Malone's life is the suffering that comes from the stirring, waking, fondling, clutching, ransacking, and ravaging of the hand—the hand, we may imagine, of Beckett's God.

Beckett's apocalypse does not have the catastrophic violence of the traditional apocalypse. The violence and suffering in Beckett's world are continuous and monotonous—without change, like the endless monologuizing of the novels themselves. Even death, which all the Beckett characters await, holds no special terror: "And there is nothing for it but to wait for the end, nothing but for the end to come, and at the end all will be the same, at the end at last perhaps all the same as before."⁵ Indeed, the difference between life and death in the Beckett world is sustained by nothing more than "a meaningless voice [which] just barely prevents you from being nothing and nowhere, just enough to keep alight this little yellow flame feebly darting from side to side."⁶ Every attempt of a Beckett character to conceive of a mode of existence alternative to the life-in-death in which he lives is baffled. Mulloy confesses that "death is a condition I have never been able to conceive to my satisfaction and which therefore cannot go down in the ledger of weal and woe."⁷ The confusion between life and death in the Beckett character is a symptom of his general disintegrated condition. Without past or future, he experiences every moment as an impossible effort to go on. "If I could learn something by heart, I'd be saved."⁸ But he cannot. So he is compelled to say "the same thing, and each time it's an effort, the seconds must be all alike and each one is infernal." The hell of a Beckett character is the unrelenting repetition of the same moment, with only the most occasional variations in suffering to raise delusive hopes. The pointless repetitions are brilliantly and comically expressed in the body of the Beckett character, which is a sort of broken-down Cartesian machine.⁹ Both body and mind have gone mechanically awry, have lost the control and perfect functioning that one expects of the machine.

The despair of the Beckett character is *almost* complete. The paralysis and futility have so thoroughly penetrated flesh and spirit that the Beckett character is in danger of losing his power to dream of a different world. But he has not quite lost the power. Though Godot never comes, he is awaited. The conclusion of *The Unnameable* (the last novel of the trilogy) suggests the ambiguity: "I can't go on, I'll go on."¹⁰ "Go on" is too strong: the Beckett character survives—barely.

Beckett's heroes are confessors in the line of Jean-Jacques Rousseau. Unlike Jean-Jacques, they have lost faith in the integrity and authority of their being, but they retain the absolute devotion to self of the modern confessor. There is no alternative to the exhaustion of the Beckett hero. Indeed, the exhausted ego constitutes the entire landscape of the novel. Beckett represents in a "classic" way a tendency in modern literature to refuse the resistances of which literature has traditionally availed itself to combat disintegration and despair.

Goethe once remarked that "every emancipation of the spirit is pernicious unless there is a corresponding growth in control."[11] This remark encapsulates an aspect of the cultural history of the past two hundred years. Rousseau, Byron, Goethe's own heroes (Werther and Faust) immediately evoke this emancipation with all its promise and danger. The poems of Whitman and Rilke, the work of Lawrence are all an effort to extend the boundaries of the self by going beyond the area of safety in order to create the adventure of the "spirit" which even risks the destruction of the self. Lawrence gives us a superb image of this adventure:

I wish we were all like kindled bonfires on the edge of space, marking out the advance-posts. What is the aim of self-preservation, but to carry us right to the firing line; there what *is* is in contact with what is not. If many lives be lost by the way, it cannot be helped, nor if much suffering be entailed. I do not go out to war in the intention of avoiding all danger or discomfort: I go to fight for myself. Every step I move forward into being brings a newer, juster, proportion into the world, gives me less need of storehouse and barn, allows me to leave all and take what I want by the way, sure it will always be there; allows me in the end to fly the flag of myself, at the extreme tip of life.[12]

But Lawrence knew the value of resistance (the preserving element) in life. At the same time that the heroes of this emancipation advance the claims of the self, they seek the controls that will secure these claims. Their efforts (heroic as they are) have ambiguous results.

Jean-Jacques' antinomian belief in the privileged status of his character (he alone of all mortals is innocent) did not prevent him from being the most guilt-ridden of men. His "sins" were sanctioned by his innocence. Stendhal's heroes, for all their energy and art (they are artists in life), are perpetually at the mercy of the instability and discontinuity of their energy. Nietzsche, devoted to the monumental task of possessing himself, becomes the victim of an irrepressibly explosive imagination of human energy. Lawrence, at once a moralist and a visionary artist, confuses the visionary and the ethical in order to achieve a specious integrity. And Dostoevsky shows again and again the slavery into which his "emancipated" heroes are led through their immoralist presumptions.

The seeds of the modern situation are already in the failures of the heroes of the cult of the ego. But the heroism of the earlier writers was precisely in their effort of resistance: moral, religious, aesthetic. With a large portion of contemporary literature, it is as though there were no leftover energy for resistance. The imagination is totally committed to the experience of disintegration: it is in conspiracy with the destructive tendency of modern life and "teaches" us to accept it with an almost perverse pleasure. The sheer impossibility of exercising our wills (in the old-fashioned way) means that there is no alternative to resignation, and resignation for the imagination is ultimately a form of collaboration.

Thus contemporary "romantics," exalting spontaneity and narcotically induced states of ecstasy, are possessed of a superstitious belief that at the bottom of the abyss a miracle awaits them, a miracle that will transform them, make them whole and powerful. The only "moral" capacity that the new romantics seem to demand is the courage to take the plunge. The miracle may be no more than an instant of "mystical" lucidity: for this they will pay the full price of disease and self-destruction. And the moment of truth belongs to a hidden self remote from the normal workaday self of which one's character is made. Behind this "romantic" attitude is the cult of the artist. *Faute de mieux,* the artist is the bearer of the spiritual life, and the sometimes disorderly *appearance* of his personal life conceals the workings of inspiration. The cult of the artist rests on a false identification between the artistic personality and aesthetic values, and on the democratic faith that everyone is creative. The contemporary situation is also characterized by a confusion of roles between the immoralist who ventures beyond the moral boundaries of the community and the preacher of morality. It was Nietzsche who cautioned against the confusion:

He, however, who would dissect must kill, but only in order that we may know more, judge better, live better, not in order that all the world may dissect. Unfortunately men still think that every moralist in his action must be a pattern for others to imitate.[13]

Norman Mailer *affirms* "the subterranean river of untapped, ferocious, lonely, romantic desires, that concentration of ecstasy and violence which is the dream-life of the nation,"[14] as if this dream-life somehow yielded a morality.* And Jean Genet, taking an aesthetic delight in the energies of perversity, devotes his imagination to the celebration of the new trinity of treason, theft, and homosexuality. Genet is like a Dostoevsky character who has pre-empted the moral authority of the novelist. Immoralism, of course, is not new to literature or life, though the literature of extreme experience seems often innocent of its tradition—perhaps unavoidably so since it depends upon a sense of its own novelty and freshness and a knowledge of that tradition might inhibit its impulse. It is true, however, that contemporary immoralist literature has explored homosexuality and drug addiction in

---

* A recent reviewer of Mailer compares Mailer's preoccupation with the underground river to Conrad's vision of "the horror." But it is the difference between Mailer and Conrad (one of many instances) that defines the contemporary situation—I am tempted to say the corruption of the contemporary situation. (See John William Corrington, review of *An American Dream* in *Chicago Review* 18, no. 1 [1965]: 58–66.)

unsurpassed detail. Moreover, contemporary immoralism is distinguished by its ideological attempt to present its values as normative. Thus Genet, and others, have tried to convert homosexuality from a clinical fact into heroism or saintliness. From the point of view of contemporary immoralism, all forms of opposition are philistine, or, in the American idiom, "square." But this treatment of the opposition is itself a kind of philistinism, for it blurs the issues and blunts discriminations.

Jaspers speaks of both Nietzsche and Kierkegaard as "representative destinies," by which he means that in venturing out into unknown seas they risked "shipwreck," and that we can mark the course of our lives by the disaster they suffered.[15] The remark is valuable, if we discount the possible suggestion that their work is cautionary in the traditional moral sense. Nietzsche's refusal to confound dissection with moral preachment marks him off from democratic nihilism. The temptation of democratic nihilism can be explained partly by the feeling that if the morals dissected are inadequate, even poisonous, to human life, then the ultimate purpose of such dissection must be to discover a new morality for everyone. But the fact that the inherited forms of reason and morality are contaminated by the sickness of the present human condition does not justify a plunge into moral and intellectual chaos. Such a remedy, from Nietzsche's point of view, would be worse than the disease. Norman O. Brown would seem to share this view when he speaks of the need to *reconstruct* the Dionysian ego, but he does not adequately distinguish between nihilistic self-abandon and the new constructive work of Dionysian energy.[16]

One may sympathize with the dream of a new powerful self resurrected from the chaos and disorder of our present lives. But the problem remains how to bridge the gap between our disordered bodies and the resurrected one. Narcotics, liquor, psychopathology, criminal self-abandonment, perversion, for all their advantages of intensity, are culs-de-sac. To say, as Mailer has said in the notorious essay "The White Negro," that the psychopath "may be indeed the perverted or dangerous frontrunner of a new kind of personality" [17] is to beg the question. To pass beyond the psychopath one must make a detour: to pass through the psychopathic condition is to come smack against a wall. Perversion, as Freud and Dostoevsky before him taught, is slavery, not freedom. To be driven by a murderous impulse or by the compulsion to be beaten may produce an ecstasy of pain and pleasure, but it is not to be confused with the repossession of one's body that one would expect in the resurrection. The paradox of the perverse rebel is that he is the most complete victim of the order against which he is revolting, that his revolt is itself a mark of his enslavement, and that, even knowing this, he has no choice but to continue to revolt. The belief that something new will spontaneously emerge is the other side of the nihilistic belief that the will is futile—that we are at the mercy of chaotic forces we can neither understand nor master.

Futile too is the impulse to moralize about this situation. There are good historical reasons for the nihilism: the atomic bomb, the incredible devastations of contemporary wars and concentration camps. Recent German literature, in particular, has taught us that the natural impulse toward immediate indignation or protest necessarily yields to a kind of resignation in the feeling that the enormities of contemporary life are not subject to the human will—that they are too deep in human character to be exorcised by conventional moral responses. As Oskar of Günter Grass's *Tin Drum* says: "You can't lock up disaster in a cellar. It drains into the sewer pipes, spreads to the gas pipes and gets into every household with the gas. And no one who sets his soup kettle on the bluish flames suspects that disaster is bringing his supper to a boil." [18]

The enormities of our present situation have conspired with the modern idea (which is based on the principle of the continuous superannuation of everything) in creating an atmosphere in which the effort of resistance seems impossible.

The forces of contemporary life are too powerful and too complex to be mastered by the human will, and the extraordinary changefulness of our life makes it impossible for us to hold onto anything. When in "Signs of the Times" (1829) Carlyle lamented the new mechanical age, he spoke with the traditional confidence that underneath the historical change there existed undisturbed realities which it was his prophetic duty to bring forth to contemporary consciousness. The very definition of the *modern* is the metaphysical character of changefulness.

This is the apology and to an extent the reality of contemporary nihilism. In studying the efforts of some of the greatest writers of the past to control the "emancipation" of the spirit during the past two hundred years, we might find some illumination of the contemporary situation (which a contemporary perspective fails to provide) and arrive at an estimate of the resources of resistance in modern literature.

I

The Antinomianism of
Jean-Jacques Rousseau

"I am not made like any of those I have seen."[1] With that announcement in *The Confessions,* Jean-Jacques Rousseau presents his reader with a strange new hero. The conviction of his uniqueness distinguishes him at once from Augustine, who would have condemned Rousseau for the sin of pride. The events of his life, the feelings and thoughts that Rousseau records in such copious detail are the consequences of a proudly extravagant sensibility and a perverse temperament. Nor is Rousseau like that other great confessor, Montaigne, crotchety and idiosyncratic on occasion, but confident of his normal human qualities. "The vagabondage and egoism," one critic has remarked of Montaigne, "are more or less superficial. What we find under the surface is a fairly firm conviction, based on the Greek, and especially the Latin, classics, as to what the true man should be."[2] Rousseau is perversely, one might say pathologically, unique. And he cherishes his uniqueness with the pride of the immoralist.

9

"If I am not better, at least I am different."[3] Even when he condemns vicious actions, the pride of the immoralist asserts itself in the fantastically indulgent descriptions of everything. The pleasure of recollection is so great for Rousseau that whatever moral impulse is contained in the work gives way to a kind of shamelessness. "I will let you off with five [anecdotes]," he remarks to the reader, "but I wish to tell you one, only one, provided that you will permit me to tell it in as much detail as possible, in order to prolong my enjoyment."[4] The anecdotes are about a happy time in his life, but the statement could as well apply to his sufferings and humiliations. Rousseau's confessional impulse seems to take as much delight in revealing the masochistic pleasures, for example, that he experienced as a child at the punishing hands of Mlle Lambercier as it does in evoking the joys of solitary walks in the country.

Rousseau's overriding passion is a need to dramatize himself, to show himself as *other*—and this passion cannot be reduced to moral or exemplary terms. *The Confessions* belongs to a side of Rousseau that made him uneasy when he thought of the role he had created for himself as citizen of Geneva, the champion of the Spartan virtues.

The line from Jean-Jacques is to Stendhal's heroes, Werther, the underground man, the immoralist of Nietzsche and Gide. What do these characters have in common? In the first place, none of them is virtuous, except perhaps in the Renaissance sense of *virtù*. They possess an energy, an impulsiveness for which we are hard put to find a name. Abbé Pirard's view of Julien Sorel (in *The Red and the Black*) is suggestive: "I see in you something that offends the common herd."[5] The energy may not be entirely free of scruples, but the scruples are obstacles to the energy, which thrives in an atmosphere free of the constraints of conventional society and morality. One hesitates to include Jean-Jacques in this discussion, for doesn't he give as the motive for *The Confessions* a desire to expiate his crimes: his accusation of a maid for a theft of a ribbon he himself com-

mitted, the abandonment of a friend in need, the surrender
of his children to a foundling hospital, and so on? The
confessions, it would seem, deliberately invite the judgment
that he had escaped when the acts were performed. But on
closer inspection the moral animus disappears, for Jean-
Jacques' guilt does not issue in remorse or contrition. The
guilt retains a residue of anxiety, but in the confessional act
it is strangely robbed of its moral quality and becomes
instead an energy, an expansiveness of the heart, a dramatic
occasion. The confession of the theft (which he had committed as a youth while in service to the Comtesse de
Vercellis) is a superb instance of this curious transformation
of guilt; after describing the incident in fulsome detail,
Rousseau, without precisely justifying himself, turns the
incident into a testimony to his uniqueness, a memorial to
Jean-Jacques.

I have behaved straightforwardly in the confession which I have
just made, and it will assuredly be found that I have not
attempted to palliate the blackness of my offence. But I should
not fulfill the object of this book, if I did not at the same time
set forth my inner feelings and hesitated to excuse myself
by what is strictly true. Wicked intent was never further
from me than at that cruel moment; and when I accused the
unhappy girl, it is singular, but it is true, that my friendship for
her was the cause of it. She was present to my thoughts;
I threw the blame on the first object which presented itself.
I accused her of having done what I meant to do, and having
given her the ribbon, because my intention was to give
it to her. When I afterwards saw her appear, my heart was
torn; but the presence of so many people was stronger than
repentance. I was not afraid of punishment, I was only afraid of
disgrace; and that I feared more than death, more than crime,
more than anything else in the world. I should have rejoiced
if the earth had suddenly opened, swallowed me up and
suffocated me; the unconquerable fear of shame overcame
everything, and alone made me imprudent. The greater my
crime, the more the dread of confessing it made me fearless.
I saw nothing but the horror of being recognized and

publicly declared, in my own presence, a thief, a liar and slanderer. Complete embarrassment deprived me of every other feeling . . . .[6]

This is hardly the language of contrition. All that Rousseau can muster at the end of this passage is a statement about "the unhappiness that has overwhelmed the last years of [his] life."[7] In that fact, Rousseau rests content that "poor Marion finds so many avengers in this world, that, however great my offence against her may have been, I have little fear of dying without absolution." The episode was to plague Rousseau all his life. We can guess this from the vividness with which he recalls it more than thirty years later. He is reliving it with all its shame. But the language of the recollection indicates a desire to displace the significance of the episode from his guilt to his suffering. Poor Marion's sufferings (she had been immediately discharged from service) had been more importantly the occasion for Rousseau's sufferings, which he would like his reader (and himself) to believe sufficient to absolve him of responsibility.

The confession itself, then, is no longer an occasion for genuine contrition and expiation. The act of confession tends to bestow forgiveness. Thus, in defense of his behavior in surrendering his children to a foundling hospital, Rousseau says: "My remorse at length became so keen, that it almost extorted from me a public confession of my error at the beginning of *Emile*; the allusion itself is so obvious in a certain passage, that it is surprising to me how anyone, after having read it, can have the courage to reproach me."[8] *

---

* "A father has done but a third of his task when he begets children and provides a living for them. He owes men to humanity, citizens to the state. A man who can pay this threefold debt and neglects to do so is guilty, more guilty, perhaps, if he pays it in part than when he neglects it entirely. He has no right to be a father if he cannot fulfill a father's duties. Poverty, pressure of business, mistaken social pressures, none of these can excuse a man from his duty, which is to support and educate his own children. If a man of any natural feeling neglects these sacred duties he will repent it with bitter tears and will never be comforted." (*Emile*, p. 17.)

He has suffered and admitted the act. But nowhere does he suggest the moral urgency to compensate by some action for the things he had done. It is of course true that the time for compensation had passed. But I am characterizing a mentality which immediately transforms the whole question of moral responsibility to one of personal suffering. Rousseau would have been incapable of admitting, though he was capable of feeling, that the failure to compensate for a crime or sin necessarily leaves its traces on the offending soul.

Rousseau's shame is very intense, but the confessions (and herein lies their originality) are not so much expressions of, as sharp reactions against, his guilt. He has felt the guilt all along and does not need the confessional atmosphere to bring it to consciousness. Rousseau is the first of those modern writers who expose their most intimate lives out of a compulsiveness that Rousseau called his "disposition [which] renders it impossible for me to conceal any of my thoughts or feelings." [9] Jean Guehenno, in his biography, mistakes the implication and truth of this statement when he speaks of Rousseau's capacity for "discretion and secrecy" as proof that Jean-Jacques was quite mistaken about himself.[10] The impassioned eloquence with which Rousseau speaks in *The Confessions* is not necessarily a guarantee of the authenticity of his statements or of his essential goodness, but it is unmistakably an expression of his compulsive need to rid himself of self-wounding feelings that might poison him if he were silent. In both *The Confessions* and *Rousseau: Juge de Jean-Jacques* he speaks of his tendency to remember only pleasurable moments in the past. The fact is that he remembers painful moments and remembers them with remarkable intensity. The apologetic writings, after all, are in part a cataloguing of the sufferings which the world has caused him throughout his life. The confession has a paradoxical effect: it recalls the past, which it tries (often unsuccessfully) to purge or liquidate through the act of expression.

If we detect the absence of genuine remorse, we cannot simply charge Jean-Jacques with sophistic self-justification.

Rousseau's "method" is too transparent, too revealing for a Jesuitical purpose. In confessing all, he has taken risks that no amount of disingenuousness (conscious or unconscious) can mitigate. What disturbs is not the disingenuousness, but the self-fascination which dissolves the moral question in the psychological analysis. "The important thing is what I felt, not what I did," Rousseau seems to tell us; he attempts to gain our sympathy by distracting our attention from his actions to his sentiments and motives. For all of Rousseau's apparent and real candor, the confessions are motivated by a desire to sustain his self-esteem at all costs. There is more than a hint of this trait in his failure to do the decent thing by Marion: "I was only afraid of disgrace; and that I feared more than death, more than crime, more than anything else in the world. . . . the unconquerable fear of shame overcame everything."

Self-esteem is, of course, a complicated idea. Rousseau himself regarded self-esteem as a "natural" feeling, which is ultimately the basis of a moral community. But he also knew that he had to distinguish it from a vice, which it closely resembled. Rousseau had developed this distinction in philosophical terms in *A Discourse on the Origin of Inequality* (1755). (He is never simply a "psychological case": he always raises his torment to the dignity of a philosophical idea.) The virtue is *amour de soi,* which translates roughly as self-respect or pride, and the vice is *amour propre,* to which egoism or vanity is probably the closest equivalent.

Egoism must not be confused with self-respect: for they both differ in themselves and in their effects. Self-respect is a natural feeling which leads every animal to look to its own preservation, and which, guided in man by reason and modified by compassion, creates humanity and virtue. Egoism is a purely relative and factitious feeling, which arises in the state of society, leads each individual to make more of himself than of any other, causes all the mutual damage men inflict on one another, and is the real source of the sense of honour.[11]

Rousseau pursues this distinction in the Dialogues,

Rousseau: Juge de Jean-Jacques. The causes of egoism are social obstacles to the simple enjoyment of self-respect.

> The primitive passions all tend directly toward our happiness, and bring before us only the objects related to that end; since they are rooted only in self-love, they are all essentially tender and loving: but when they are deflected from their goal by obstacles, they become more preoccupied by the obstacle they must overcome, than by the object they seek to attain. At this point their nature changes, they become irritable and hateful; that is how self-love which is a good and absolute emotion, becomes vanity; that is to say, a relative emotion which leads one to comparisons, requires preferences, whose enjoyment is purely negative, no longer seeking satisfaction for our own good, but rather in the harm of others.[12]

The obstacles in his own life (real and imaginary) made it impossible for Rousseau to rid himself of the self-righteous and egoistic tone. He did, despite himself and unwittingly, "make more of himself than of any other."

Jean-Jacques is caught in a conflict between his wish to speak the truth and his desire to satisfy his pride. The two desires are not necessarily opposed to each other, since it is an essential part of Rousseau's program to justify his singularity, to convince the reader of its significance and therefore of its worthiness of an audience. Rousseau must establish at once the truth and value of his singularity. But he is deluded about himself: he insists forever on his innocence and sincerity because he cannot endure admitting the duplicities to which he has been compelled by character and circumstance. So he transforms the truth to serve his self-esteem. Rousseau's love affair with Sophie d'Houdetot (the model for Julie of *La Nouvelle Héloïse*) reveals, perhaps more than any other episode in his life, what a devious thing his heart was. It is the story of "alienation of affections" under the guise of platonic love. While Saint Lambert, Mme d'Houdetot's lover and Jean-Jacques' friend, was away, Rousseau read passages from *La Nouvelle Héloïse* (which he was then writing) aloud to her. As Guehenno remarks: "Saint Preux [the hero of the novel] said for him what he himself had not yet the courage to say."[13] Sophie found it difficult to resist Rousseau's eloquence and fell in love. Whether Jean-Jacques slept with her is beside the point. He had compromised her and betrayed a friend while protesting solipsistically and irrelevantly the purity of his feeling for her. It is the kind of episode that occurred daily in the aristocratic life of France in the eighteenth century. But the episode is particularly damaging to Rousseau, because such equivocal behavior was anathema to the honesty and forthrightness that he cherished.

And yet the eloquence with which Rousseau defends himself on almost every occasion of wrongdoing springs from genuine conviction, however deluded. The basis of the conviction is *amour de soi*—in the sense of self-preservation. Beleaguered by enemies and by guilty memories, Rousseau creates the impression that the confessions are acts of self-preservation. He feels himself to be *in extremis,* for the man with the highest conception of himself who feels his self-respect menaced at its very foundations is like a man threatened by physical destruction.

II

"That I was a great transcendent sinner I confess. But still I had hopes of forgiveness, because I never sinned from principle, but accident."[14] This is not Jean-Jacques speaking, but the antinomian "hero" of James Hogg's curious and fascinating *Confessions of a Justified Sinner*, originally published in 1824, approximately sixty years after the publication of Rousseau's apology. Hogg's hero has unwittingly summed up the moral burden of Jean-Jacques' apology.

Antinomianism has an ancient lineage. As old as Christianity, it can be traced to certain gnostic cults. It appears in Christianity at various times and in various forms as a heresy. Hogg's book re-creates a peculiarly Scottish atmosphere of the sixteenth and seventeenth centuries: Calvinist and fanatical. The antinomianism of the *Justified Sinner* can be understood as a perversion of Calvinist (and for that matter Lutheran) doctrine of the superiority of faith over good works. Both Calvin and Luther found man's spiritual connection with God in an invisible bond (the bond of conscience), not in the activities of the practical life. Calvin valued the practical life more than did Luther, but he placed a similar emphasis on the invisible connection, and he too understood the practical sphere as the uncertain arena for the religious drama. Good works were possible signs of grace, but not unmistakable confirmations. Both Luther and Calvin meant to dramatize the superior importance of the inward disposition of the soul to divine light, for the unbounded mercy of God is reflected in the unearned grace which the sinner might receive. Though they regarded good works as at best extrinsic marks of the graced condition of the soul, they did not intend to sanction laxity in the moral life. Antinomianism sanctions laxity. Hogg's hero, assured of his salvation, feels free to commit the most terrible crimes, as if the crimes themselves were expressions of divine authority.

In his description of gnosticism as a doctrine, the theologian Anders Nygren gives a lucid account of the antinomian rationale.

The tendency to asceticism . . . readily turns into its opposite, the tendency to *antinomianism*. If the divine Pneuma is our innermost being, our true self, then the main thing is to save this, whatever happens to our lower, inferior part, our outward man. It is of sole importance to free Pneuma from the chains of sense. But this is done less by ascesis than by Gnosis, not by a moral life, but by the rebirth which takes place in the Gnostic Mystery-cults. Hence arises great indifference to ethical life in general. A pure ethical life is for the lower, merely psychical man, who is preserved by ascesis and good works from total corruption, but it is not for the pneumatic

man, who is *by nature* above the risk of corruption and can
live in the world as he pleases. As things material are by nature
incapable of salvation, so pneumatic things by reason of
their nature simply *cannot* be overtaken by corruption—quite
independently of how the pneumatic man conducts his life.[15]

In this view, intention (an expression of pneuma) and deed
(a fact of the sensuous and corruptible world) are separated,
joined only by the power of a graced intention to transform a
deed (even a vicious one) to signify whatever it wishes.

Like many heresies, antinomianism has modern secularized
equivalents. Rousseau, for all the vagaries of his religious
"career," was bound by blood, as it were, to the Calvinist
church of Geneva. (Born a Genevan, he underwent a dubious
conversion to Catholicism—a conversion pleasing to his
petite maman, Mme de Warens—returned to the Church of
Geneva—again dubiously—and finally espoused the romantic
theism of the Savoyard Vicar—in *Emile.*) There is hardly
an attitude or feeling in Rousseau that is not tied in some
way to his Calvinism. His famous celebration of conscience
in the voice of the Savoyard Vicar is the acting out of his
Calvinist demon.

Conscience! Conscience! Divine instinct, immortal voice from
heaven; sure guide for a creature ignorant and finite
indeed, yet intelligent and free, infallible judge of good
and evil, making man like to God! In Thee consists the
excellence of man's nature and the morality of his actions;
apart from Thee, I find nothing to raise me above the beasts—
nothing but the sad privilege of wandering from one error to
another, by the help of an unbridled understanding and a
reason which knows no principle.[16]

And so paradoxically is that contrary laxity of soul that makes
for his antinomianism.

The ethical imperative is more essential to Rousseau's
thought than to his feeling, a sort of check to his self-
acknowledged moral indolence. Antinomianism can be
found in Rousseau's judgment of Mme de Warens:

All her faults were due to her errors, none to her passions. She was well born, her heart was pure, she loved propriety; her inclinations were upright and virtuous, her taste was refined . . . instead of listening to her heart, which always guided her aright, she listened to her reason, which guided her wrongly . . . but, unfortunately, she rather prided herself on her philosophy, and the morals which she drew from it corrupted those which her heart dictated.[17]

In his self-judgments, Rousseau repeatedly distinguishes his "pneumatic" sanctity: "After the most ardent and most sincere researches that perhaps had ever been made by any mortal, I decided for the rest of my life on the feeling which it was necessary for me to have; and if I may have been deceived in my results, I am sure at least that my mistake cannot be imputed to me as a crime."[18] More striking is his refusal to consider the *effect* of an action in moral terms: "To judge of the speeches of men by the effects they produce is often to appreciate them wrongly. Apart from the fact that these effects are not always felt and easy to understand, they vary as infinitely as the circumstances in which the discourses are held; but it is solely the intention of him who holds them that gives them value and determines their degree of malice or good will."[19] And again in the Dialogues: "My conscience tells me that no crime has ever come near my heart."[20]

Rousseau's defense of his own conduct is precisely his justification of Mme de Warens': if his conduct is reprehensible, it is not because of an evil intention, but because of an incapacity to determine his behavior by reason or duty.[21] This is what Rousseau learns in his curious imaginary meeting with Jean-Jacques in the Dialogues. Earlier in the Dialogues, Rousseau had insisted against the scepticism of Jean-Jacques' accuser that Jean-Jacques "resembles no other man I know: he requires a separate analysis, one made for him alone,"[22] an analysis that would transform reprehensible actions into inconsequential expressions of the essential goodness of Jean-Jacques.

The subject of the analysis, which follows closely, is Jean-

Jacques' solitary condition—or rather the morality of that condition. Haunting the analysis is Diderot's famous remark (directed at Rousseau) that solitude is a condition that only the wicked seek. Rousseau argues the contrary: that solitude is the correlative of the premoral state, in which the sentiments of *amour de soi* and natural compassion are at play. Jean-Jacques fled Paris because he wanted to protect himself from the predatoriness of Parisian society and because his natural impulse for friendship and companionship was continually and painfully baffled by others. The moral danger of solitude (of which Rousseau himself is aware) is the vacuum it creates for the impulses of his heart and the consequent bizarre aspect that it puts on his conduct. However bizarre that conduct may seem, it can nevertheless not be construed (in Rousseau's view) as immoral or vicious:

> Therefore our man will not be virtuous, because he will not have to be, and for the same reason he will be neither vicious nor wicked. For indolence and laziness, which in society are such great vices, no longer are so for anyone who has been able to give up its advantages in order to avoid its obligations. The wicked man is wicked only because of the need he has for others; some are not favorable enough to him, others block his way, and he can neither use them nor push them aside at will. The solitary man needs only the bare minimum, which he prefers to obtain by working in his retreat, than by intriguing in society, which would be an even harder labor for him.[23]

In a society which does not concern itself with the moral development of its citizens, which indeed even encourages their vices, there is no alternative to solitude for the man of integrity—to a life in which the individual, uncorrupted by social influences, obeys the sentiments of his heart.

Jean-Jacques' solitude, Rousseau is at pains to make clear, is the result neither of egoism nor of malice: it is the result of his baffled social impulse. The source of that impulse is compassion or pity, the *natural* sentiment, in Rousseau's view, on which society is based. By compassion Rousseau does not mean Christian charity; he means rather a sentiment complementary to and expressive of *amour de soi.* Rousseauian compassion moderates but does not cancel the love of self, and it serves the self as well as the species by diminishing human destructiveness.

It is then certain that compassion is a natural feeling, which by moderating the violence of love or self in each individual, contributes to the preservation of the whole species. It is this compassion that hurries us without reflection to the relief of those who are in distress: it is this which in a state of nature supplies the place of laws, morals and virtues, with the advantage that none are tempted to disobey its gentle voice: it is this which will always prevent a sturdy savage from robbing a weak child or a feeble old man of the sustenance they may have with pain and difficulty acquired, if he sees a possibility of providing for himself by other means: it is this which instead of inculcating the sublime maxim of rational justice, *Do unto others as you would have them do unto you,* inspires all men with that other maxim of natural goodness, much less perfect indeed, but perhaps more useful: *Do good to yourself with as little evil as possible to others.*[24]

But this philosophical formulation of compassion does not fully convey the role it plays in Jean-Jacques' drama. As an element in the character of Jean-Jacques, it is inextricably bound up with his egoism.* The egoism is of such a nature that it requires an audience which can sympathetically vibrate to it. It is driven by an imperialistic desire to extend its circumference and include within its orbit as much of the outside world as it can contain. For Jean-Jacques, compassion, pity, intimacy provide an atmosphere in which the ego can expand, display itself, and delight in itself. In his last work, *Reveries of a Solitary Walker,* Rousseau reproaches himself for the exhibitionism of *The Confessions* (its betrayal of a need for an audience), and he tries to prove his contention that, unlike Montaigne, he writes the book only for himself.[25]

---

* Neither *amour de soi* nor *amour propre* will do here.

But the strain of the attempt gives Rousseau away. The *Reveries* constantly lapses into the apologetic mode of *The Confessions,* and the capacity of the reveries to stimulate memories of a golden time and purge pain is limited by Rousseau's consuming need for approval. Montaigne's manner, by contrast, is aloof and self-possessed, for he needs his audience less than does Rousseau. Rousseau requires the solitude which will make it possible for him to cultivate his self-esteem in imagination without censure by public opinion. He speaks in *The Confessions* of "doing his utmost to root out of his heart everything, which from fear of censure might turn me aside from that which was good and reasonable in itself." [26] But shortly afterward, in a somewhat rueful tone, he speaks of a letter he wrote in his own defense which he regarded as unique, which "for some reason or other, has made less stir than my other writings." [27] Rousseau needs an audience for his solitude, an audience that will sympathize and not judge, that will confirm his value and never doubt it. For Jean-Jacques, compassion is the self-enhancing tie between himself and the world. It has none of the humility or asceticism of Christian sentiment; it has the emotional atmosphere of an uninhibited self-regard.

Rousseau's feeling that he writes only for himself (in the *Reveries*) is his illusion of privacy. He needs the belief that what he is doing is without reference to an audience and hence without the accompanying impulse to justify himself. And yet the public confession of feeling is always modified by an anticipation of the response of the audience. The translation of feeling into language, the heightened character of language, that is, its eloquence, suggests that the romantic cult of sincerity (the writer speaking to himself) is a kind of myth that sustains the writer in his work without really explaining what he is doing.

The irony of Rousseau's performance is that his confessions expose him to punishment as often as they win him admirers. The unveiling of the self is based on the presumption that he is unmasking the god in himself, for which he can expect only love and admiration. But as Dostoevsky has so impressively shown, a man may unveil the self because the horror in his soul needs to be judged. Rousseau's "mania of drawing people's attention to himself" (D'Alembert's phrase)[28] proceeds consciously from a conviction of his value, though one suspects from his talent for making enemies that Jean-Jacques unconsciously sought the punishment against which he complained.*

This curious ambiguity is very strong in antinomian psychology. Hogg shows how the conviction of grace in the "justified sinner" is born of an acute sentiment of original sin, the legacy of Calvinism. So strong is the sentiment that the antinomian must utterly expel the conviction of guilt or sin in order to "justify" himself—or better, to *save* himself. Despite the protestations of innocence by the antinomian (and Jean-Jacques), the sentiment of sin and the provocations of punishment remain very strong, which helps explain Rousseau's chronic habit of provoking his enemies.

The motive for *The Confessions* is neither expiation nor self-justification in a conventional sense—not expiation because, as we have seen, the moral urgency, the recoil from deed and self are missing, and not self-justification because

---

* As Jean Starobinski has shown in a persuasive essay on Rousseau*
(*L'Oêil Vivant*, pp. 93–190), Rousseau's conviction of his
innocence and his paranoid projection of evil onto his environment
reflects an unconscious sentiment of sin, the "birthright" of
every Genevan, which Rousseau tried vainly to escape. Rousseau's
Calvinist heritage as a Genevan was reinforced by the particular
events of his life: the death of his mother, for which his birth
was responsible; his father's ostracism from Geneva; his orphaned
and abandoned state. Starobinski shows that the conviction of
innocence is strangely mixed with episodes in which Rousseau
seems to dramatize a general unspecified feeling of culpability, as if
he were deliberately inviting punishment. There is, for instance,
the flagrant episode of self-exposure. More subtle and
complicated is Rousseau's timid entrance into the chamber
of Mme Basile in order to gaze on her without being perceived—
only to find himself standing before a mirror accessible to
Mme Basile's view. (See *L'Oêil Vivant*, pp. 109–112.)

the admissions are too damaging in one sense and the casuistic impulse to reconcile an action to an accepted standard of behavior is absent. The motive—if one may call it that—is more subversive and more insidious, for it is nothing less than an attempt to revolutionize our standard or mode of judgment. Rousseau wants to be judged by a standard derived from those very feelings and motives responsible for actions that we—and even Rousseau—deplore. "I am now again coming to one of those confessions, in regard to which I feel sure beforehand that those readers will be incredulous, who are always determined to judge me by their own standard, although they have been compelled to see, throughout the whole course of my life, a thousand inner emotions which have not the least resemblance to their own."[29] He reminds us that he is unique, so that judgments of him in accordance with any commonly accepted ethical norm are impertinent. In fact, judgment itself becomes impossible, for judgment presupposes something with which the thing judged can be compared, and Rousseau is presenting us with something *incomparable*.

The incomparable quality is his innocence. Says Rousseau of Jean-Jacques (in the Dialogues): "He can regard his misfortunes with a dry eye, but he cries, contemplating his innocence and the rewards his heart should have received."[30] After lamenting (in the preface of the Dialogues) the absence of anyone capable of sympathizing with his situation (would there were another like himself in the world capable of such understanding and sympathy!), he presents his plight through the analogy of paradise and the fall. The men of Rousseau's world can as well understand Jean-Jacques as the creatures of the fallen world can understand the behavior of the children of paradise.

All the reader can do, then, is to place himself imaginatively within the consciousness of Jean-Jacques and respond to him with sympathy. There is an analogue for this kind of demand in romantic theory about literature. In Coleridge's words, the reader is to suspend his disbelief and enter sympathetically into the alien consciousness of the poet. Perhaps the analogue is clearest in the case of the novelist who creates for his "hero"—that is, the character in whom he has made a special investment—an aura which distinguishes him from other characters. The hero may have no other virtues but the glow of the novelist's attention and sympathy. Often the reader revolts against the novelist (against the arbitrariness of the aura), refusing him the assent he demands for his hero. The novelist, by dramatizing the singularity of the hero and by lavishing so much attention upon his feelings, ideas, and vibrations, has made for his hero the claim that earlier poets made for kings and princes. Oedipus, Hamlet, Lear: no one denies their right to be heard. They are the princes of the earth, who *command* our admiration and sympathy. But Jean-Jacques and the antiheroes of the novel belong to the anonymous and the invisible, and now they demand to be heard, to be known, to be loved, to be hated as if they too were the princes of the earth. In *The Confessions* Rousseau has supplied, so to speak, a sanction for the claims of every anonymous and unheroic life. That Jean-Jacques' career was heroic is incidental, for the aspect of his life that he dramatized and in which he gloried in *The Confessions* was not.

III

Behind Rousseau's claim for love, for happiness, for justice, are centuries of apocalyptic striving, heretical Christian movements whose ambition was the immediate realization of the millenial expectations of the meek, the poor, the disinherited. The paradisiacal theme in Rousseau's work is almost too obvious to require exposition. In the apologetic writings, it appears in early childhood memories, in his feeling of having been expelled from paradise, in the strenuous effort to regain (in solitude, *faute de mieux*) the happiness he thought he had enjoyed in the golden age of infancy; in the political and educational writings, it appears in the form of the state of nature, on a higher level the (ideal) social contract, a condition of happiness all men will enjoy. Rousseau exhibits the gnostic tendency to split the world between absolute good and absolute evil; just as the corruption of the material world, in the gnostic view, is something *external* to man, the corruption of society, according to Rousseau, is caused by something outside his nature, thereby absolving man of the radical culpability one finds in Christian doctrine. Rousseau, in secular and sophisticated terms, reawakens the apocalyptic yearnings that characterized certain heretical movements in the centuries of the Christian hegemony.

By connecting Rousseau with the chiliastic tradition, I do not intend the disparagement that seems to attend every discussion of chiliasm. (In *The Pursuit of Millenium*, Norman Cohn, for instance, repeatedly exposes the charlatanism, the ideological fakery of the medieval apocalyptists and sees the appetite for millenium as primitive, though understandable, desire for release from extreme misery.) Even if we are to grant the prevailing conservative view of the charlatanism and brutality of the medieval apocalyptic expectation, Rousseau's version of it discovers, so to speak, the valuable aspiration contained in the apocalyptic idea. Medieval chiliasm offends, on the ideological level, because it uses Christian mythology to mask its essential egoism and materialism. Rousseau and modern utopian thinkers disengage the dream from the mythological setting. Rousseau affirms his egoism—as does Nietzsche, who speaks of the ego as the *primum mobile*[31]—because it is for him the main repository of value, the "place" out of which and for which a new world will be created. (Christian myth and image may be part of the texture of modern utopian thought, but its use is symbolic, not literal.) At least two consequences issue from the secularization of apocalyptic striving: (1) chiliasm loses its heretical character; it need not define itself casuistically in relation to values opposed to it—that is, the values of a religion of altruism and self-abnegation—it makes value of its own true desires; (2) it no longer reflects the crude materialism that inevitably grows out of economic misery (a materialism which has its modern equivalent in crude versions of Marxism). The ego must refine and complicate its appetites as the price for its "emancipation." Not that the arbitrary and rapacious element in egoism can be wholly eliminated. But it is precisely the recognition of the ego as the ground of value which compels any *human* speculation to reconcile it to a conception of justice.

One of the major links between Rousseau's apologetic writings and his political writings is a passion for justice. In the apologetic writings we cannot escape the concern with motive: the passion for justice often becomes an expression of resentment, a solipsistic desire to adjust the world to Jean-Jacques' own imperious needs. The political writings are not free of the motives that complicate the confessional works. In a sense, they are the political expression of the themes of the apologetic writings.* But in the political and educational works, Rousseau's thought achieves a disinterestedness which compels us to view it in its own terms.

The political and educational writings represent Rousseau's effort to make the *I* worthy of its revolutionary claim. In order to appreciate what Rousseau achieved as a political thinker, it is important to keep in mind the immediate tradition of political thought in which he worked. It is a

---

* Starobinski has brilliantly demonstrated that the apologetic and political writings express in common a desire for transparency. Whatever is dark or concealed or subtle constitutes an obstacle to happiness and truth. The hatred of darkness and concealment was to achieve the intensity of paranoia in Rousseau's later years. Rousseau reveals himself to the world as he would expect everyone to reveal himself. In this view, the concept of the general will (in *The Social Contract*) can be regarded as a harmony of individual wills joined together in their transparency. The darkness of the particular will (*la volonté secrète*) has been overcome in the true social contract. Thus Rousseau's attachment to his singularity is not final: it is required by the historical circumstance of his being the only transparent self in a world of darkness and intrigue. (See Starobinski, *Jean-Jacques Rousseau: La Transparence et L'Obstacle*.)

tradition inhabited by such thinkers as Grotius, Pufendorf, Burlamaqui, Bayberac, and, of course, Hobbes and Locke. Its vocabulary consists of terms like social contract, the state of nature, the civil state, natural law, sovereignty, individual rights. As Robert Derathé has shown in his excellent study of Rousseau's political ideas,[32] the force and intention of many of Rousseau's statements can be appreciated only after disentangling his debts to the tradition from what is original.

Rousseau's unique conception of the state can be seen at once in comparing it with the conceptions of Hobbes and Locke, the most distinguished of the social-contract thinkers. In both Hobbes and Locke, the state is considered a necessity, which hinders the destructiveness of human egoism. Opposed as they are in their political allegiances, Hobbes and Locke see the state in its negative function: it protects the security and (in Locke) the property of the individual against the predatory incursions of other individuals or groups of individuals. For Rousseau, on the other hand, the state in its ideal form is justified by its capacity to develop the moral and intellectual character of the citizen. Antisocial qualities (cruelty, envy, etc.) are, in Rousseau's view, products of a corrupt civilization: they are not to be found in the state of nature (Jean-Jacques' solitude) or the ideal community based on the social contract. The aim of true communal life is to develop the virtues which already exist in germinal form in nature and eradicate the vices of civilization in its present form. In *Emile* especially, Rousseau tries to show how a natural *and* moral development occurs in a community congenial to such growth. The "totalitarian" tendency in Rousseau's thought is precisely in his extension of the provenance of the state beyond the area of security—to include the whole life of the person. Implicit in this tendency is an identification between the idea of the state and the idea of community. The view rests on the assumption that a genuine conciliation between the interests of the self and the communal idea is possible. Without that assumption, the general will (*la volonté générale*) is an intolerable idea. The point to emphasize in the conception of the general will is not its coercive character, but rather its insistence on the political significance of the people—of all the Jean-Jacqueses that compose the political community.

If Rousseau intends totalitarianism when he makes the alienation of individual rights to the whole community a condition of the social contract, he would be, as Derathé points out, in contradiction to repeated declarations throughout his life that individual liberty is of supreme importance. Derathé argues convincingly that the formula (of alienation) is a philosophical device (aphoristically expressed) for effecting a conversion of natural rights to civic liberty.[33] Rousseau has a conception of liberty which holds that man is free not when he is in isolation, in a state of nature, but when he has the advantages of communal life to develop his own personality. Contrary to the stereotype, Rousseau does not exalt the state of nature above the social state. He values the state of nature as a critical standard for judging the corruptions of society in its contemporary forms, but he is fully alive to its deficiencies as a human state. Thus in the *Discourse on the Origin of Inequality* he can speak of "the pure emotion of nature, prior to all kinds of reflection, [as] the force of natural compassion, which the greatest depravity of morals has as yet hardly been able to destroy."[34] But in *The Social Contract* he envisages the superiority of the civic state to the state of nature.

Although, in this state, he deprives himself of some advantages which he got from nature, he gains in return others so great, his faculties are so stimulated and developed, his ideas so extended, his feelings so ennobled, and his soul so uplifted, that, did not the abuses of this new condition often degrade him below that which he left, he would be bound to bless continually the happy moment which took him from it forever, and, instead of a stupid and unimaginative animal, made him an intelligent being and a man.[35]

In establishing the intentions of Rousseau's political thought we do not absolve him of its unintended consequences. One might object, for instance, that Rousseau may

intend the society he envisages to foster the development of
the individual, but that the general will, with its power to
"force" one to be free and its absolute sovereignty, invites
totalitarianism. J. L. Talmon has argued with some force
that the decline of the religious sanction, and in particular
the decline of belief in the doctrine of original sin, leads to a
conception of man as capable of becoming anything, which
in turn makes possible the totalitarian hubris of attempting
to remake man in the image of some political ideal.[36] The
issue is partly historical and partly logical. Is the Rousseauian
idea of the natural goodness of man a historical source of
totalitarianism? Is totalitarianism a necessary logical consequence of Rousseau's conception of human nature? There
are no fully convincing answers to these questions. The very
abstractness of Rousseau's formulations, among other
things, leaves the matter in doubt.

But it is certain the the Rousseauian conception inaugurates
modern utopian speculation: I mean the imagination of a
historically realizable community based on a harmony between
individual self-development and the communal ideal. More's
Utopia and Bacon's New Atlantis are mythic constructs,
nowhere in place or time. Neither More nor Bacon has illusions
about the possibility of historically realizing his utopia. *

---

* See *Daedalus* (Spring, 1965) on Utopia, in particular Judith N.
  Shklar, "Political Theory of Utopia," pp. 367–81, and George
  Kateb, "Utopia and the Good Life," pp. 454–73. Rousseau's
  belief in the historical possibility of the social contract is
  equivocal. Thus he writes in a despairing mood: "If unhappily
  this form cannot be found, and I declare candidly that I believe it
  cannot be found, my advice is that it is necessary to go to the
  opposite extreme and put man as much above the law as possible,
  and in consequence establish an arbitrary despotism and the
  most arbitrary possible: I would wish this despot to be God. In a word,
  I do not see an endurable middle way between the most austere
  democracy and the most complete Hobbesianism: for the
  conflict between men and laws, which makes for a continual
  internecine war, is the worst of all political conditions."
  (From a letter to Mirabeau, July 26, 1767, quoted in
  C. E. Vaughan, *The Political Writings of Jean-Jacques Rousseau,*

Rousseau recognizes the utopian character of his political speculation (without using the word) when, for instance, he criticizes Grotius for establishing the validity of his principles on the basis of historical fact. "His usual method of reasoning is to establish right by fact. It would be possible to employ a more logical method, but none could be more favorable to tyrants."[37] Rousseau's method is (deliberately) more abstract: he will establish the validity of his principles from the point of view of Platonic perfection, of ideal justice. Here again Rousseau parts company with the tradition. Grotius, Pufendorf, Hobbes, and Locke may argue in the abstract principles of political community, but at the same time they are rationalizing an existing state of affairs. Hobbes is the apologist for absolute monarchy, Locke for constitutional monarchy. Rousseau's political community is in the heaven of his own mind. When Rousseau descends to practical political considerations, as in his work on the constitutions of Poland and Corsica, he is inevitably forced to modify his principles.

IV

The moral animus of Rousseau's writings is very strong. Kant paid Rousseau the supreme compliment when he referred to him as the "Newton of the Moral Universe."[38] However, Kant was performing an act of appropriation and thus ignoring contrary tendencies in Rousseau. The apologetic writings often point in another direction, for the moral idea depends on a conversion of the natural or un-inhibited self to a higher social self—a conversion contrary to the spirit of the apologetic writings. In the Dialogues, for instance, against the diabolic version of Jean-Jacques proposed by the Frenchman, Rousseau offers a sentimental Jean-Jacques, whose innocence consists partly in his moral

2: 160–61 [my translation].) Rousseau's "advocacy" of despotism is a paradoxical way of expressing his pessimistic sense of the social contract as a historical possibility.

indolence, his incapacity for acting according to reason or duty. (It is the evil man, we are told, who reasons and calculates.) This moral indolence is reinforced by a view of conscience that has no reference to anything outside itself, neither God nor law. Kant embodies the Categorical Imperative in law; for Rousseau it tends to remain a sentiment, a state of being or feeling. To be sure, Rousseau implies a criticism of Jean-Jacques' moral inadequacies, but this is secondary to his affirmation of his sincerity and capacity for feeling (irrespective of the consequences). In the apologetic writings, Rousseau prides himself on his compulsive honesty, his intransigent refusal to compromise what he is (whatever he may be or do). *

Sincerity and integrity are, of course, not devoid of moral content. But in Rousseau's case they are not, as we have seen, to be accepted at face value. "Sincerity," La Rochefoucauld noted a century before Rousseau, "is a desire to compensate for one's defects and even to reduce their importance by winning credit for them" [39] Indeed, the very need for Rousseau to think himself sincere and innocent often betrays him into duplicity, as in the affair with Sophie d'Houdetot.

The value and interest of Jean-Jacques' character are not in its moral simplicity, as Rousseau would like his readers to believe, but in its ungovernable complexity. In the act of self-

---

* From the historical point of view, Rousseau's pride in his honesty is a tonic. The age in which he performed his version of Alceste was corrupt and complaisant. One has only to read accounts of *la vie Parisienne,* in which back-biting, envy, dishonesty, intellectual servility, and smugness were the order of the day. The salons, dominated by women of meager intellectual attainment and deplorable character, set the tone of much of the intellectual life of the time. This judgment of salon life is not a projection of Rousseau's paranoia, though no doubt he saw the corruption with a paranoid intensity—that is to say, exaggerated many of its features. (See Kingsley Martin, *French Liberal Thought in the Eighteenth Century,* ed. J. P. Mayer (London: Turnstile Press, 1954), pp. 103–16.)

dramatization, Rousseau discovered a real self rather than the logically prefabricated selves that were his immediate inheritance. In rationalistic and materialistic conceptions the person tends to be a logical entity. The elements of this entity can be arranged in a variety of ways, but the variety is fixed according to permutations and combinations set beforehand. For instance, Dryden's definition of character: "A character, or that which distinguishes one man from all others, cannot be supposed to consist of one particular virtue, or vice, or passion only; but 'tis a composition of qualities which are not contrary to one another in the same person: thus, the same man may be liberal and valiant, but not liberal and covetous . . . yet it is still to be observed, that the virtue, vice, or passion, ought to be shown in every man as predominant over all the rest."[40] In a preface to *La Nouvelle Héloïse* (written in the form of a "Dialogue between A Man of Letters and M. J. J. Rousseau on the Subject of Romances"), Rousseau challenges the presumption that one can fix the bounds of human nature: "Can you be ignorant how widely human nature differs from itself? how opposite its characteristics? how prejudice and manners vary according to times, places, and ages? Who is it that can prescribe bounds to nature and say, thus far shalt thou go and no farther?"[41] From a rationalistic point of view the nature of Jean-Jacques is uneconomical, gratuitous, unpredictable. He presents his caprices and follies as marks of a plenitude of being that cannot be reduced, in the words of Dostoevsky's underground man, to the arithmetical operation of two plus two equals four. Ambivalent, self-contradictory, even pathological, the character of Jean-Jacques is a psychological—if not moral—discovery that has not been superseded.*

---

* Diderot discovered the new self in *Rameau's Nephew,* but the fantastic ungovernable Rameau is contained by the dialogue. He exists as a possibility in the consciousness of Diderot, but though he threatens to take over, he never does. *The Confessions* is, so to speak, *Rameau's Nephew* written from the point of view of Rameau.

(Freudian theory, in a sense, represents the extension, refinement, and consolidation of what Rousseau had in part discovered.)

If the complex and passionate self that Rousseau dramatized in his apologetic writings could not be actually contained by the moral community that he envisaged, he could uninhibitedly present that self in literary works—as he does, for instance, in *The Confessions,* the *Reveries,* and *La Nouvelle Héloïse.* Rousseau's "antinomianism," his voluptuous willingness to confess himself lead to the romantic cult of the artist, which we find first in Germany and England. It is, of course, a consummate irony that Rousseau appears as an enemy of art. In the first discourse and the *Letter to D'Alembert,* he re-enacts the Socratic attack on the arts as a source of social corruption. It should be kept in mind, however, that the target of Rousseau's attack is a specific kind of art: the sophisticated drama of seventeenth- and eighteenth-century France. Had Rousseau known the English romantic poets he might not have written his first discourse, and he would have been forced to modify his attack on art in the *Letter to D'Alembert.* Indeed, even in these ostensible attacks on the freedom of the arts, one finds the most extraordinary sensitivity to the (necessary) radical power of literature. Thus in the *Letter to D'Alembert* Rousseau criticizes with uncommon severity the conventional aspect of Molière's vision. Molière's drama, according to Rousseau, is penetrating but never radical, the measure of its limits being Molière's willingness to undercut the romantic and demonic Alceste (in *The Misanthrope),* with whom Rousseau himself so strongly identified. This willingness springs from the central core of Molière's art, for its balance and wit depend upon the sophistication of a Philinte, not the boorishness of an Alceste.[42] The censorious character of the *Letter to D'Alembert* derives not from a mistrust of the radical character of art, but from Rousseau's aversion to the sophisticated and conventional art that prevailed in his society: it was lacking in spiritual purity. This art was for him the expression of a civilization that he hated, itself a symptom of the general corruption.

Rousseau's attack on art, then, is a sort of historical accident, for he is kin to the romantic poets who came after him. He himself never possessed the discipline, the self-restraint, the impersonal devotion to art that made Wordsworth and Keats, for example, great poets. He was too passionately committed to his own immediate and immoderate needs—the need to confess, the need to escape from reality—to make of his powerful imaginative tendency a successful poetry. Repeatedly, Rousseau presents himself as a man given to reverie, to the random association of sentiments, incapable (even mistrustful) of the organizing and creative activities of the higher forms of reason and imagination. This self-image is not entirely accurate: he did produce *The Social Contract,* and *La Nouvelle Héloïse* with all its faults is a work of art. But Rousseau does dramatize a weakness which prevented him from realizing his imaginative gifts. His importance (an importance of the first magnitude) is not in the achievement of a work of art, but in the creation of a character, a sensibility, a vision that has revolutionized our consciousness.

2

The Aesthetic Morality
of Stendhal

I am making every effort to be matter of fact. I want to
impose silence on my heart, which wants to say too much.
I am always afraid of only having put down a sigh when I
imagine myself to have recorded a truth.[1]

At first glance nothing could be further from Rousseau's
Confessions than this brief aside by Stendhal. Until, that is,
we resist the temptation to take Stendhal at his word. He
has revealed himself, uttered the sigh, while speaking of
the need for silence and concealment. The complication is
characteristic. The impulse to self-dramatization is as strong
in Stendhal as in Rousseau, but its route is less direct—*la voie
oblique*, as one critic puts it.[2] This route has its detours: at
moments it seems that Stendhal is moving in an opposite
direction, away from self-revelation to a quasi-asceticism.
In Rousseau there is also a countermovement to self-
exhibition: Jean-Jacques retreats into nature and reverie, but
never without a dramatic indication of where he is going.

He must always make his presence felt, even if in ascetic retreat.[3] The exhibitionism in Rousseau, however, is without calculation, unless one wants to speak of the calculations of the unconscious. He genuinely wishes to separate himself from the egoism of self-dramatization ("making more of himself than of any other"), but his temperament, his very being prevents the separation. In *Reveries of a Solitary Walker*, Rousseau lapses continuously against his better judgment into self-exhibition and apology. He is not content simply to be the solitary walker. Alone, he suffers a kind of vertigo; when in the "Seventh Promenade" he comes upon a factory, he discovers to his surprise the joy of finding himself once more among human things. Rousseau remains to the end mastered by his egoism. Driven into solitude by a combination of real persecution and paranoid sensitivity, Jean-Jacques cannot endure the deprivation of not having his presence felt by others. It is not enough to say that Rousseau simply wants the company of men: he wants it on the condition of a recognition of his own uniqueness, that is, that his inordinate claim upon the sympathy of others be met. The claims of Stendhal's egoism are certainly as large as those of Rousseau, but Stendhal differs in having mastered his. He has found a unique way of asserting and protecting the *I*.

Stendhal mistrusts autobiographical egoism at the same time that he is drawn to it: "I have felt, during a month of thinking about it, a genuine repugnance at writing solely to speak of myself, of the sum total of my shirts, of the mishaps to my self-esteem."[4] He anticipates the difficulties: "This same idea of writing my life occurred to me lately during my journey to Ravenna; to tell the truth, I have often thought of doing so since 1832, but I have always been discouraged by the appalling difficulty of the *I*'s and *me*'s which will make people take a dislike to the author."[5] And again in *The Life of Henri Brulard*: "Where will the reader be found who, after four or five volumes of *I* and *me*, won't long for a bottle of ink, rather than a glass of dirty water, to be thrown at me?"[6] Stendhal elsewhere distinguishes himself from some of the egoists of his acquaintance: "What distinguishes me from these silly self-important journalists . . . is that I have never thought society owed me the slightest thing."[7] If Stendhal wants to avoid self-importance, he cannot, however, escape his fundamental egocentricity.

Stendhal's solution to the problem of *I*'s and *me*'s is suggested in a passage in *Brulard*: "All the harm lies simply in the seven letters B, R, U, L, A, R, D, which form my name and interest, my self-love. Supposing I had written BERNARD, this book would cease to be anything more than a novel written in the first person."[8] Of course, the matter is not so simple. As we know, self-love can persist in a novel ostensibly about a character who is not the novelist. Moreover, Brulard is as different from Beyle as Bernard is: Stendhal (*né* Beyle) has for some private reason attached himself to Brulard rather than Bernard. Robert Martin Adams gives a *partial* list of eighty-seven pseudonyms that Stendhal used. [9] The pseudonyms reflect Stendhal's passion for secrecy; they also express his desire to see himself fully and without illusion. Thus Dominique when he saw himself as young and romantic, and Bombet when he saw his grossness and clumsiness. And Stendhal had more than desire: he had the happy faculty of ironic disengagement, which permitted him to see himself as clearly as he saw others. This faculty is, of course, indispensable to the novelist, particularly to the novelist who makes a large personal investment, as Stendhal did, in his heroes.

Though primarily an instinct in Stendhal, self-irony has its method and its *raison d'être*. Behind the self-reproach is an even stronger self-love. If irony permits a detachment, an objectivity which works against the overinvestment in the hero, it is also a way of protecting that investment. Stendhal disarms his reader from making negative judgments on his hero by anticipation—that is, by ironizing with affection qualities in the hero that the reader would deplore. I have purposely refrained from characterizing these qualities as faults, because whether or not they are faults is a matter of one's point of view. Extreme sensitivity, an easily wounded pride, ruthlessness: these are qualities that are immediately suspect in the eyes of a democratic society. Whatever the artist may personally think about these qualities (he may be in secret complicity with his hero), he cannot permit himself the luxury of simply cherishing them.

Irony, from this point of view, is the artist-aristocrat's concession to the *demos*. In a democratic society, the private man who singles himself out as extraordinary and especially deserving (e.g., Julien Sorel, Stephen Dedalus) is vulnerable to mockery and scorn: he lacks the egalitarian complacency of the crowd. Irony satisfies the plebian mistrust in the reader, allows him to get beyond it to an appreciation of the hero. Stendhal is probably the most brilliant and most successful practitioner of this kind of irony. Its problems can be seen in the work of Joyce, who moved from an extreme romantic involvement in his hero (in *Stephen Hero*) to an ironic distance from him (in *A Portrait of the Artist as a Young Man*). Joyce's disengagement from his hero has created problems for many of his readers, who cannot make up their minds about his attitude toward Stephen. Joyce, it seems to me, wanted (and failed to achieve) that same delicate balance between sympathy and irony that Stendhal achieved.

In any event, when we think of the Stendhal hero, we do not experience the same uncertainty about the hero's value that we do in thinking about Stephen Dedalus, whose coldness, priggishness, and hypersensitivity often seem to undercut the impassioned prose that represents his consciousness. The value of a Stendhal hero is unmistakably communicated by the radiances that emanate from him almost without interruption. Energy, *brio,* the imagination of love and happiness, ambition for glory: these among other elements mix to constitute the indefinable Stendhalian essence. ("One cannot deny," the imaginative Marquis de la Mole remarks, "that Julien shows . . . audacity, perhaps even brilliance . . . But at the back of the character I find something alarming.") [10]

The drama of a Stendhal novel is the strategy through which the hero asserts, protects, and cherishes the elusive, magical, and "alarming" quality in his soul. And that drama is most elaborately and most imaginatively enacted in Stendhal's greatest novel, *The Charterhouse of Parma*. The choice of *The Charterhouse* as the focus for a discussion of egoism in Stendhal may seem odd in the light of his *journal intime, The Life of Henri Brulard*, and *Memoirs of an Egotist*. The reason for the choice may become clearer when we consider the connection between the *journal intime* and the novels.

The journals show Stendhal to be like other *intimistes,* a prisoner of his consciousness of himself. This self-preoccupation greatly troubled Stendhal. He regarded it as an obstacle to his ambition to become a great playwright and poet. He felt that his egoism impoverished his imagination, prevented him from moving outside the circle of his own ego into an imaginative awareness of other people, other situations. Stendhal exaggerated the case, for he did become a great imaginative novelist; we need only note his capacity for creating characters who are not merely projections of himself.* Nevertheless, for Stendhal the *journal intime* was something that had to be transcended. Unlike Amiel, the *intimiste* par excellence, whose whole life and work is the *journal intime*, Stendhal regarded his journal as at best a preparation for the novels: it provided him with an opportunity to cultivate the habit of analysis. As Jules Lemaître remarks: "Stendhal's journal is not a casual and voluntary effusion; it is a useful labor. For him it was a way of changing himself, of shaping himself little by little with a precise goal in mind . . . in his eyes, to analyze oneself is to act."[11] The "activity" of analysis is one of Stendhal's main activities as a novelist.

But the journal also reveals why Stendhal wanted to,

---

* Alain Girard's point that Stendhal never invented his own plots is gratuitous support to Stendhal's self-doubt. What would Girard have to say about Shakespeare? (See Girard, *Le Journal Intime*, p. 293.)

indeed had to, escape from the perpetual consciousness of himself into a more imaginative form of activity. The journal is filled with expressions of ennui, apathy, depression. Stendhal's cult of energy represents his continual effort to overcome these feelings. It is a significant though hardly surprising fact that there is an inverse proportion between the activity of writing novels and the activity of keeping the journal. As Alain Girard remarks: "When the literary work awakens, the journal is silenced, and the journal comes to life again when literary productivity stops."[12]

The *journal intime* gives the writer the physiological bases, so to speak, of his behavior. Amiel somewhere speaks of his journal (and he is speaking of all true journals) as capturing the palpitations, convulsions, trepidations, and undulations of the interior life. Elsewhere he says in a manner that resembles La Rochefoucauld that "the basis of our virtues is not virtue."[13] The *journal intime*, when successful, reveals the true motives and the real shape of behavior. Conventional moral life, from the "physiological" point of view, is not much more than the perturbations, scruples, worries, and anxieties of daily life. Real moral life occurs when one has to make a significant choice, when one has to make oneself, so to speak. At that moment, adventure and morality become synonymous. The novels show the power of art and imagination to redeem man from his primitive "moral" condition: ennui, inertia, distraction, timidity, inconsequence. It is the journals, which present the primitive condition, that the novels transcend.

II

The tendency toward "asceticism," which we have already noted as a characteristic of Stendhal, seems to dominate Fabrizio, the hero of *The Charterhouse*. Fabrizio's romanticism is connected with the absence of "a real passion for anything in the world,"[14] and it is identified with the renunciation of the pleasures of life.

"Can't you see yourself on the *Corso* of Florence or Naples,"
said the Duchessa, "with thoroughbred English horses?
For the evenings a carriage, a charming apartment, and so
forth." She dwelt with exquisite relish on the details of this
vulgar happiness, which she saw Fabrizio thrust from him
with disdain. "He is a hero," she thought.[15]

Fabrizio, joyfully accepting his imprisonment in the Citadel
(only there can he truly love Clelia!), is merely fulfilling his
deeply held ascetic ambition. Elsewhere Stendhal speaks of
Fabrizio's lofty nature, which "prevented him from copying
other young men he saw, to wish, for example, to play with
any degree of seriousness the part of lover."[16] Fabrizio, of
course, will soon become the lover of Clelia, on the highest
plane of Stendhalian *crystallization,* and the condition of that
love will be such as to fortify the ascetic tendency. This
tendency is particularly strong in Fabrizio but by no means
peculiar to him. His imprisonment and death soon afterward
repeat the great renunciation of Julien, who, in rejecting
Mathilde de la Mole and the brilliant life she represents,
chooses the "pure" love of Mme de Renal and death. There
is the suggestion of martyrdom and saintliness in Julien's
final moments on earth.

The bad air of the cell became insupportable to Julien.
Fortunately on the day on which he was told that he must die,
a bright sun was gladdening the earth, and he himself was
in a courageous mood. To walk in the open air was a delicious
sensation to him, as is treading solid earth to a mariner who
has long been at sea. "There, all is well," he said to himself,
"I am not lacking in courage."
Never had that head been so poetic as at the moment it
was about to fall. The most precious moments that he had
known in the past in the woods of Vergy came crowding into
his mind with an extreme vividness.
Everything passed simply, decorously, and without
affectation on his part.[17]

The ascetic impulse, however, can be sustained only by a
religious conception of an afterlife, and despite Fabrizio's

nominal piety, there is little reason to regard him differently from Julien and Stendhal himself. I refer to their atheism, an atheism that does not exclude a certain otherworldliness. We see this strange blend, for instance, in Julien's "mystical" experience in the monastery as Besançon:

> The silence, the profound solitude, the coolness of the long aisles, made Julien's musings all the sweeter. He had no fear of being disturbed by abbé Chas, who was occupied in another part of the building. His soul had almost quitted its mortal envelope, which was strolling at a slow pace along the north aisle committed to his charge. He was all the more at rest, since he was certain that there was nobody in the confessionals save a few devout women he saw without observing.[18]

Fabrizio's "religious" aspiration is perfectly expressed by the sonnet he composes in the margins of one of the books that Don Cesare lent him in prison.

> *To die near what one loves!* expressed in a hundred different fashions, was followed by a sonnet in which one saw that this soul parted, after atrocious torments, from the frail body in which it had dwelt for three-and-twenty years, urged by that instinct for happiness natural to everything that had once existed, would not mount to heaven to mingle with the choirs of angels as soon as it should be free, and should the dread Judgment grant it pardon for its sins; but that, more fortunate after death than it had been in life, it would go a little way from the prison, where for so long it had groaned, to unite itself with all that it had loved in this world. And "So," said the last line of the sonnet, "I should find my earthly paradise."[19]

Fabrizio can find happiness only in this life, and he cannot afford to follow out his ascetic tendency, so long as he remains committed to the idea of earthly happiness. He must adopt stratagems, play the game of politics (of which Mosca is the indubitable master), negotiate various ruses in order to win his happiness.

We must avoid the temptation of seeing the ruse as a

traitor to the self and the drama of the Stendhal novel as the knowledge learned through suffering of the soul's diminishment in its practical involvements. Certainly Fabrizio is uncompromised by his employment of ruses to advance his courtship of Clelia while in prison. In prison he finds not only a "real passion" but the instinct and method to foster it. Fabrizio becomes an adept at the politics of love, evoking at moments Mosca's finesse in the sphere of power. Fabrizio's attempt to correspond with Clelia by means of letters which he traces in charcoal, his pretense at not hearing her give a warning about a danger to his life so that she is forced to communicate with him after he has uttered the taboo words "I love you," show him in complete command of the ruse.

Fabrizio was transported with joy to see at length established, after three months of effort, this channel of correspondence for which he had so vainly begged. He had no thought of abandoning the little ruse which had proved so successful, his aim was to write real letters, and he pretended at every moment not to understand the words of which Clelia was holding up each letter in turn before his eyes.[20]

The long passage about Fabrizio in prison (it runs to several chapters) is filled not only with elaborate descriptions of various ruses (fostered by Clelia, the Duchessa, Fabrizio, Grillo, the jailer), but also with a psychological and passional complexity to which the ruse is in a sense the external counterpart. It is Stendhal's peculiar insight (in which he anticipates Freud) that love has its politics (one has only to observe the history of love since the troubadours): its hot and cold wars, manoeuvers, negotiations, and armistices. The animations as well as the enervations of love derive from its various ruses.

For this reason alone, the ascetic recoil from the world is not enough. Stendhal and his heroes take pleasure in the ruse, in its artful and artistic element, its wit and gaiety and daring. And this is of no trivial significance. In his generally perceptive essay on *The Charterhouse*, Judd Hubert underestimates the importance of the ruse when he remarks that "likable characters, such as Mosca, Gina and Fabrice, owe much of their superiority, in the eyes of the reader, to the fact that they can play the game of politics without becoming the least involved."[21] Not so. Though they are not defined entirely by the game, they would be diminished without it. The ascetic element is present in Stendhal and his heroes, but it is often connected with a quite un-Pascalian predilection for the *divertissement*. Even the Stendhal hero who does not feel the attraction of the game is inevitably drawn into it. Thus Lucien Leuwen encounters the "brilliant" conversation of Mme de Grandet's salon with silence. "How can one talk of true virtue, fame, beauty in front of fools who misunderstand everything that is fine with their degrading jests?"[22] But he knows that silence leads to boredom, and "boredom made [Lucien] ill-humored, and he was never sure he would be able to resist the temptation of launching some amusing sally by way of diversion."[23] Even the sincere and "naïve" Clelia and her counterpart in *The Red and the Black*, Madeleine de Renal, are remarkably capable of the ruse, as they both help their lovers and deceive in one case a father and in the other a husband. Madeleine becomes perhaps the most competent Machiavellian in *The Red and the Black* by an instinct identical with her love for Julien. But the most graphic image of this strange combination between asceticism and the ruse is Fabrizio, passionately in love while in prison. Outside of prison ("in life")—at the battle of Waterloo, at court, in the intrigue with Marietti and Gilletti—Fabrizio seems possessed of an almost fatal aloofness.

The combination of *erotic* asceticism and *divertissement* assumes an interesting form in Mosca. Mosca is the reverse of Fabrizio in his instinctive predilection for the ruse. In Mosca, the attitude toward the practical life is antinomian rather than ascetic: he is drawn to action but is indifferent to its ethical consequences. Indeed, so keen is his commitment to the political game that he seriously compromises his higher loyalty to the Duchessa and his love for her by striking out the phrase "unjust proceedings" from a document, thereby endangering Fabrizio's life. The instinct from which

this gesture proceeds is the instinct of his craft: he is Prince
Ernesto's peerless prime minister. The Duchessa judges him
harshly; she sees him at that moment as the political animal,
the complete courtier. But he is not simply that and the
Duchessa knows it. He is capable of shucking off his political
role and leaving Parma with the Duchessa, with whom he is
"madly" (a favorite Stendhalian word) in love. Early in *The
Charterhouse* we catch Mosca in the act of disengaging his
erotic interests from his political concerns: "[Gina] was
tenderly attached to the Conte, who was literally mad with
happiness. This pleasing situation had bred in him an absolute
impassivity towards everything in which only his professional
interests were concerned."[24] But the impassivity in no wise
destroys Mosca's political competence. On the contrary, in
the same paragraph in which we are told of Mosca's happiness
and his political impassivity, we are also told that he soon
becomes prime minister, receives "honors which come very
near to those paid to the Sovereign himself," and achieves
"complete control of his master's will."

That the fascination with the political game is no sin in the
Stendhalian code is confirmed by the Duchessa herself, who
has her joy in the game which Mosca has invited her to play
at Parma. The Duchessa establishes her ascendancy at the
court when she starts her Thursday parties. The Prince
attends the parties, thereby breaking precedent, the effect
of which is a defeat of the Duchessa's rival, the Raversi. The
Duchessa expresses to Mosca her pleasure in the triumph:
"All this owing to a thoroughly rash idea which came into
my mind. . . . I should be more free no doubt in Rome or
Naples, but should I find so fascinating a game to play there?
No indeed, my dear Conte, and you provide me with all my
joy in life."[25] The difference is that the Duchessa's actions
(her disguises as well as her confessions) appear to be
creatures of pure impulse, uncalculated and unpredictable.
She is constantly risking her safety, courting madness (like
the poet Ferrante Palla), because her loves and her personal
happiness (which includes the happiness of those she loves)

are always of first, immediate, and burning importance to her. Only Mosca has been able to find what seems like a balance, a *modus vivendi* between his love and the world, between erotic asceticism and political involvement.

Problematic as this *modus vivendi* is, Mosca's "solution" contains a wisdom (peculiarly Beylist) which is missing from the more attractive solutions of Fabrizio and the Duchessa. If happiness for Mosca is a life with the Duchessa away from Parma, "where he is bored to death," [26] he nevertheless knows how contingent that love is upon the ruse, in Mosca's case the extraordinary game of power that he plays. It is almost impossible for us to contemplate Mosca and Gina away from the scene at Parma. How quickly they would grow into domestic middle age!* Mosca's erotic quality derives in large measure from his political charisma. Only in his Machiavellian-Metternichian capacity can he hope to rival Fabrizio.

Mosca lacks the contempt for mere survival shared by the Duchessa, Fabrizio, and Ferrante Palla—it is this contempt which enables them to be so madly heroic—because he knows the elementary truth that happiness is impossible without survival. Despite the Duchessa's criticism of him, Mosca's presence is magical, like that of a duke in Shakespearean comedy (*Measure for Measure* or *The Tempest*, for instance). He embodies and sustains (alone among the major characters) the twin comic principles of survival and happiness. Without the conditions that he creates, the world of Parma would be one of unrelieved misery.†

Mosca's position is, to be sure, a painful one. His will remains tense in the art of playing a game that in one sense does not count in order to foster and protect a happiness in which there is supposed to be no strain, only the gay com-

---

* One thinks of Antony and Cleopatra in the ripeness of middle age, radiating power as well as passion.

† Harry Levin is on the right track, it seems to me, when he says that "Mosca's debonair maturity is the quintessence of Beylism." (*Toward Stendhal, Pharos,* no. 3 [Winter, 1945], p. 68.)

munion of kindred and happy spirits, what Stendhal called the "happy few". The ruse is a scaffolding (a kind of erotic foreplay), necessary to the achievement of happiness, abandoned at the moment of bliss, but not everlastingly abandoned, because the moment of happiness is transient and the pursuit of it must be constantly renewed. Mosca must play the game of power to win his happiness, though at the same time instructed by the ascetic need to keep himself pure of the more corrupt expressions of power, that is, power that demeans itself, that betrays its original inspiration in the happy energies of men and becomes bourgeois politics, the exchange of privileges and favors unillumined by an idea or a gracious emotion. In valuing the *modus vivendi* that Mosca embodies, we must not, however, ignore its inadequacy: the discontinuity between the inner and the outer life (intense happiness and outer impassivity, exquisite sensitivity and cruelty) may be a necessary condition in the post-Napoleonic world of Stendhal, but it is at the same time a tragic condition. The dreaming, fantasy-making part of Stendhal's imagination tries to overcome the discontinuity, to imagine moments when power and happiness are one. Stendhal's favorite figure for this fusion is Napoleon, who is both fact and metaphor, and Stendhal's favorite historical time is a sort of combination of the court of Louis XIV and the Italian Renaissance. The Napoleonic era itself is too close to Stendhal in its factuality to be easily transmuted into dream. The opening pages of *The Charterhouse*, in which Fabrizio achieves a disillusioned knowledge of the Napoleonic wars, are a kind of justification of Stendhal's retreat into the temporal synthesis that he has created. But even in the dream world of Parma, the "marriage" between power and happiness is untenable. The usual condition is a dualism, a bifurcation between power and happiness.

Only Mosca among the major characters manages to create a balance between erotic reverie and the rigorous demands of the ruse. The Duchessa and Ferranta Palla, as I have already remarked, are always verging on madness, and their ruses are finally hardly ruses. They are extravagant caprices, wild and uncontrollable acts of spirit. The Duchessa's plan to flood Parma by opening the gates of the reservoir, for instance, is presented to us as sheer madness, "horrible from the moral point of view," "fatal to the tranquillity of the rest of her life." [27] To be sure, in the madness we are given glimpses of the *élan* and gaiety of the Duchessa. "Wine for the people of Sacca and water for the people of Parma." [28] The laughter of the Duchessa and her henchman Lodovico rings through the madness.

Not that the "moral point of view" is adequate to the Stendhalian ethos: it is narrow, tainted with the *esprit bourgeois*, it cannot compass the splendor of the Stendhalian hero. Even Mosca, whose *virtù* is governed by a classical conception of prudence (a prudence, one might add, that does not exclude courage), is hardly to be judged morally. "He is a thoroughly good man, deserving to be loved," the Duchessa remarks of him. [29] But it is doubtful that this is a conventional moral judgment. Mosca is capable of severities, which the liberals call cruelties, [30] and he can speak rather casually of a conscience vaguely troubled by the memory of two alleged spies whom he once shot in Spain, perhaps "a little lightly." [31] This ruthlessness is part of the Stendhalian ethos, a trait that belongs to most of Stendhal's heroes and heroines. The Duchessa, for instance, believes quite naturally that "the death of a ridiculous creature like Gilletti [was not] the sort of thing that could be seriously charged against a del Dongo." [32]

And yet it is possible to judge the actions of a Stendhal character. In the cultivated Stendhalian atmosphere, the tyranny of the Prince is severely condemned: "People with brains who are born on the throne or at the foot of it, soon lose all fineness of touch; they proscribe in their immediate circle, freedom of conversation, which seems to them coarseness; they refuse to look at anything but masks and pretend to judge the beauty of complexions; the amusing part of it is that they imagine their touch to be the finest." [33]

"Fineness of touch," "freedom," "beauty": the terms here suggest an aesthetic standard of judgment. To negotiate the issues of power in a manner that would not degrade him, the Stendhal hero instinctively consults his sense of style. Style may have its attendant cruelties—as it has in the actions of Mosca and the Duchessa—but it also has the aristocratic virtues: nobility, spontaneity, magnanimity, *brio*. There is instinct in the Stendhal hero, a compassion for victims of injustice, for the sufferings of the poor. The Duchessa is constantly bestowing her largesse on the needy ("wine for the people of Sacca") while she contemplates her revenge upon Parma. (Julien Sorel's sensitivity to injustice is as keen as Rousseau's.) The magnanimity of the energy proscribes the kind of gratuitous cruelty that proceeds from weakness. "Never hurt anyone unnecessarily," a precept of Lucien Leuwen's moral code, can be generalized to the other Stendhalian characters. (Lucien is extraordinarily sensitive to insults offered to his moral person. Reviled by the multitudes rioting in Blois, Lucien struggles to overcome the humiliation of the insult: "But how can I ever get rid of the mud I'm covered with, morally as well as physically? I have tried to be useful." [34] Lucien never really rids himself of the feeling that the mud is on his face.)

Style, however, is the ultimate term of the Stendhalian moral code. Henri Beyle had some affection for the ornamental behavior and appearance of the dandy, but style for him is ultimately not a matter of decoration, but a function of energy. Nietzsche's conception of style as a sublimation of energy applies perfectly to Stendhal. Sublimation is both expression and suppression, and style has its aspect of concealment as well as of revelation. The barbarian (or Jacobin) energy in Stendhal's heroes is necessarily refined and to some extent attenuated. The element of calculation, the sense of duty to one's appearance (indeed, the whole activity of masking), which are ingredients of style, in some cases distort the energy. Consider, for instance, Julien's seduction of Mme de Renal:

But, in the most delicious moments, the victim of a freakish pride, he still attempted to play the part of a man in the habit of captivating women: he made incredible efforts to destroy his natural charm. Instead of his paying attention to the transports which he excited, and to the remorse that increased their vivacity, the idea of *duty* was continually before his eyes. He feared a terrible remorse, and undying ridicule, should he depart from the ideal plan that he had set himself to follow. In a word, what made Julien a superior being was precisely what prevented him from enjoying the happiness that sprang up at his feet. He was like a girl of sixteen who has a charming complexion and, before going to a ball, is foolish enough to put on rouge.[35]

There is unquestionably an irony in speaking of a superiority that destroys natural charm, but the object of irony should not be generalized to include the very idea of duty or of calculation or of any of the artful elements that create style. Julien at this moment shows bad form: but the incongruity between appearance and impulse that Julien here exhibits is a personal failure, not a Rousseauian illustration of the corruption of artifice.

Indeed, *The Charterhouse of Parma* is a celebration of style. In *The Charterhouse*, Stendhal devalues reality and creates opportunities for unexampled expressions of energy.* The ease with which the characters move across the stage of the novel (its affinities with opera, which Stendhal loved, have been often noted), the absence of resistance to their remarkable energies: this is not the realistic world of the nineteenth-century novel. Consider only Mosca's extravagant offer to Gina of a marriage with the Duke de Sanseverina, which will

---

* In his essay "The Devaluation of Reality in *The Charterhouse of Parma*" Judd Hubert shows an exceptional sensitivity to the utopian quality of the novel, though he does not, in my opinion, always draw the right conclusions from it (see ed., *Stendhal,* Victor Brombert, pp. 95–100). Harry Levin casually and misleadingly suggests the utopian aspect when he refers to Parma as "the ultra-reactionary utopia" (*Toward Stendhal,* pp. 62–63).

confer upon her an almost limitless freedom and power of action and no corresponding obligations.[36] Too much has been made of the corruptions of the Parmesan world. The Prince, Rassi, the spineless liberal Fabio Conti, Mosca himself are, of course, all signs that the nineteenth century is still very present in Stendhal's imagination, but it is there reduced to farce, overcome by the dream of power and happiness. In no other novel by Stendhal are characters permitted to explode their magical essences so brilliantly and so uninhibitedly to the surface as they are in *The Charterhouse of Parma*. In the Duchessa particularly, the distinction between energy and the ruse, between happiness and the game, is almost obliterated. In her (and in Ferrante Palla) style tends to be simply the radiance of energy. Almost, but not quite: for that way lies madness. (The words "mad," "madly," "madness," as I have already remarked, constantly recur in *The Charterhouse* and often in connection with happiness.)*

The sanity of Mosca is precisely in his instinct for suppression (both moral and political). He loves the "Jacobinism" of the Duchessa,† but his behavior is characteristically Metternichian: style asserting itself against or containing energy. At times Mosca is infected with the Duchessa's enthusiasm and relishes the subversive possibility. Thus Mosca on the prospect of abandoning Parma with the Duchessa:

"But you will make me the immense sacrifice," he added, laughing, "of exchanging the sublime title of Duchessa for one

---

* Elsewhere as well: "Where can I find words to paint a picture of perfect happiness, enjoyed with ecstasy and without satiety, by a spirit sensitive to the point of annihilation and madness?" (*Life of Henri Brulard,* p. 117.)

† The intellectual and imaginative energy of the Duchessa makes the Princess suspect her of being Jacobin, despite her ultraroyalist opinion: ". . . the Princess . . . felt that the Conte and his friend had too exclusive a regard for brains, always slightly akin to Jacobinism" (p. 237).

greatly inferior? For my own amusement, I am leaving
everything here in inextricable confusion; I had four or five
workers in my various Ministries, I placed them all on the
pension list two months ago, because they read the French
newspapers; and I have filled their places with Blockheads
of the first order.[37]

But the principle of Mosca's being is to change the metaphor
"Apollonian": the cool, reverent containment of the energies
embodied by the Duchessa and Ferrante Palla. Mosca has
learned the art of imposing silence on his heart, of suppressing
the sigh when necessary. He is the supreme incarnation of
Stendhal's famous *logique*. Not to deny the heart, but to
"derousseauize" it, to make it intelligent in order to advance
its interests all the more, is a characteristic Stendhalian
effort.* Nietzsche's statement about our mixed nature in
Human, All Too Human illuminates the Stendhalian dialectic
between intelligence (or intellect) and passion:

... [our] mixed nature, alternately inspired with ardour and chilled
through and through by the intellect. . . . The *fire* in us
generally makes us unjust, and impure in the eyes of our
goddess; in this condition we are not permitted to take her
hand, and the serious smile of her approval never rests upon us.
We reverence her as the veiled Isis of our life; with shame we
offer her our pain as penance and sacrifice when the fire
threatens to burn and consume us. It is the *intellect* that saves
us from being utterly burnt and reduced to ashes. . . .[38]

Fabrizio, who is given to tears—Stendhal knows well the
temptations of Rousseauism—makes the *dry* effort toward
self-mastery.

[Hearing Cimarosa,] Fabrizio stood firm throughout the
opening bars, but presently his anger melted away, and he
felt a compelling need to shed tears. "Great God!" he said
to himself, "what a ridiculous scene! and with my cloth, too!"
He felt it wiser to talk about himself.[39]

---

* There is some truth (and some oversimplification) in Levin's
  remark: "Whatever the Ideologues may have put into Stendhal's
  head, he remained a Rousseauist at heart" (*Toward Stendhal,* p. 40).

Logique (the intelligence that informs the ruse) douses fires and dries tears.

The dryness of Stendhalian logic scarcely indicates its sensitivity to that which it controls. The logic of Mosca, for instance, is no careful, step-by-step movement through an inexorable series of statements and actions. It is itself an art, full of surprises, suddennesses, and leaps. It is the artful counterfoil to energy, appropriate to it when it gets out of hand. But this is not all: the paradox of Stendhal's passion for logic and his romantic enthusiasm dissolves at least partly in the realization that logic serves as a method for locating the region of mystery into which it cannot enter. Like reason in the Christian dispensation, Stendhalian logic is the servant of an intelligence (or spirit) which surpasses it. Unlike the Laclosian intelligence (of *Les Liaisons Dangereuses*) with which Stendhal's logic has certain affinities and which tends to be mechanical and chesslike, a brilliant process of cold motive and pure calculation, Stendhalian logic is informed with a passional energy that also transcends it.* "Love, that passion which is so visionary, demands in its language a mathematical exactness. It cannot make do with a kind of diction that always says either too much or too little (and which always recoils before the right word)."[40] But exactness is not to be confused with exhaustiveness: one must avoid "deflowering the happy moments . . . by describing and dissecting them."[41] The role of logic is essential but limited.

III

In an influential essay, Irving Howe makes a misleading contrast between the *espagnolisme* of the Duchessa and the calculated ruse of Mosca.

---

* See Stendhal's preference for Werther over Don Juan in *On Love*, pp. 232–33.

Sanseverina dominating Mosca represents the victory of
espagnolisme over calculated ruse, the power of desire to elbow
aside the restraints of caution. In drawing her with an affection
seldom matched in literature, Stendhal suggests that wherever
passion is vital and full, morality must suffer some consequence.
Sanseverina seems to move beyond the margin of morality,
though one is less inclined to suppose that she has achieved a
Nietzschean transvaluation of values than that she is impervious,
like some majestic natural force, to moral argument.[42]

If the Duchessa is triumphant, it is highly doubtful that
Stendhal would have endorsed the victory. In *The Life of
Henri Brulard*, we are told that it was Aunt Elizabeth who had
"infected" Henri with *espagnolisme* as a child, from which
"arose a ridiculous series of follies committed through
overscrupulousness and nobility of soul."[43] And elsewhere
he complains that this "accursed Castilianism [a synonym
for *espagnolisme*] prevents me from having the genius of
comedy."[44] In logic (particularly the "ideology of De
Tracy), Stendhal tries to find the way to control his *espagnolisme*. "Until I was 25, nay even today, I often have to grip
myself with both hands, in order not to be completely swayed
by the impressions things make on me, and to be able to
judge them rationally, on the basis of experience."[45] Moreover, the issue between the Duchessa and Mosca is not moral.
Mosca as well as the Duchessa "move[s] beyond the margin of
morality." What distinguishes them are their different styles
(both amoral) with which they dispose their energies.

From the point of view of the Duchessa, Fabrizio, and
Ferrante Palla, there is perhaps something commonplace
about the soul of Mosca. But this judgment is excessively
severe. Mosca's political skill is nothing short of art (he has
Stendhal's "genius of comedy"), and it is based on the finest
psychological perceptions and on a courage that perfectly
matches these perceptions. Mosca shares the Duchessa's
contempt for the bourgeois spirit, her love of beauty and
nobility, her dream of happiness. They are *natural*, a word
always intended as praise by Stendhal.

In appropriating the word "natural" to Mosca, we are suddenly reminded of how different Stendhal's conception of the natural is from Rousseau's. Stendhal does not conceive of an opposition between nature and society, critical as he may be of the vices of a particular society. The natural for Stendhal is identical with the genuine, which develops in sophistication (vile word for Jean-Jacques): it is opposed to the meretriciously artificial but not to the artful, to which it is closely allied. The opposite of sophistication and urbanity is not the natural, but the provincial, the atmosphere that constrains and cramps the free spirit.* Naturalness is the fruit of sophistication, the art that conceals art, cultivated in the great cities, Paris and Milan, for instance, not in the drawing rooms of Nancy and Grenoble.

Like every seeker after grace, the Stendhalian hero wants to be relaxed in his freedom, undisturbed and uncompromised by an alien element. But this cannot be achieved by the simple recognition of the natural substratum of one's being. Though Stendhal values naturalness and sincerity (like Rousseau), he is keenly aware of the enormous obstacles that confront the would-be sincere and natural man. Naturalness and sincerity are comparatively unproblematic for Rousseau, who castigates himself for various things, but rarely for the failure to be sincere and natural. Stendhal, on the other hand, impressed with the instability of the energy that composes the self, makes the natural and the sincere the

---

* "Provincial Frenchmen set up an absurd standard of the qualifications necessary for a gentleman in Society and they lie in wait and spend their lives watching to see if anyone transgresses this standard. Thus there is an end to naturalness, they are always in a state of pique, and this mania makes even their love ridiculous. It is this which, after envy, makes living in small towns so unbearable, and one should bear this in mind whenever one admires the picturesque surroundings of some of them. The most generous and noble emotions are stifled there by contact with the basest of all the products of civilization. To put the finishing touch on their repulsiveness, the respectable citizens talk of nothing but the corruption of great cities" (*On Love*, pp. 116–17).

object of a strenuous quest. In his "treatise" *On Love*, Stendhal indicates the difficulties that attend the effort to be natural.

We say a thing is *natural* if it does not depart from the usual methods of procedure. It goes without saying that we must not only never lie to the person we love but we must not even exaggerate the least bit in the world or tamper with the strict outline of truth. . . .

Reverting to the word *naturalness,* I maintain that naturalness and habit are two different things. For if we confuse the meaning of these two words, it is evident that the more sensitive we are, the more difficult it is for us to be *natural*, for our way of life is less controlled by habit and more by our individuality at every fresh circumstance that arises. . . .

A sensitive man, as soon as his heart is touched, no longer finds in himself any trace of habit to guide his actions. . . .

How can he avoid laboring to say the right things. . . .

A passionate man can only, as his sole refuge in the storm, strongly embrace the vow never to alter the truth in any way and to interpret clearly the feelings in his heart; if the conversation is lively and disjointed, he may hope for some delightfully natural moments, otherwise he will only be perfectly natural during those hours when he is a little less madly in love.

When we are actually with the person we love, even our movements hardly remain natural, even though the habit of them is so firmly rooted in our muscles. . . .[46]

The above passages constitute an antiromantic account of the relation between strong feeling and naturalness. In Stendhal's paradoxical view, the natural is the fragile flower of self-possession and sophistication: when feeling is strong and uncontrolled, man becomes unnatural. This is the fallen state. In a character like Madeleine de Renal we glimpse an Edenic harmony between strong feeling and natural behavior. The corresponding adverse judgment of Julien when he tries to seduce Madeleine suggests Stendhal's mistrust of the excesses of sophistication. But Mosca is excepted from this kind of judgment: his sophistication is the ripeness of civilization, his behavior the graceful and energetic performance of a man who knows himself and acts in the fullness of his knowledge.

IV

The significance of style for Stendhal is ultimately a matter of the metaphysics of the self. What is it to be a man, what is it to be a self? The questions may not be directly posed by Stendhal, but they are implicit in Abbé Pirard's statement about the "something [in Julien's soul] that offends the common herd,"[47] in the presentation of the *brio* of the Duchessa and Ferrante Palla as proceeding from incalculable and unpredictable energies, in the artful calculations of Mosca, his utter mastery of appearances. In Rousseau, there is a natural substratum of self, an authentic natural self, which a man must recover if he is to achieve salvation. For Rousseau, this self is a *given,* an act of grace. Not so with Stendhal. The self for Stendhal is composed from moment to moment: it resides in its capacity for self-multiplication, that is, into pseudonymns, elaborate disguises, discontinuities of being: for instance, quick movements from enthusiasm to *sang-froid,* from Rousseauian sentimentalism to icy bravery. No single moment or role catches the full essence of a Stendhalian character: the magical, indefinable element hovers above the hero as he acts, but it is never exhausted by any moment.

In the Stendhalian view the self is an artistic creation or a series of creations. When Rousseau desires transparency, he is, of course, presupposing a natural self that must be recovered from the corruptions and artifices of a civilization which overlie it. Concealment is the enemy of the authentic in the Rousseauian view, and style for Rousseau would be one of the more sophisticated versions of concealment, a way of darkening the truth. There is in Stendhal a vestigial Rousseauism, which expresses itself in such statements as: "The only crime at which one can take offense in love is want of candor." [48] Elsewhere Stendhal knows that love has its necessary politics. For Stendhal, there is no self without style, without the force that shapes energy and makes it vivid and beautiful and thrilling. Style is what the Duchessa and Mosca share, though their particular styles are different. It is a mistake to see the Duchessa simply as the incarnation of pure energy: she is finally an artist at extravagance and caprice, like Mathilde de la Mole (in *The Red and the Black*). Her behavior would be unthinkable outside the sophistications of a society like Parma.

What Stendhal has discovered is a *moral* idea greater than conventional morality. The *art* of making and ordering selves requires extraordinary sensitivity to the uniqueness, the volatility, the instability of the energy that composes the self. Conventional morality rests in absolutes, in fixed ideas about what the self is or should be: it attempts to predetermine the destiny of the self, to fix its behavior according to ideas of good and bad set beforehand. Conventional morality is always anterior to the self, always a morality-in-itself. "There was no act of human life, serious or frivolous, which was not imprisoned in advance, as it were, in the imitation of a model." [49] Stendhal is here complaining, as Rousseau before him had complained, against the "immorality" of Molière. "It is precisely this dread of not being like everybody else that inspires Molière, and that is why he is *immoral*. To resist oppression—not to dread a danger because it is hidden— this is what may be called not being like everybody else." [50] The aesthetic morality of Stendhal and of those who followed him is "inspirational": the form that the self takes at any moment is governed or should be governed by the *vital* direction of the energy, regardless of the hidden dangers. This is the cult of the ego which Stendhal is said to have created, the cult that issues finally in supermen and nihilists and immoralists. The cult is already implicit in Rousseau's

self-exaltation, the special value that he placed on his uniqueness. But Rousseau never finds a vocabulary adequate to his
singularity: the language of traditional morality is insensitive
to the new mode of feeling that Rousseau principally created.
The aesthetic morality of Stendhal justifies and is justified
by the energy: it is constantly and keenly sensitive to its
motions and vagaries. Out of the agreements and quarrels
between art and energy, Stendhal has produced a varied,
witty, and beautiful world.

Stendhal's aesthetic morality is extraordinarily generous.
There is a nice instance of this in Stendhal's own creative
process. The model for the Duchessa was the promiscuous
wife of a minor clerk who fascinated and exasperated
Stendhal for several years. Robert Martin Adams succinctly
marks the distance between Angelina Pietragrua and the
Gina of *The Charterhouse*: "Between the promiscuous wife
of a minor clerk in the Milanese bureaucracy, who happened
to exist in historical flesh and blood, and the eternal duchess
of Stendhal's imagination, there lies an evident abyss."[51]
The point to be made about the transformation of this bitch
who plagued Stendhal for years is not the cliché that art
converts or shapes life to its uses, but that Stendhal chose to
make of her a magical creature. The transformation in the
opposite direction is the more usual occurrence in fiction.
The novelist has the most enviable of ways to work his
revenge for some unhappy love affair. But this was not
Stendhal's way. In imagining or re-creating the life of
Angelina, Stendhal with his immoralist sensitivity to energy
and beauty generously discovered in her a grace of being that
transcended moral judgments. In Stendhal we see one of the
very rare moments in the history of modern literature in
which immoralism presents itself as humanism: a vision of
the vital energies of man, fulfilling the values of a humanized
civilization.

3

Goethe, Carlyle, and "The Sorrows of Werther"

In *Biographia Literaria* Coleridge makes the suggestive statement that "there have been men in all ages who have been impelled as by an instinct to propose their own nature as a problem, and who devote their attempts to its solution."[1] Such a man was Goethe. Unlike Rousseau (or Byron), who was impelled as by an instinct to propose his nature as a dramatic fact, Goethe attempted to understand the spiritual revolution that men like Rousseau and Byron had made. I have already suggested Goethe's ambivalence in his remark: "Every emancipation of the spirit is pernicious unless there is a corresponding growth in control."[2] He is the first great writer to be aware of the problematic nature of Rousseauism or Byronism.*

---

* See Matthew Arnold's portrait of Goethe in *Memorial Verses*. Arnold overemphasizes Goethe's classical mistrust of the romantic revolt. The Goethean response is more complex and more catholic.

Goethe's awareness is to be distinguished from hostility in any sense. It is in contrast, for instance, to Irving Babbitt's view that this spiritual revolution was simply an aberration,[3] a seduction from the proper concerns of men. This kind of hostility characteristically greeted every new effort of Byron, and Goethe's response to the hostility *distinguishes* his own view. Thus in reply to the doubt of Eckermann that "a positive gain for pure human culture" could be won by Byron's works, however brilliant they might be, Goethe remarks:

There I must contradict you. Byron's boldness, audacity and grandeur, are they not formative in themselves? We must beware of seeking for that quality only in what is decidedly pure and moral. Everything great promotes culture as soon as we are aware of it.[4]

E. M. Butler has documented what she calls Goethe's obsession with Byron ("Byron inspired in the mind of Goethe an overriding passion."[5]) But it would be misleading to regard Goethe's view of Byron as sheer personal fascination. For Goethe, Byron was an instance of the demonic, a force at once amoral and beneficent. Goethe describes his discovery of the demonic in his autobiography.

He thought that he discovered in Nature, animate and inanimate, with soul and without soul, something which was only manifested in contradictions, and therefore could not be grasped under one conception, still less under one word. It was not godlike, for it seemed unreasonable; not human, for it had no understanding; not devilish, for it was beneficent; not angelic, for it often showed malicious pleasure. It resembled chance, for it exhibited no consequence; it was like Providence, for it hinted at connection. Everything which limits us seemed by it to be penetrable; it seemed to sport in an arbitrary fashion with the necessary elements of our being; it contracted time and expanded space. Only in the impossible did it seem to find pleasure, and the possible it seemed to thrust from itself with contempt.[6]

Though it is an ambiguous power, Goethe stresses its positive side.

Although that Daemonic element can manifest itself in all corporeal and incorporeal things, indeed even in animals it expresses itself most remarkably, yet it stands especially in the most wonderful connection with man, and forms a power which, if not opposed to the moral order of the world, yet crosses it so that one may be regarded as the warp and the other as the woof.[7]

If Goethe was drawn to Byron's demonic power, he was ambivalently responsive to Byron's sentimental side. With the instinct of the doctor, Goethe also saw this sentimentality as hypochondria (a mixture of morbidity and self-pity). Before Byron had awakened to find himself famous, Goethe had already anatomized this hypochondria in *The Sorrows of Werther,* a work that has close kinship with *Childe Harold.* What makes Goethe's testimony about hypochondria so interesting and convincing is the fact that he had been on intimate terms with its charms and that his imagination of those charms remained keen even after he had learned to master them. In his reflections on *Werther* many years afterwards, he describes the Werther period with great affection:

That resolution to let my inner nature go according to its peculiarities, and to let my inner nature influence me according to its qualities, drove me to that strange condition in which "Werther" was designed and written. I endeavored to free myself outwardly from all that was foreign to me, to regard lovingly that which was external, and to allow all creatures from man downwards, so far as they could be comprehended, to work upon me each in its own way. Thus arose a wonderful affinity with the individual objects of Nature and an inner accord, a harmony with the whole, so that every change, whether of places and regions, or of days and seasons, or whatever else might happen, affected me most inwardly.[8]

Goethe goes on to speak of that time as "the precious days of [his] youth," when "the genius of inspiration" worked boldly and impetuously. He is referring to his own creative effort in writing *Werther,* but his reflections curiously blend the reminiscences of that effort and the sentiments and atmosphere of the book itself.

Werther's filial relationship to Jean-Jacques is apparent at once. Like Jean-Jacques of the *Reveries*, he is the solitary walker in fields of beauty, away from the squalors of the town. ("The town itself is not attractive, but I find ample compensation in the indescribable beauties of nature surrounding it.")[9] The feeling of "marvelous gaiety" that fills his "sweet spring mornings" is a token of his spiritual uniqueness. "I am alone and glad to be alive in surroundings such as these, which are created for a soul like mine." And shortly afterward, writing to his friend William, he distinguishes himself from the rest of the human race:

. . . You ask what the people are like here. All I can say is, as they are everywhere else. There is something coldly uniform about the human race. Most of them have to work for the greater part of their lives in order to live and the little freedom they have left frightens them to such an extent that they will stop at nothing to rid themselves of it. Oh, human destiny![10]

The imaginary editor who presents the letters and narrates the portions between has little authority to counteract the effusions of Werther. He may be best described as an amanuensis: a humble, admiring, and sorrowing friend, who will allow Werther the full range of his grief and his claim. Goethe's choice of this kind of editor suggests a protective impulse.

But there is also a strong and persistent criticism directed toward Werther throughout the book, a criticism that is generally accomplished without the direct intrusion of the narrator. The ironic contrast between Werther's early moral pronouncements and the unfolding of his destiny is not lost upon the reader. Thus Werther inveighs against moodiness, the tendency of the soul to surrender its authority to adverse circumstances:

People often complain . . . that there are too few good days and too many bad ones, and as far as I can see, they do so unjustly. If we always kept our hearts wide open to receive the good things God has in store for us daily, we would soon have strength enough to bear the bad when they come.[11]

It is the vicar's wife who objects with a wisdom that turns out to be deeper than Werther's that "our spirit is not ours to shape." Werther agrees that moodiness or ill humor is an ailment of the soul, but he insists that there is a cure, which resides in every man—the will to be happy. He chastises preachers for not sermonizing against the vice of ill humor. In his impassioned plea for happiness, Werther betrays a nervous sensibility that belies his words and which carries a dim anticipation of his own destiny.

> My heart was full. Memories of things past brought the
> tears to my eyes too. 'If only man would tell himself daily:
> you owe your friends nothing but to leave them their joys and
> increase their happiness by sharing it with them.'[12]

The tears in Werther's eyes are tears of compassion. With a fatal ease he enters into the feelings of others, whether they be in books or in life. Thus he distinguishes himself invidiously from Albert, Lotte's husband:

He is not the man to fulfill all her desires. A certain lack of
sensitivity, a lack. . . . Oh, put it any way you like, his heart
does not respond to certain passages in a book in which Lotte's
and mine would meet and on a hundred other occasions. . . .[13]

This is no idle self-congratulation. Werther proves his capacity for sympathy in the most astonishing manner when he takes on himself the burden of the young peasant who has murdered his faithless mistress:

The impact of his horrifying experience created a state of chaos
in his mind. For a moment he was torn out of his grief, his
despondency and indifference to things, and sympathy for the
young man overwhelmed him. He could feel the man's
misery. . . .[14]

And in his defense "Werther set forth in the liveliest fashion and most passionately and truthfully anything and everything that one could possibly say to excuse his neighbor." In his sympathy for the peasant boy, however, Werther is lamenting the loss of Lotte to Albert. The peasant's action—at once a murder and a suicide—is a premonition of Werther's own suicide. The self (the *I*) is the ultimate referent of all of Werther's feelings and actions. His acts of sympathy are forms of self-indulgence: his compassion is the obverse of his egoism.

The antinomian tendency that we have noted in Jean-Jacques is explicitly brought out in Werther. His defense of the young peasant is based on an appeal beyond the law. According to Werther's lights, the young man's misery is sufficient evidence of his innocence (Werther is converting an emotional or spiritual condition into a legal one), and the authority to which he appeals is his own empathic capacity to put himself in the place of the young peasant. "He would feel the man's misery; even as a criminal—he felt the man was innocent; and he could put himself so wholeheartedly into the poor wretch's position that he could make others feel the same way." [15] But the judge is "understandably" unmoved, though he and his sons sympathize with Werther.

He didn't even let Werther finish what he had to say, but disagreed heatedly and reproved him for defending a murderer. He explained that all law would be voided and the security of the state destroyed if Werther's standpoint were accepted, adding that he was in no position to do anything about it without taking grave responsibility upon himself. Everything would have to take its prescribed and orderly course. [16]

Albert, who is present at the hearing, concurs with this view. Indeed, he gives to the judgment a special resonance when he says, "the man is doomed." With characteristic egoism, Werther detects resentment against himself in these words.

The "editor" delicately intrudes at this point to endorse the view of Albert and the judge: "After giving the matter more thought, the fact could not have escaped him that both men were right." But the narrator also perceives that Werther could never have admitted this. To do so he would have had to deny his "innermost" self. Werther's defense of the peasant does not spring from any conviction about justice or morality: it is rather based on the bond of compassion or sympathy, a feeling (like his egoism) that goes to the very roots of his vitality. "Werther's vain effort to save the unfortunate man was the last flickering flame of a light that was dying."[17]

Despite the fact that Werther's suffering is vague and unfocused and that he does not avoid cliché ("Yes, I am a wanderer on this earth—a pilgrim. Are you anything more than that?"), we are moved by the authenticity of the suffering. One of the achievements of *The Sorrows of Werther* is the deftness with which Goethe suggests the sociological basis of the suffering. Werther has the sensitivity of the aristocrat without the status and authority. Like Jean-Jacques, he is exquisitely sensitive to insult. (Jean-Jacques' paranoia creates it when he cannot discover it.) Werther's conviction that he is spiritually unique is insufficient sustenance to his ego. He needs the assurance that he is loved by those who matter. "Count von C. is very fond of me. He singles me out—but you know all that. I have mentioned it a hundred times."[18] Werther himself is aware of the contradiction in his attitude. After the rude rebuff that he suffers at the Count's party, he writes to his friend: "I could run a knife into my heart! Because people can say what they like about being independent—show me the man who can stand being raked over the coals by scoundrels."[19] The image of the knife is not fortuitous. Werther's agony over the rebuff at the Count's party continues to mount, and his imagination returns to the knife, this time in connection with another extraordinary image.

Oh, I have picked up a knife a hundred times with the intention of plunging it into my heart! I have heard tell of a noble breed of stallions who, when they are overheated and run wild, instinctively open one of their veins to relieve themselves. I feel like that often. I would like to open the veins that would give me eternal freedom.[20]

He is soon to obtain this "freedom."

Werther's connection with the aristocracy suggests that the real theme of the book is his uncertain self-esteem, not his love for Lotte. The passion for Lotte intensifies Werther's uncertainty; it is not the cause of the uncertainty. In an early letter to William, Werther writes: "One thing is certain—nothing justifies a man's existence like being loved."[21] The statement pertains to Lotte, but is equally pertinent to the Count von C. and all those whose affection Werther needs if he is to survive. He is one of those creatures, soon to become legion in European literature, who *live* in their capacity to love and be loved. "When [Lotte] speakes of her betrothed with warmth and love, then I am a man degraded, robbed of his honor, title and sword."[22] Lotte herself perceives Werther's weakness when she exhorts him to "be more manly." [23] Werther retains his nobility and beauty to the end, but he is a hero or martyr of love, and the heroism of love is essentially feminine, as Flaubert and Tolstoy knew—a heroism of intense passivity, of willed disintegration. One of the great illuminations in *Anna Karenina* is Vronsky *diminished* by his passion for Anna. In order to recover his manly purposes, Vronsky must break with her.

Though Goethe's perception of the trouble in Werther is penetrating and unequivocal, he does not mean to be didactic. Albert judges Werther rather severely (he shows a distaste for emotional excesses and makes a harsh anticipatory judgment of suicide), but Werther's own perception of Albert as an insensitive though good man seriously qualifies Albert's authority. We have already noted Lotte's cautionary words to Werther and her severe reproach of unmanliness; yet they are so informed with sympathy and love that we are more aware of the solicitude than of the judgment. Everything in the tale seems to cherish Werther without sanctioning his behavior. It is therefore not puzzling that *The Sorrows of Werther* should have been taken up by the youth of Goethe's time as a program for a mode of feeling rather than as a dramatic critique of a phenomenon that Goethe had observed in himself and others.

But the motive of Goethe's sympathy has yet to be understood in the light of his unillusioned view of Werther. The sympathy is not that of a diagnostician or clinician. There is comparatively little analysis in the tale: Goethe allows Werther to bear the major burden of narration, and there is a cherishing lyricism throughout. The tale is not governed by a cautionary intention: what a waste of splendid gifts to indulge oneself in this manner! Werther has value in what he is, in the fate that he enacts. When Werther proclaims the virtues of the heart over those of the mind, he speaks with the authority of Goethe. "[The Prince] seems to value my mind and my various talents more than this heart of mine, of which I am so proud, for it is the source of all things—all strength, all bliss, all misery."[24]

Goethe's sympathy for Werther—and for all the Werther characters in his work*—comes out of his conception of psychology. In a letter to Schiller on the death of his daughter, Goethe writes:

> One knows not whether in such cases it is better to let sorrow take its natural course, or to repress it by the various aids which culture offers us. If one decides upon the latter method, *as I always do*, one is only strengthened for a moment; and I have observed that nature always asserts her right through some other crisis.[25]

The vulnerability of the moral idea makes the *insistence* on the control of natural energies a sort of blasphemy against life. This does not mean that the moral idea is done away with. Quite the contrary, every means should be found to strengthen it, but a rude disregard for the rebellious energies will not accomplish that purpose. As Goethe's Tasso remarks:

> 'Tis somewhat perilous to have to seem
> For ever sage and moderate. There lurks
> An evil genius, always at one's side,
> Who will, what'er we do, from time to time
> Seize on his victim.[26]

---

* He speaks somewhere of Eduard (the hero of *Elective Affinities*), for instance, as a heightened Werther.

Goethe himself exhibited a remarkable capacity for subduing the rebellious energies—as he says, it is his habit to avail himself of the various aids which culture offers—but he did not propose this habit as a universal model. As he suggested in the letter to Schiller, he suspected its efficacy. It is for this reason that he was so responsive to a character like Byron, who in contrast to Goethe allowed nature always to assert her rights. At the same time, Goethe repudiates willful exacerbations of rebellious energy. Nature must be allowed to assert her "right," but the deliberate cultivation of new extravagant rights should not be encouraged. Thus Goethe qualifies his admiration for Bryon when he criticizes "his perpetual negation and fault-finding," which are "injurious even to his excellent works."[27] Goethe separates himself from the nihilistic tendency in romanticism, not because it is immoral, but because it is destructive. "The great point is, not to pull down, but to build up; in this humanity finds pure joy."

One of the great themes of Goethe's work is the tension between natural energies and the forms of civilization. For all of Goethe's faith in the beneficence of nature, he sees the tension as essentially tragic. It is true that his masterpiece *Faust* is characterized, as Eric Heller has remarked, by an avoidance of the tragic.[28] But to say that Goethe *avoids* the tragic implies that the tendency of his imagination is tragic. And there is certainly no avoidance in *Werther* or, say, *Elective Affinities*.

Goethe is able to take the edge off the tragic in *Elective Affinities* by exploring the possibilities of accommodation.

"If your resolution to renounce Eduard is so firm and unalterable," Charlotte retorted on this occasion, "you must be careful of the danger of seeing him again. When we are far from the person we love, and the deeper our affection is, the more we apparently succeed in controlling ourselves, because the whole force of our passion, formerly directed outward, is now turned inward; but how soon and how quickly do we discover our self-deception when the person we thought we

could renounce stands suddenly before us and seems more
indispensable to us than ever. You must now do what you
think is most suitable in your case. Examine your heart; you
may even change your present resolution; but do it of yourself,
with a free, determined heart. Do not let yourself be drawn
back into the former state of things, either by chance or by
surprise, because this would destroy your inner harmony and
be unbearable for you. As I have said: before you take this step,
before you leave me and start a new life which may lead you
no one knows where, think once more can you really give
Eduard up for good and all?"[29]

The didactic tone of this passage should not mislead us about
the objectivity with which Goethe views the career of passion.
Charlotte's "injunction" to Ottilie, intelligent as it is, is of
no avail, because it does not account for Eduard's behavior,
which makes for tragedy. To convert *Elective Affinities,* as
Victor Lange does, for instance, into a morality novel is to
fail to see its exploratory and tragic character. Lange writes:

For marriage—and here, if anywhere, emerges the main theme
of the novel—is the most conspicuous instance (and the most
confounding) of a form, a symbol which to experience in its
total cultural significance, requires the complete exertion of
man. In marriage, Goethe means to say, civilization fulfills
itself because it is there that we are led to recognize and realize
the dynamic interplay of reason and submission, of natural
instinct and of faith in the presence of spirit.[30]

The novel is not a lesson in the benefits of marriage. On the
contrary, it explores the problematic and tragic nature of
marriage. As much as his imagination seeks to discover the
possibilities of fulfillment and harmony, Goethe is (at his
best) fully conscious of the hostile demons that circumscribe
those possibilities. Indeed, the character of Mittler, with his
Benthamite practical wisdom, is intended as a parody of the
moralistic response to passion.

If Goethe's wisdom irritates the modern sensibility, it is
because the self-possession on which it is based is old-
fashioned. I have spoken of Goethe's sensitivity and suscep-

tibility to the new spirit that Rousseau and Byron had created, but (as Goethe reveals in his letter to Schiller) the sensitivity is under check. One gets the impression from his life and his utterances that he would permit nothing to disturb his painfully achieved equilibrium. Mann somewhere speaks of Goethe's "endangered friendship" with life.[31] (Late in life he strenuously avoided the sight of a dead body.) Though Goethe's remark about controlling every new "emancipation of the spirit" may be an ideal remark, the modern reader may wonder whether Goethe was aware of the possibility that certain extreme "liberations of the spirit" are insusceptible of control—whether, in other words, the disorder they bring into the world may not be their ultimate condition. In Goethe (despite his sensitivity to the demonic) there is an eighteenth-century faith in cosmic beneficence, which is relatively untouched by the new "emancipation of the spirit." The faith in cosmic beneficence is the philosophical counterpart of the psychological self-possession that permitted him to enjoy with reservations the Werther destiny.* This stiff self-possession, which makes for didacticism, qualifies Goethe's fundamental perception of the tragic tensions in human life.

To return to Werther, though the path of suicide was not for Goethe (the book is an act of exorcism of the demons that threatened his own life), he acknowledges and even respects the fate which Werther was driven to enact. There is even a demonic element in Werther's "sentimentality." Finding pleasure in the impossible, Werther is a driven man, enacting a necessity that he can undo only if he undoes himself. And for all his vulnerability, he exerts an extraordinary power over his reader—as do men of demonic power.

Goethe's compassion (in *Werther*) is not Olympian, for to be Olympian is to condescend from a superior vantage point of wisdom, and the wisdom of *The Sorrows of Werther* is precisely in Goethe's self-possessed nearness to his hero.

---

* In his maturity he thought the book and the character immature.

Nobody belongs to the world as a moral being. These fine, general demands are to be made by each of himself; whatever is lacking in them he should make right with God and his own heart, and he should convince his neighbor of what is true and good in him. On the other hand, in the character which Nature has given him in particular, as a man of force, activity, intellect and talent, he belongs to the world. Everything that is excellent can work only for an infinite sphere, and so let the world accept it with gratitude and not imagine that it is entitled to sit in judgment in any other sense than that.[32]

This passage cannot be read as an endorsement of Werther, because Werther has withheld from the world the force, activity, intellect, and talent which belong to it. In Goethe's mature view, man is born to be a doer, and activity for Goethe involved a certain self-renunciation. But with his extra-ordinary imaginative flexibility, Goethe would never permit the value of activity to harden into a dogma, and therefore he is free to respond to the passive and lyric character of Werther. Goethe personally recoils from the excess of Werther's commitment to the needs of his heart: his un-willingness, indeed inability, to compromise the inevitable outrage that the sensitive soul feels in an obtuse and un-comprehending world. This is the blasphemy of the cult of feeling: the implicit belief that personal suffering has no boundaries. God, society, morality: all give way to an all-encompassing suffering. Werther's suicide is a supreme manifestation of this exaltation of suffering. Goethe developed an armor to protect himself from his own Wertherian propensities, and he earned a reputation in his later years for coldness and aloofness, but he never denied the value of the Werther destiny.*

---

* There is no finer, no more incisive statement about Werther's value than the passage in Schiller's justly celebrated essay "On Naive and Sentimental Poetry." The view is sympathetic but unillusioned, very much in the spirit of the narrative voice and point of view of Goethe's book. Schiller sees *The Sorrows of Werther* as the supreme embodiment of sentimental poetry, which risks the poetic hubris of ignoring the limitations of human life in order to realize or inhabit the atmosphere of some impossible dream. (See Friedrich Schiller, *Essays Aesthetical and Philosophical,* pp. 306–7.)

Goethe is distinguished by his capacity for assimilation and development: his life confirms the legend of his catholicity. He made rejections, but he absorbed—or tried to absorb—everything of value that he had experienced. He passes beyond his Werther period, but without leaving it behind. The exquisite, delicate, even feminine nature of Werther is a permanent legacy in Goethe's thought and feeling, to be found again and again, for instance, in his lyric verse.

II

This is not how Carlyle, the midwife of Goethe's poetry and thought in England and America, understood Werther. *Sartor Resartus* (1834) turns *The Sorrows of Werther* into a tendentious exhortation to self-renunciation in work.*

The importance of *Sartor Resartus* is in its capacity to generalize the experience of its hero into a cultural destiny. Much of the book is hard to penetrate, a curio of style with flashes of remarkable perception and charm; however, in the chapters concerning the spiritual crisis of its hero ("The Everlasting No," "The Center of Indifference," and "The Everlasting Yea"), Carlyle managed for the first time in English literature the accommodation of romanticism to society. That accommodation helped create the ethos that we call Victorianism. The main interest of *Sartor Resartus* is in the unromantic decision of its romantic hero, Teufelsdröckh, to surrender the claims of the self to what he conceived to be the higher claims of society. Teufelsdröckh suffers from Wertherism (one of the chapters is entitled

---

* Goethe's admiration for Carlyle's early essays on German literature should not be taken as an endorsement of Carlyle's philosophical views. Carlyle's major work was written after Goethe's death.

"The Sorrows of Teufelsdröckh"), that spiritual disease * to which Goethe gave classic expression: self-absorption, a yearning for the infinite, isolation from the world out of a thwarted sense of one's superiority and the corresponding unworthiness of the world.

It is clear from the manner of *Sartor* that we are not to expect the same responsiveness to Teufelsdröckh's claims that Goethe exhibits toward those of Werther. The author has come into an edition of Teufelsdröckh's writings, so we hear three voices: the voices of the narrator, Teufelsdröckh, and his editor, Hofrath Heushrecke. Carlyle's distance from his hero enables him to direct a steady stream of irony toward him: "Professor der Allerly-Wissenschaft who had never delivered any course."[33] The philosophy itself is characterized as an " 'extensive Volume,' of boundless, almost formless contents, a very Sea of Thought; neither calm nor clear, if you will; yet wherein the toughest pearl-diver may dive to his utmost depth, and return not only with sea-wreck but with true orients."[34]

The irony is never destructive, nor is the extravagant manner of presenting Teufelsdröckh necessarily an indication that Carlyle intends irony. He presents some of his favorite ideas in an extravagant verbal manner, the extravagance often being a matter of personal idiosyncrasy. At the same time, the manner enables Carlyle to cast Teufelsdröckh's romantic *schwarmerei* and Byronic hypochondria in an absurd light. Thus Teufelsdröckh's melancholy view of his beloved Blumine in the company of Herr Towgood—"With slight unrecognizing salutation they passed me; plunged down amid the neighboring thickets, onwards to Heaven, and to England; and I, in my friend Richter's words, *I remained alone, behind them, with the Night*"—is followed by a typical satiric stroke:

---

* In "Characteristics" (1831) Carlyle defines health as the full integration of the individual in the life of the community. The medical metaphor is pursued throughout the essay. (*Critical and Miscellaneous Essays*, vol. 3.)

Were it not cruel in these circumstances, here might be the place to insert an observation, gleaned long ago from the great *Clothes-Volume*, where it stands with quite other intent: 'Some time before Small-pox was extirpated,' says the Professor, 'there came a new malady of the spiritual sort on Europe: I mean the epidemic, now endemical, of View-hunting. Poets of old date, being privileged with Senses, had also enjoyed external Nature; but chiefly as we enjoy the crystal cup which holds good or bad liquor for us; that is to say, in silence, or with slight incidental commentary: never, as I compute, till after the *Sorrows of Werther*, was there man found who would say: Come let us make a Description! Having drunk the liquor, come let us eat the glass . . .'[35]

Carlyle's view of Byron is a measure of the difference between him and Goethe—a difference that Carlyle himself never perceived. In an early essay on Byron, Carlyle writes:

Byron was our English Sentimentalist and Power-man; the strongest of his kind in Europe; the wildest, the gloomiest and it may be hoped the last. For what good is it to 'whine, put finger i' the eye, and sob' in such a case? Still more, to snarl and snap in malignant wise, 'like dog distract, or monkey sick.' Why should we quarrel with our existence, here as it lies before us, our field and inheritance, to make or to mar, for better or for worse.[36]

For Carlyle, Byronism was a form of selfishness and a source of misery: "the school of Satan"[37] (in the denunciatory mood of *Sartor*) or the cultivation of idle, visionary dreams (in the chiding mood of "Signs of the Times").[38] Or consider Carlyle's judgment of Rousseau in *Heroes and Hero-Worship*. Reluctantly conceding him a place as a heroic Man of Letters, Carlyle quickly discovers his fault, *Egoism,* and the result is that "his books, like himself, are what I call unhealthy, not the good sort."[39] (Rousseau, for Carlyle, is little more than the sincere man par excellence.) The passage on Rousseau is incisive in discovering Jean-Jacques' malaise, but in judgmental puritan fashion, Carlyle is unwilling to concede it any value. Goethe would have been incapable of striking this harsh puritan note. His vision was of a more catholic and generous order.

The difference is again apparent in the different fates of Teufelsdröckh and Werther, and in the conclusion that Carlyle draws from his hero's experiences. The alternative to the Werther fate (suicide) is some form of self-renunciation. We find it in stoicism, in Christianity, in Goethe himself— but with a difference. In a famous passage, Carlyle gives us his moral formula:

. . . *the Fraction of Life can be increased in value not so much by increasing your Numerator (of Satisfaction) as by lessening your Denominator (of desire).* Nay, unless my Algebra deceive me Unity itself divided by Zero will give *Infinity*. Make thy claims of wages a zero, then; thou hast the world under thy feet. Well did the wisest of our time* write: 'It is only with Renunciation (*Entsagen*) that Life, properly speaking, can be said to begin.'[40]

The *Entsagen* of Carlyle should not be confused with stoicism, despite that part of his mathematical metaphor which exhorts the reader to reduce the denominator of desire to zero. If we pursue the metaphor, as Carlyle does, the resulting quotient is infinity. And what stoic, we may ask, ever conceived the rewards of self-renunciation to be infinity? Nor is it possible to reconcile the grimness and essential pessimism of stoicism with the exaltation of Carlyle's *Entsagen*.

. . . the Self in thee needed to be annihilated. By benignant fever paroxysms is Life rooting out the deep-seated chronic Diseases and triumphs over Death. On the rearing billows of Time, thou are not engulfed, but borne aloft in the azure of Eternity. Love not Pleasure; love God. This is the EVERLASTING YEA, wherein all contradiction is solved: wherein whosoever walks and works, it is well with him.[41]

The ecstasy of losing oneself to find oneself seems closer to Christianity, but here again a distinction must be made. Elsewhere in *Sartor,* Carlyle makes it clear that the traditional

---

* Goethe, of course.

Christian embodiment (mythos) of the spiritual life of man is no longer possible and speaks of the necessity of creating a new mythos. What remains to Carlyle is a belief in the values of the spiritual life, but he can, significantly, express those values only in the language of German transcendentalism. The concretely ritualized experience of the Christian on his way to salvation yields to an abstract conceptualization of the experience. Carlyle himself is, in this respect, guilty of the spiritual nakedness that he understood to be characteristic of Byronism.

Teufelsdröckh's crisis is the crisis of romanticism—that of the spirit nakedly contemplating itself, unable to embody itself in the practical life. "The authentic Church-Catechism of our present century has not yet fallen into my hands: meanwhile, for my private behoof, I attempt to elucidate the matter so." [42] Carlyle may not have found the new mythos, but he has indicated its locus in *Sartor*. "I had learned to look into the business of the World in its details." [43] For Carlyle, the new godhead is society, and the new form of worship is doing the work of the world.

The romantic self, then, has been converted from its total claim upon the world to a self-denying participation in the work of the community. Goethe seems to have been beforehand in all this, having gone from the Wertherism of his youth to the classical serenity of his manhood and old age. And in *Sartor,* as we know, Carlyle gives Goethe his due: "Close your Byron, Open your Goethe." [44] Goethe's conversion to an Olympian repose (a repose that permitted him a sympathy with alien modes of thought and feeling), however, scarcely suggests the dramatic resolution of Teufelsdröckh's crisis. The exultation of Carlyle's language in describing the rebirth into "selflessness," his characterization of it as blessedness (rather than merely freedom from pain, as one might expect), his suggestion in the mathematical metaphor that the rebirth into selflessness is a movement from the finite to the infinite: all this strongly implies that romanticism has survived, though in an inverted form. Carlyle's romanticism is complicated by the fact that he is rejecting a purer version of it. In behalf of a spiritual idea of the *conditioned* character of human existence, Carlyle rejects the romantic aspiration for infinity.

That the Thoughtforms, Space and Time, wherein, once for all, we are sent into this Earth to live, should condition and determine our whole Practical reasonings, conceptions, and imagings or imaginings—seems altogether fit, just and unavoidable.[45]

If accompanied by the knowledge that man can never escape the conditions of his finitude, the gesture toward the infinite becomes a mark of a man's greatness. "Nay, what is Philosophy throughout but a continual battle against Custom; an ever-renewed effort to *transcend* the sphere of blind custom, and so become Transcendental?"[46] The impulse to dramatize the self survives, paradoxically, in the act of self-renunciation.

. . . When your Ideal World, wherein the whole man has
been dimly struggling and inexpressibly languishing to work,
becomes revealed, and thrown open; and you discover,
with amazement enough, like the Lothario in Wilhelm Meister,
that your 'America is here or nowhere'? The situation that has
not its Duty, its Ideal, was never yet occupied by man.
Yes here, in this poor, miserable, hampered, despicable
Actual, wherein thou even now standest, here or nowhere
is thy idea: work it out therefrom; and working believe,
live, be free. Fool! The Ideal is in thyself, the impediment too
is in thyself: thy Condition is but the stuff thou art to shape
that same Ideal out of: what matters whether such stuff
be this sort or that, so the Form thou give it be heroic,
be poetic? . . .
    'I too could now say to myself: Be no longer a Chaos,
but a World, or even Worldkin. Produce! Produce! Were it
but the pitifullest infinitesimal fraction of a Product, produce
it, in God's name! 'Tis the utmost thou hast in thee: out with it,
then. Up, up! Whatsoever thy hand findeth to do, do it with
thy whole might. Work while it is called Today;
for the Night cometh, wherein no man can work.'[47]

The style in its unabated frenetic quality suggests that the resolution is something of an abstraction. The self will continue giddily to impose itself upon the world, will suffer the pain of rebuff (or indifference) with a jauntiness learned from long battle with the universe. But the self, craving its happiness, will not be satisfied. We must feel uneasy, then, about Carlyle's claim that *Entsagen,* as it is imaginatively rendered in *Sartor Resartus,* is, to use the modern idiom, the only therapy for the diseased romantic soul. There is something to be said for what Mill called the anti-self-consciousness theory of happiness, and Mill has said it. The habit of referring everything to one's desire for happiness may produce the feeling of emptiness that possessed Mill in his early manhood. By absorbing oneself in activity, one may be surprised by happiness. Mill found the idea in *Sartor Resartus,* and much of our appreciation of the book comes from Mill's statement about it in the remarkable chapter on "The Mental Crisis" in his *Autobiography*. But the idea is an appropriation from the full meaning of the experience. For the anti-self-consciousness theory can work only if the objects and activities are adequate to the energy. It is a fine theory for an impoverished temperament like Mill's, or for a harmonious nature like Goethe's. For Carlyle-Teufelsdröckh, however, suffering from an overabundance of feeling, the conversion to "the business of the world" might exacerbate rather than subdue the energy.

III

Carlyle's claim to have discovered the secret of psychic and moral health mistakes the significance of Teufelsdröckh's conversion. For one of the effects of the social imperative which Carlyle was the first to exalt is the imaginative schizophrenia of the Victorian poets. E. D. H. Johnson has shown how the major Victorian poets (Tennyson, Browning, Arnold) were torn between the exigencies of their romantic demon and the utilitarian demands that Victorian society had imposed upon them.[48] The split is the most marked in Tennyson—between the socially useful laureate poems and the shrill romantic antisocial poems uttered through the personae of madmen. This split is already implicit in Teufelsdröckh's conversion—the failure to subdue the old romantic energy to the self-renunciation. The failure is never formulated in *Sartor Resartus*, for Carlyle-Teufelsdröckh believes that the conversion is a success. But the reader experiences the enormous strain of Teufelsdröckh's attempt to commit the energy to the social ideal. The tempestuous Teufelsdröckh confines his impulse toward self-dramatization within the moral role only at the price of gnashing of teeth, exasperation, and recurrent accesses of feelings of impotence. Throughout Carlyle's work we are given exhibitions of the will strenuously and eccentrically trying to deny itself.

It should be noted here that Goethe's conception of self-renunciation is not in the service of a narrow social ideal. Goethe had a vision of the organic wholeness of life. Though Carlyle shared Goethe's view of the world as an organism, Carlyle's doctrine has a decidedly social and political emphasis. For Goethe, nature was an intricate harmony of flora and fauna, which he observed with a combination of "scientific passion" and romantic love. Goethe never tired of scientific observation; indeed, at times he valued it above his poetic achievements.[49] Carlyle is responsive to the natural world, but his real interest is in the social and political community of men. In this respect, Carlyle is closer to Burke than to Goethe.

The social cast of Carlyle's thought helps explain his mistrust of the egoism of the romantic poets. "For a great while yet, most of them will fly off into 'Literature,' into what they call Art, Poetry and the like; and will mainly waste themselves in that inane region."[50] Carlyle's philistinism—for this is what his mistrust of romantic egoism amounts to—is betrayed in his paeans to work.

All work, even cotton-spinning, is noble; work is alone noble: be that here said and asserted once more.[51]

> On the whole, we do entirely agree with those old Monks, *Laborare est Orare*. In a thousand senses, from one end of it to the other, true Work is Worship. He that works, whatsoever be his work, he shows forth the form of things unseen; a small Poet every Worker is.[52]

> The vulgarest Plugson of a Master-worker, who can command Workers, and get work out of them is already a considerable man.[53]

Our sensitivity to the work ethic is perhaps sharper than that of Carlyle's contemporaries, because of our experience of the inadequacies of the work ethic in a technological society. Carlyle, to be sure, distinguished between the ennobling creative work of the hero-worker and the degrading work of the factory operative. But the frenetic emphasis on work at a moment when all of society is in a frenzy of material growth and achievement betrays a failure in Carlyle to perceive exactly where his interests lay. Carlyle wanted to exploit the opportunities of the new society, and he deserves praise for seeing human opportunities in the mechanical revolution; but his overeagerness to exploit them compromised his achievement. It is an ironic commentary on Carlyle's view of the social-political situation that his vision of a heroic alliance between the captains of industry and the aristocracy should materialize in the inglorious Victorian compromise.

Carlyle reveals his philistinism in a more oblique manner in his uneasiness in the presence of the demonic. Carlyle knew what it was to be pursued by demons (of Rousseau: "his ideas *possessed* him like daemons; hurried him so about, drove him over steep places";[54] there is not a little of this in Carlyle himself, whose own demonic drive was somewhat offset by a jocose humor). In Carlyle, however, the demon is socialized in the form of the hero-worker, who competently performs his social and historical tasks: Abbot Samson, Sir Robert Peel, and the Captains of Industry (potentially, at least). Unlike Goethe, who saw the demonic and the moral order as crossing each other like "warp and woof" (the tapestry of life itself), Carlyle sees the world as chaotic and abysmal, if the demons are not governed by the moral order. In his judgment of Napoleon, a touchstone of the demonic, Carlyle betrays the strenuous Hebraism of his moral temperament:

The fatal charlatan-element got the upper hand. . . . Self and false ambition had now become his god. . . . This Napoleonism was *unjust,* a falsehood and could not last. It is true doctrine. The heavier this Napoleon trampled on the world holding it tyrannously down, the fiercer would the world's recoil against him be, one day. Injustice pays itself with frightful compound-interest.[55] *

The subordination of the demonic to the moral is the basis of Carlyle's belief in the organic community. Like Burke, Carlyle attacked the spirit of innovation which proceeded from the Enlightenment belief in a progressive combat between the moral imagination and the traditional and natural resistances of the community. For Carlyle, the demon—that is, the unconscious—of the community was wise, healthy, and moral. Having socialized the demon, Carlyle was able to characterize the unconscious as the repository of social motive and moral impulse. The destructive element was introduced when the theoretic mind prevailed. In the early essay "Characteristics," Carlyle envisages the healthy organic community in the metaphor of the physical body:

To figure Society as endowed with life is scarcely a metaphor. . . . Look at it closely, that mystic Union, Nature's highest work with man, wherein man's volition plays an indispensable yet so subordinate a part, and the small Mechanical grows so mysteriously and indissolubly out of the infinite Dynamical, like Body out of Spirit—is truly enough vital, and bears the distinguishing character of life. In the same style also, we can say that Society has its periods of sickness and vigour, of youth, manhood, decrepitude, dissolution and new birth; in one or

---

* Napoleon is, of course, not above criticism. It is with Carlyle's manner that I am concerned.

other of which stages we may, in all times, and all places
where men inhabit, discern it; and do ourselves, in this time
and place, whether as cooperating or as contending, as healthy
members or as diseased ones, to our joy and sorrow,
form part of it.[56]

Carlyle's subsuming of the demonic under the social
category in his imperious and strident way was an arbitrary
act, an expression of will rather than of intelligence. The
demonic, denied in this fashion, was bound to reassert and
avenge itself for such disrespectful treatment. The aestheticism
of Wilde and Swinburne can be understood as the revenge of
the demonic against the presumption that it could be contained in this manner. The demonic force of English
aestheticism, however, was extremely attenuated—as if the
long hegemony of the social conscience had taken the heart
out of the demon. There is a disquieting tameness about
Wilde and Swinburne: after an encounter with them one
longs for their French counterparts, Baudelaire and Rimbaud,
who had happily never suffered the tyranny of a Victorian
moral aesthetic.

"Spirit," "vitality," "dynamic": these are characteristic
words in Carlyle's vocabulary. He meant to restore to them
the meaning they had lost in the decaying institutional life
of Christianity. But the words retain for Carlyle their conventional moral meanings (despite the rhetorical fireworks)
and emerge almost as emasculated as before the effort of
rejuvenation. This is precisely the effort of romanticism, and
Carlyle, it would seem, inadvertently contributed to its defeat.

IV

The political counterpart of Carlyle's antiromanticism is an
antilibertarian position. His abhorrence of Mill's essay *On
Liberty* is consistent with his general position, but it does
betray an inconsistency within the position. One might think
that Carlyle would have found Mill a kindred spirit when

Mill disparages the modern "tendency in the best beliefs and practices to degenerate into the mechanical" or when he insists "emphatically on the importance of genius, and the necessity of allowing it to unfold itself freely both in thought and practice."[57] With all his faith in the hero and hero worship, Carlyle failed to see (as "the logic-chopping" Mill saw so clearly) that the vividness and greatness of society are reflected in the socially antithetic individuals that inhabit the society—that an individuality that is profound and courageous is not necessarily a menace to social life, but may even be an enrichment of it. It is ironic that the supreme rationalist of the age should have written perhaps the definitive *political* rationale for romanticism. And it is a complementary irony that one of the great apologists for heroism and the organic community should have harbored what can only be characterized as a repressive, one might say mechanistic, social doctrine. In Carlyle's view, the individual automatically had a social role, which he rejected only at the price of losing his soul.

This is perhaps to put the case against Carlyle's "moral earnestness" too strongly. His authentic visionary power can be found in the portraits of heroic historical personages and in his perception of historical situations. These perceptions are often penetrating, and without moral blinders. But the Hebraistic tendency in Carlyle tends to undermine his own antiutilitarian bias. In some of his early essays, Carlyle shows himself sensitive to the poet's claim for autonomy. "Art is to be loved, not because of its effects, but because of itself; not because it is useful for spiritual pleasure or even for moral culture, but because it is Art, and the highest in man, and the soul of all beauty."[58] But this fine implicit defense of the poet's right to follow "selfishly" the bent of his own imagination, wherever it may lead, must be contrasted with the judgment of Byron, the mistrust of the demonic, the impatience with literature in "Shooting Niagara."

In endorsing the romantic view of the autonomy of the poet, I am aware that I am precariously skirting a banality about the freedom and integrity of the artistic imagination. I should want, however, to separate myself from the comfort which the slogan of artistic freedom gives. For the slogan is a banality when it is attended by a belief in the innocuousness of art. Thus the characteristic effort of "liberal" critics to justify an interest in Swift, Nietzsche, or Lawrence by showing them to be conventional after all. And if they are conventional, what harm can they do? Modern criticism too has provided an easy justification for artistic freedom, by arguing for the intransitive and self-enclosed character of art. Censorship is thus an irrelevant response to art. The critic does not feel that he has to defend *Ulysses* or *Lady Chatterley's Lover* against substantive charges like obscenity and immorality. The defense need only concern itself with the artfulness of the work.

It is to the credit of Carlyle and the other Victorian critics that they perceived the explosive spiritual *substance* of literature. Literature made a difference and had to be taken seriously as a social force. What Carlyle failed to grasp—what his Calvinism prevented him from grasping—was that the spiritual interest could express itself as a social threat, an impossible demand; that a demonic art, for instance, might teach us the value of cultivating certain passions at the expense of every social obligation.

One might want to mediate between a visionary (antisocial) art and society. This has, in fact, been part of the task of the social criticism of the nineteenth and twentieth centuries. But a genuine and mutually enriching mediation cannot occur if either term of the mediation is canceled. (Arnold saw the preservation of the tension as one of the tasks of criticism: "It must be apt to study and praise elements that for the fulness of spiritual perfection are wanted, even though they belong to a power which in the practical sphere may be maleficent. It must be apt to discern the spiritual shortcomings or illusions of powers that in the practical sphere may be beneficent." [59]) Out of an extraordinary insensitivity to the claims of the poet—one might add to the claims of his own raging imaginative energy—Carlyle prematurely committed the poetic imagination to the social conscience. In doing so, he unwittingly subordinated the spiritual to the practical interest and revealed himself not as the sage, but as a sign of the times.

I am here anticipating later chapters on the artist-hero, for that is where the argument for the value of egoism (in its lyric and demonic forms) inevitably leads. It was Goethe's wisdom, distorted and vulgarized by Carlyle, to see both the value and the problems in the new egoism.

A final word about the respective attitudes of Goethe and Carlyle toward politics. Carlyle, without political power, was drawn to it. His admiration for Sir Robert Peele, a kind of hero worship (occasioned by Peele's courageous leadership in the repeal of the Corn Laws), had to suffer Peele's untimely death. Carlyle's increasing disenchantment with the possibility of political salvation within the frame of existing possibilities turned him in the direction of authoritarianism, of which *Latter-Day Pamphlets* is an expression. Goethe, on the other hand, had a long career as the "prime minister," so to speak, of the small duchy of Weimar. At one time or other, he had experience of virtually every position of political power. But he remained indifferent, almost militantly indifferent, to political ideas. Or, one might say, his indifference itself constitutes an idea.

George Henry Lewes, one of his earliest and best biographers, remarks that since Germany never really constituted a nation in the nineteenth century, its fierce nationalism and patriotism were actuated by negative motives: for instance, its envy and hatred of France. Goethe wanted no part of the vulgarity of this patriotism. He even thought that the strength of the Germans might be in their freedom from nationalist passions. He wanted to see them develop as individuals and citizens of the world. Thus he advocates the development of inward culture and an indifference to the burning nationalistic questions of the day.

This indifference provoked a judgment against which

Goethe's admirers (Lewes among them) tried hard to defend him. It is amusing to see Lewes adduce evidence of Goethe's kindness and generosity to friends and acquaintances in an effort to combat the charge of egoism. The case is complicated. It is impossible to deny the coldness and self-centeredness of Goethe in his later years. In the image of Mann's *Lotte in Weimar,* he was the taper to which the moths were attracted and by which they were sometimes consumed.[60] There is a vivid imaginative account in Mann's novel of how Goethe prevented his son from enlisting in the Prussian cause, because he required him for secretarial duties. This was only the most notable episode in the unmanning of August, about which Goethe seems to have had little conscience. August, of course, shared the extravagantly worshipful attitude of the circle and lent himself to the unmanning. And yet it is also hard to deny the feeling that the ultimate wisdom about the Prussian cause was Goethe's, and that the real interest of his attitude toward it has little to do with whatever private selfishness motivated him. Mann is very sensitive to the complication: he does not blink the egoism, but the wisdom is reserved for Goethe. Mann has Goethe reproach the idealistic young schoolmaster, Dr. Passow:

Nothing is less my wish, Herr Doctor, than to hurt your feelings. I know you mean well. But it is not enough to mean well, or even nobly. One must also be able to see the consequences of one's activities. I shudder at yours, because they are the first manifestation, as yet quite high-minded and harmless, of something frightful, to be displayed some day by us Germans in the form of the crassest follies. You yourself, if you could know of them, would turn in your grave.[61]

Mann is imagining Goethe with the retrospective knowledge of naziism. The nationalism that Goethe condemned may have enlisted the idealistic sentiments of noble and generous spirits, but the content of that nationalism, as Goethe divined, was a megalomaniac form of egoism—which is the dream of personal power in a nationalistic guise. Goethe responded to the incipient megalomania by refusing to be involved in the national political life.

It is not fair to see in Goethe's indifference to political thought (as some have seen) the polarization between the intellectual life and the common life in modern Germany. It might perhaps be more accurate to say that this polarization is a distortion or an exaggeration of something in Goethe, for as I have already noted, Goethe's indifference to political thought was accompanied by an intense political career. Indeed, his own life might be taken as a model for the place of politics in one's life. A necessity like housing and nutrition, politics is a necessary condition for sustaining what is most significant in human life—culture. Goethe's political quality can be seen in his effort to establish in Weimar the conditions for a new Athens. The remarkably fruitful friendship of Goethe and Schiller, which among other things produced the theater in Weimar, owes its success in part to the atmosphere that the political Goethe created in Weimar. In his *Social History of Art,* Arnold Hauser speaks of the cultural backwardness of the German people in the nineteenth century, citing Goethe's relative artistic unpopularity even in Weimar and the notorious incident of the dog-trainer's performance in the theater of Weimar, despite Goethe's energetic attempts to prevent the performance.[62] But Weimar as an idea is more important than the empirical reality of its social and cultural history. Goethe's regime is one of the happiest events in the modern cultural history of the West.

4

Dostoevsky and the
Hubris of the Immoralist

Notes from the Underground (1864) inaugurates Dostoevsky's
great creative period. There are anticipations of the underground man in earlier work, but he emerges full blown as a
type for the first time in *Notes*. He haunts Dostoevsky's
major novels in a way that makes it impossible to come to
grips with them without first settling with him and with the
tale that he inhabits as hero—or antihero. (He is present in the
characters of Raskolnikov, Stavrogin, and Ivan Karamazov.)

Apart from the abrupt interruption at the end of the tale
and a "footnote" at the beginning, Dostoevsky never appears
in the traditional novelist's role of narrator and commentator.
The story is completely occupied by the confessions of the
underground man. This in itself is not extraordinary: many
tales and novels of the eighteenth and nineteenth centuries
are narrated by the hero or another character. In those cases,
however, there is a coincidence between the moral vision of
the novelist and the moral vision of the character—or if not

coincidence, at least a sympathy which makes it possible without too much difficulty to identify the "point of view" of the tale or novel. The underground man, on the other hand, does not express the views of Dostoevsky.

Some of Dostoevsky's best critics have precipitously translated the underground man's powerful presence and intelligence into evidence of Dostoevsky's approval of him. Edward Wasiolek, in a recent study, admits the underground man's obnoxious qualities, but claims (with Berdayaev and Ivanov) that Dostoevsky "approves" of him because "in the very marrow of that cold and malignant spite [of the underground man] is a principle that is precious for him and for Dostoevsky: freedom."[1] Philip Rahv, in an earlier influential essay, states outrightly: "When it came to writing *The Brothers Karamazov,* Dostoevsky had wholly surmounted the standpoint of defiant and obdurate individualism exhibited in *Notes from the Underground.* . . . This type of individualism, with its stress on the unfettered human will and the inexhaustible intransigence of self-pride, is not really consonant with the religious valuation of life."[2] The identification between Dostoevsky and the underground man at the time that he wrote *Notes* certainly cannot be derived from external evidence. The simple fact that Dostoevsky valued freedom is too tenuous as evidence for such an identification. Freedom itself is a battleground of conflicting views.

It is, however, evident at the outset that the immediate effect of *Notes* is to upset the kind of moral and intellectual equilibrium that the reader enjoys when his assumptions are not being attacked or undermined.* Dostoevsky, it would seem, wants to preempt the moral authority of the reader for the underground man and use him as an "instrument" for

---

*Only Joseph Frank has properly caught the paradoxical moral spirit of the tale in what is surely the best American essay on the subject—though, as will become presently evident, my interpretation differs significantly from his (see "Nihilism and *Notes from the Underground*" in *Sewanee Review* [Winter, 1961], pp. 1–33.

judging the reader—without necessarily endorsing his views. The reader may loathe the underground man throughout the tale, but he will find it hard, if not impossible, to resist the underground man's final judgment of him.

For my part, I have merely carried to extremes in my life what you have not dared to carry even half-way, and, in addition, you have mistaken your cowardice for common sense and have found comfort in that, deceiving yourselves. So that, as a matter of fact, I seem to be much more alive than you. Come, look into it more closely! Why, we do not even know where we are to find real life, or what it is, or what it is called. Leave us alone without any books, and we shall at once get confused, lose ourselves in a maze, we shall not know what to cling to, what to hold on to, what to love and what to hate, what to respect and what to despise. We even find it hard to be men, men of *real* flesh and blood, *our own* flesh and blood. We are ashamed of it. We think it a disgrace. And we do our best to be some theoretical "average" men. We are stillborn, and for a long time we have been begotten not by living fathers, and that's just what we seem to like more and more. We are getting a taste for it. Soon we shall invent some way of being somehow or other begotten by an idea. . . .[3]

The judgment is persuasive, mainly because it develops out of the experience and "wisdom" of the underground man.

There is, to be sure, the reader who is untouched by the tale, who sees in it little more than the peevish outburst of a sick and spiteful man. (This is a view—false, I think—that the underground man himself perversely provokes.) The tale may have failed of its effect. But the failure may be that of the reader, who for various reasons (personal or ideological) exhibits a moral and spiritual obstinacy which prevents him from responding to the strange vitality of the underground man. The question of why Dostoevsky should want us to respond—though he himself cannot be taken as an exponent of the character or polemical position of the underground man—remains to be answered. Whatever the reasons, the sense of disequilibrium is immediately experienced by the sensitive reader.

The "confessions" begin with our hero's admission that he is a "sick man . . . a spiteful man." He goes on to speak of his nastiness as a civil servant, and though he soon qualifies this by saying that he is exaggerating his spitefulness, the inconsistency only bewilders the reader and intensifies the unpleasantness that the underground man has deliberately (it would seem) created at the outset. But the reader is not allowed the rather comfortable feeling of revulsion to which he is constantly tempted, for the "confessions" modulate almost at once to paradoxical statements that arrest the reader's attention, statements to which the reader may not be able to give his immediate assent, but which have at least the resonance of profundity:

And now I've been spending the last four years of my life in my funk-hole, consoling myself with the rather spiteful, though entirely useless, reflection that an intelligent man cannot possibly become anything in particular and that only a fool succeeds in becoming anything. Yes, a man of the nineteenth century must be, above all, a characterless person; a man of character, on the other hand, a man of action, is mostly a fellow with a very circumscribed imagination.[4]

The paradoxical character of such a statement inhibits any impulse to reject the statement peremptorily. We hesitate if only to understand, and the hesitation is fatal, for we find ourselves drawn into the logic and feeling of the underground man.

In this case, the paradox is in the identification of stupidity and character, on the one hand, and of intelligence and characterlessness, on the other. By intelligence, the underground man means acute consciousness, an activity that he characterizes as a "disease, a real honest-to-goodness disease."[5] He distinguishes acute consciousness from ordinary consciousness, "which is quite sufficient for the business of everyday life." He speaks of an acute consciousness of "the sublime and the beautiful" which virtually caused him to commit contemptible and degrading actions. "The more conscious I became of goodness and all that was 'sublime and beautiful,' the more deeply did I sink into the mire and the more ready I was to sink into it altogether." [6] Added to this is the strange feeling of delight *in the intense awareness* of his degradation. From this the underground man deduces the dubious proposition that "whatever happened, happened in accordance with the normal and fundamental laws of intensified consciousness and by a sort of inertia which is a direct consequence of those laws." [7] He implicitly identifies paralysis of the will and self-degrading actions, that is, actions which are not willed.* Acute consciousness, paralysis of the will (hence characterlessness), self-degrading actions, feelings of delight: this is the puzzling dialectic of the underground man's psyche.

The dialectic is illuminated by the contrast the underground man makes between the man of acute consciousness and the man of action.

You see, people who know how to avenge themselves and,
generally, how to stand up for themselves—how do they,
do you think, do it? They are, let us assume, so seized by the
feeling of revenge that while that feeling lasts there is
nothing but that feeling left in them. Such a man goes straight
to his goal, like a mad bull, with lowered horns, and only
a stone wall perhaps will stop him. (Incidentally, before such a
stone wall such people, that is to say, plain men and men of
action, as a rule capitulate at once. To them a stone wall
is not a challenge as it is, for instance, to us thinking men, who,
because we are thinking men, do nothing; it is not an excuse
for turning aside, an excuse in which one of our sort does

---

*After Ferdyshtchenko confesses in the *petit jeu* that is played early
in *The Idiot* to having urged a maid to admit a theft that he himself
had committed (echoes of Jean-Jacques), Totsky judges it quickly
as "a pathological incident, rather than an action," for action has
a moral quality (pp. 142–43).

not believe himself, but of which he is always very glad.
No, they capitulate in all sincerity. A stone wall exerts a
sort of calming influence, and perhaps even a mystic one . . .).[8]

Though the underground man can do nothing, he refuses
to reconcile himself to the stone wall paradoxically because
"I have to deal with it and haven't the strength to knock it
down." The inability to cope with the stone wall and the
refusal to reconcile himself to it become the source of self-
contempt and pride. In his imagination, where his courage
mainly resides, he can conceive grandiose defiant gestures
and refuse to submit to the inevitable. At moments the underground man wants us to regard this refusal as an act of will,
but it is clear that the refusal grows out of his impotence,
not his will. Indeed, he asserts at one point the fact that "the
direct, the inevitable and the legitimate result of consciousness
is to make all action impossible."[9]

The image of the stone wall is an analogue for scientific
consciousness: "the laws of nature . . . the conclusions of
natural science, mathematics." The stone wall that science
rears is its denial of individuality and freedom. Laws of
nature, determinism, abstractions (Petersburg, we should
remember, is the most "abstract" and most "premeditated"
of cities) deny the individual life by rationalizing it as an
instance or an effect of these laws. The underground man's
inertia *seems* like an effective refusal to participate in this
abstracting process, but he himself knows that this inertia
is part of the process of abstraction. Thus he regards himself
as "the antithesis of the normal man . . . who of course has
sprung not out of the lap of nature, but out of a test tube . . .
then this test-tube begotten man sometimes capitulates to his
antithesis to such an extent that for all his intense sensibility
he frankly considers himself a mouse and not a man."[10]

The underground man's most powerful weapon is his
suffering. The suffering man proves his individuality and
freedom by refuting through his very being the "scientific"
(utilitarian) law that the enlightened man pursues pleasure
and avoids pain. The underground man tells us that he will

suffer and with full consciousness if only to prove that he has freed himself from the tyranny of "a law of nature." "One's own free and unfettered choice, one's own whims, however wild, one's own fancy, overwrought though it sometimes may be to the point of madness—that is that same most desirable good which we overlooked and which does not fit into any classification, and against which all theories and systems are continually wrecked."[11] But is this really freedom? Though the underground man's fancy is often overwrought to the point of madness and his actions are whimsical and wild, we are never under any illusion that he is free—unless freedom is understood to be simply another word for perversity. In his relations with his friends and with the prostitute Lisa, the underground man behaves as if he has no will—as if his actions proceed from diabolical energies over which he has no control. The underground man himself is aware of his own *compulsive* nature: one might say that in "defying" the pleasure-pain calculus and taking delight in suffering, the underground man is being victimized by the laws of his own nature.

The underground man's suffering is a *necessity* of his nature. For this reason, Joseph Frank's view that the underground man's "masochism" is an indication not of pathology, but of his "paradoxical spiritual health," is dubious. Mr. Frank's reading simply masks the compulsive-pathological nature of the underground man's reaction under the opaque phrase: "moral-emotive response of his *human nature* to the blank nullity of the laws of nature."[12] The delight which the underground man experiences from his self-degrading acts is a compulsive response (or so *we* experience it in reading the story).* Though we might want to claim for it a

---

*The "freedom" of the underground man is characteristic of "Western nature" as Dostoevsky understood it and which he distinguishes invidiously from the freedom in fraternity of "Russian nature." In *Winter Notes on Summer Impressions* (1863), Dostoevsky writes: ". . . in Occidental nature in general . . . you find . . . a principle of individualism, a principle of isolation, of intense self-preservation,

certain value, normative language like "spiritual health" will not do. Indeed, at the end of his confessions, the underground man stresses his typicality in a manner which makes the claim for "spiritual health" impossible. His distinction, we may recall, consists in his having dared to carry "to extremes in my life what you have not dared to carry even half-way." But he is like everyone else in his confusion, abstractness, and lack of flesh-and-blood reality. The underground man enacts the laws of nature, but he has discovered "laws" that are truer than those of the pleasure-pain calculus. The underground man has anticipated Freud.

If we admit to the compulsive-masochistic character of the underground man, then we should hesitate about viewing the story as a dramatic embodiment of the conflict between the competing principles of freedom and determinism— because the protagonist of "freedom" is himself unfree. Dostoevsky has perceived the enslaving nature of capricious or unlimited "freedom," but he has not as yet presented us with an image of true freedom. He makes us aware of the compulsive motives behind every action: all moral and religious attitudes undergo a psychological inspection. Thus whatever moral judgment we make must be informed by sensitivity to the psychic energy that creates the moral disposition of a character. (In general, to speak of freedom,

---

of personal gain, of self-determination of the *I*, of opposing this *I* to all nature and the rest of mankind as an independent, autonomous principle entirely equal and equivalent to all that exists outside itself. Well, fraternity could scarcely arise from such an attitude. Why? Because in fraternity, in true brotherhood, it is not the separate personality, not the *I*, which should be concerned with its right to equality and equilibrium with everything else, but rather this *everything else* which comes *of its own volition* to the individual who is demanding his rights, to that individual *I*, and of itself, without his asking, should recognize him as possessing the same value and the same rights as it does, i.e., as everything else on earth. And what is more, this demanding, rebellious individual ought first of all to offer the *I*, to offer himself entirely to society, not only without demanding any rights but, on the contrary, offering these up unconditionally to society." (Pp. 110–11.)

good and evil—i.e., moral categories—in isolation from the psychic energy that informs moral behavior is to miss the essential in the Dostoevskian ethos.) *

The condition from which the underground man suffers has been analyzed by Nietzsche in masterly fashion. Max Scheler considers the discovery of *resentment* to be one of Nietzsche's great achievements, perhaps his greatest, and he has devoted a book to the subject.[13] Scheler is right in crediting Nietzsche with the discovery in the sense that Nietzsche was the first to formulate the phenomenon in a conscious philosophical manner.† But Dostoevsky had a profound novelist's grasp of resentment before Nietzsche. In his early novel *The Insulted and the Injured,* Dostoevsky gives us a very incisive portrait of the resentful man in the character of Natasha's father, Nikolay Sergeyvitch. The narrator of the novel describes him:

> I am convinced that everything was topsy-turvy and aching in his heart at that moment, as he looked at his poor wife's tears and alarm. I am sure that he was suffering far more than she was, but he could not control himself. So it is sometimes with the most good-natured people of weak nerves, who in spite of their kindliness are carried away till they find enjoyment in their own grief and anger, and try to express themselves at any cost, even that of wounding some other innocent creature, always by preference the one nearest and dearest. A woman sometimes has a craving to feel unhappy and aggrieved, though one has no misfortune or grievance. There are many men like women in this respect, and men, indeed, by no means feeble, and who have very little that is

---

*The "freedom" espoused by the underground man is already exposed for what it is in Milton's rendering of Satan's "unconquerable will."

†A characteristic Nietzschean analysis of the resentful man: "For the indignant man, and he who perpetually tears and lacerates himself with his own teeth (or in place of himself, the world, God or society) may indeed, morally speaking, stand higher than a satyr, but in every other sense he is the more ordinary, more indifferent, and less instructive case. And no one is such a *liar* as the indignant man." (*Beyond Good and Evil,* p. 40.)

feminine about them. The old man had a compelling impulse
to quarrel, though he was made miserable by it himself.[14]

This is a condition to which Dostoevsky was to return again
and again. The man of resentment suffers from a physiological
malaise—weak nerves. He is a man constitutionally incapable
of expressing or controlling a strong emotion. When he does
give vent to his feelings, he is often wild and chaotic, hurtful
both to the object of the feeling and to himself. He tries to
relieve himself of his misery, and in the process wounds an
innocent creature and is made even more miserable. When
he does not give vent to his feeling, his resentment is, in the
memorable phrase of Scheler, "an evil secretion in a sealed
vessel, like prolonged impotence."[15] This characterization
fits the underground man, who differs from Natasha'a
father in that he has turned his resentment into an ideological
program and is therefore without the good intentions of
Natasha's father, who merely suffers from weak nerves.

In Nietzsche's view, the man of resentment is the product
of the habit of repression that was trained into Western man,
principally by Christianity.* The expression of strong feeling
has been regarded in the Christian world as a form of pride,
and so it has been taken as a mark of spiritual power to be able
to repress strong feeling. This habit, which has had an
inevitably deleterious effect on the physical constitution, has
resulted, paradoxically, in the weakening of the power of
repression and consequently in wild, uncontrolled emotional
displays. To the man of resentment Nietzsche contrasts the
aristocrat, the man of strong feeling who has cultivated the
power of expressing it. He acts immediately on every impulse
of revenge or anger or love without fear of the social consequences. In doing so, he is merely honoring the laws of
life, which consists of "injuring, annihilating, oppressing."[16]
We respond to this image of the aristocrat to the extent that
we accept the concept of resentment: for if we harbor

---

*Scheler, in his book, defends Christianity against the accusation.

Christian and democratic sympathies for the victims of injury, annihilation, and oppression, we must nevertheless cope with the fact that the repression of the impulse to injure is often a losing battle. Not only does it poison the life of the man who has the impulse, but the rebellious impulse (refusing to brook repression any longer) may express itself with a destructiveness surpassing the violence of aristocratic anger. In this view, the man of resentment lives in an atmosphere of negation: he defines himself through envy, jealousy, and repressed anger. He exists solely in relation to his antithesis. The aristocrat, on the other hand, lives in an atmosphere of affirmation. He affirms himself: his negations simply enforce the distinction he makes between what is valuable (i.e., what he values) and what is not. *

The underground man makes an equivalent distinction between the man of action and the man of thought, but since he is a resentful man, the contrast that emerges is not favorable to the man of action. What Nietzsche might have called the innocence of the aristocratic hero is, from the point of view of the underground man, a species of stupidity.† The man of action is a kind of archaism, in the idiom of the tale, at once impossible and undesirable in the modern world. By permitting the underground man to expose the stupidity of the man of action (he has no more than animal intelligence about the stone wall) and to affirm by contrast his own moral penetration (in spite of the fact that he is also cowardly), Dostoevsky disequilibrates the reader, making the underground man fascinating and persuasive at the same time that the reader finds him repulsive. However deformed and corrupt he may be, the underground man seems near to some

---

* See chapter 5, pp. 119–26.

† "I call an animal, a species, an individual corrupt, when it loses its instincts, when it selects and *prefers* that which is detrimental to it" (*Anti-Christ,* p. 131). Nietzsche would have joined the utilitarians in condemning the perversity of the underground man.

truth about human life, a nearness that both parodies and reveals the truth.

To be true to the moral intention of the story, we should preserve Dostoevsky's own conception of the underground man's activity—he *suffers*—without suppressing the idea of masochism altogether. If we simply convert the suffering into masochism, we conceal the affinities between the career of the underground man and the Christian drama. That those affinities were in Dostoevsky's mind is revealed by a letter he wrote in which he spoke of his intention in the *Notes* to present Christ as an alternative idea both to the doctrine of reason and self-interest and to the underground man's "freedom." [17] He never realized this intention, and indeed it is hard to see how he could have accomplished this within the orbit of the underground man's confessions. Nevertheless, the underground man does choose to dramatize his "freedom" through suffering, an activity in which he at least resembles the Christian penitent.

But with a difference! For the Christian, suffering is a mode of purification. By suffering, the Christian (ideally) exercises his freedom (with the grace of God) in order to win the greater freedom of communion with God. He suffers in order to purge himself of all the worldly things that *enslave* and *paralyze* the human will. For the underground man, on the other hand, suffering is mainly a mode of negation. As the antithesis to the laws of nature, it is the source of chaos and disorder. For the underground man, suffering is an end in itself: nothing new in the moral or spiritual order emerges from it. It does not purify or re-create, and what the underground man needs and desires is to be re-created into authentic being. All his gestures in that direction are doomed to failure (his encounters with the officer who denies his very existence, his absurd and pathetic attempts at self-dramatization in the presence of his "friends," and the series of fiascos with Lisa), because they pretend to a selfhood that the underground man simply does not possess. In his need to to demonstrate his reality, to refuse the anonymity which seems to be his fate, he behaves aggressively to his friends, he exalts himself. Yet every moment of self-exaltation is followed by humiliation and self-abasement, because the self-exaltation cannot be sustained. Thus in a characteristic moment the underground man consoles himself with the sentiment that as a hero he is too "exalted a person to be entirely covered with dirt, and hence I could wallow in dirt with an easy conscience."[18] But he knows not only that the self-exaltation is untenable, but also that it proceeds perversely from an experience of his own degradation: he speaks of it as an attack of the "sublime and beautiful," a form of self-romanticizing, which comes upon him "when [he] was touching bottom."

It should be noted that the form of self-exaltation is antinomian: that to justify contemptible feelings and actions, the underground man imagines himself to be in a state of grace, which no action of his could possibly compromise. The claim is absurd, because the underground man's deepest conviction is that he is utterly without grace. The strongest emotion of his egocentricity is self-hatred; yet by that paradoxical logic which is peculiarly his own, he is able to contrive, if only sporadically, a kind of antinomianism without grace.

From the Christian point of view, the underground man is the archsinner, obsessed with his self-esteem, parodying the Christian idea of suffering, because his "martyrdom," after all, is in behalf of his self-esteem. As Joseph Frank points out in refuting the vulgar view of Dostoevsky as an exponent of "the religion of suffering," the underground man's suffering is a species of egoism. The underground man utterly lacks Lisa's capacity for sacrificing herself to alleviate the suffering of others. Thus after she has been insulted and humiliated by our hero, she shows an understanding of "what a woman who loves sincerely always understands first of all, namely that I was unhappy," and she "flung her arms around my neck."[19] In contrast, the underground man, who has the capacity to imagine the suffering of the others, sophistically justifies his cruelty to Lisa (for the humiliation of being the object of her compassion, a mark of her superiority to him) by viewing the insult as "a sort of purification. . . . I should have wearied her heart by thrusting myself upon her while now the memory of the insult will never die in her, and however horrible the filth that lies in store for her, the memory of that humiliation will raise her and purify her—by hatred, and, well, perhaps also by forgiveness."[20]* This is the sophistry of the devil, for what evil cannot be justified in this manner? It is the angel, not the devil, who should speak of the good that comes out of evil.

But again we must equivocate, for the underground man's identification of freedom and negation has its basis in a genuine nihilistic vision of false law and order. The cardinal sin of scientific consciousness—according to the *Notes*—is that it is a false consciousness, that its laws do not truly explain human consciousness. The very fact of the underground man's suffering consciousness is proof of this. We respond unequivocally to this aspect of the underground man's claim. We are at a difficult juncture in Dostoevsky's "thought." Though our knowledge of Dostoevsky's Christian orthodoxy as well as our own moral sentiments would seem to suggest a repudiation of what the underground man stands for, such a reading of the *Notes* does not account for the reader's fascination with, even admiration for, the vitality of the underground man. As the underground man himself says at the end of the tale:

For my part, I have merely carried to extremes in my life what you have not dared to carry even half-way, and, in addition, you have mistaken your cowardice for common sense and have found comfort in that, deceiving yourselves. So that, as a matter of fact, I seem to be much more alive than you.

The final lament is not that man has become immoral or evil,

---

* One hears echoes of Jean-Jacques' "apology" for what he did to Marion.

it is a lament over lost vitality: "We even find it hard to be men of *real* flesh and blood, *our own* flesh and blood." The underground man has value, one is tempted to say, *because* of the absence of the normal compromised qualities of men. He is a brilliant negation of these qualities (as he says, he has gone the whole way), and the fascination that he holds for us is in his capacity to create an intense life from this negation. "Suffering means doubt, negation . . . a man will never renounce real suffering, destruction and chaos." [21] He is, paradoxically, the most vital of men.

II

The underground man has gone the whole way only in his mind. He is a fearful, resentful man whose "bold" acts are revulsions from self-contempt and timidity. Dostoevsky was to create characters possessed of the capacity to act out the violent imagination of the underground man.

In *Crime and Punishment* (published in 1866, two years after the publication of *Notes from the Underground*), the hero Raskolnikov not only commits a murder but supplies a justification for it in terms that recall the underground man's complaint against the laws of nature. The essay that he writes before the murder is concerned with the less powerful laws of the community, but it contains the same intense imagination of resistance to the coercive element in life.

In the essay Raskolnikov divides the world into two categories: "the first category, that is to say the masses, comprises all the people who, generally speaking, are by nature conservative, respectable, and docile . . . The men belonging to the second category all transgress the law and are all destroyers, according to their different capacities." They are, in Raskolnikov's view, the benefactors of mankind, who must destroy existing law (and in the process commit bloodshed) in order to pass beyond the law. These spiritual heroes transgress the law and kill when they have to, just as the mob, refusing to acknowledge their right to do so, "goes on beheading or hanging" them "with the proviso, however, that in the subsequent generations this same mob places the executed men on a pedestal and worships them (more or less)." They are both necessary, Raskolnikov insists, for "the first preserves the world and increases its numbers; the second moves the world and leads it to its goal." The harmony of the world, tragically, subsists in *la guerre éternelle*.[22]

The essay does not tell us why Raskolnikov committed the crime. Not only does he fail to be a hero in the manner of Napoleon (to whom he repeatedly compares himself), but the murder has none of the generosity which informed the actions of the great transgressors: Lycurgus, Solon, Mahomet, Napoleon. It is a purely personal action. Nevertheless, though Raskolnikov abandons his argument *as a justification* of his crime, he does so not because he no longer believes in the existence of these two categories of men and *la guerre éternelle,* but because he has discovered that he is no Napoleon.

> The old woman was only an illness—I was in a great
> hurry to step over—I didn't kill a human being—I killed a
> principle! Yes, I killed a principle all right, but I did not step
> over—I remained on this side. All I could do was kill![23]

Though he renounces the murder and even seems to undergo something like a Christian conversion, he never achieves Sonia's sentimental view of the dignity of human life, of all human life. Raskolnikov never renounces the feeling that "the old hag is rubbish." Toward the end of the novel, in an exchange with his sister Dunya, he insists on preserving the distinction between his intention in committing the murder and the act of murder itself, and it is clear that he is interested not in the act, but in the intention.

> Crime? What crime? he exclaimed in a kind of sudden frenzy.
> That I killed a nasty, harmful, wicked louse . . . do you call that
> crime? I'm not even thinking of it, and I'm not thinking of
> wiping it out. . . . It is only now that I see clearly the

> whole absurdity of my cowardliness, not that I've made up
> my mind to accept this unnecessary disgrace! I've made
> up my mind to do it simply because I'm a mean and
> second-rate fellow. . . .[24]

Dunya responds (as Sonia would have responded) by remind-
ing him that he had shed blood. But Raskolnikov is unim-
pressed and reminds her in turn that "all men shed blood."

Sartre's description of Baudelaire evokes Raskolnikov's
plight in language similar to that of Raskolnikov's essay.
"If [Baudelaire] departs from the norm, it is to suffer more
keenly the power of the law." [25] It was, of course, Raskolnikov's intention "to step over" and free himself from the
imposition of the old law. But he discovered that (like
Sartre's Baudelaire) he did no more than bring the law down
upon his head. Raskolnikov's behavior subsequent to his
crime, particularly in relation to Porifory, the police in-
spector, suggests an invitation to punishment. Far from
transvaluing values as his doctrine proposes, he exists in a
negative and self-destructive relation to the law. Without
knowing it, he wanted the suffering and punishment that
resulted from his crime.

Philip Rahv has remarked in connection with *Crime and
Punishment* that "Dostoevsky is the first novelist to have
fully accepted and dramatized the principle of uncertainty or
indeterminacy in the presentation of character." [26] Hunger,
the assumption of the role of transgressor, the claustrophobia
of his coffin-like room: all these "motives" by themselves
fail to satisfy. But the motives do add up, and the very impression of indeterminacy (with which Rahv rests content)
expresses the "motivation" of the crime.

Reduced to penury, living a ghostlike existence, Raskolnikov craves reality. His intense experience of nullity produces
the desire for an intense experience of reality, and as the
underground man teaches, suffering is reality. Dostoevsky's
melodramatic manner indicates complicity in his hero's
search for a heightened sense of reality. The "most terrible"
or "most astonishing" or "most amazing" things happen:

Dostoevsky's love of the superlative betrays his extreme fascination with the suffering that Raskolnikov and other Dostoevskian heroes seek.

If we understand Raskolnikov's career in the novel as the pursuit of states of suffering, then the motivation of the murder is suddenly illuminated. For what suffering is greater in a moral being than the guilt of having committed a murder? There is no more radical violation of one's character than the act of murder. This, it seems to me, is the ultimate perversity of Raskolnikov's act. Without knowing it, he murdered in order to increase his sense of reality; to enjoy, so to speak, the sheer passional quality of guilt.

Raskolnikov's "motivation" is not eccentric in the Dostoevskian canon: it is the fulfilment of the underground man's doctrine of suffering, and it is made explicit in a remarkable story published toward the end of his life "The Dream of the Ridiculous Man." The hero is another Petersburg version of the underground man, "for whom nothing in the world made any difference."[27] After a sentimental chance encounter with a crying, poverty-stricken little girl, the ridiculous man dreams that he has entered paradise only (to his shame) to corrupt the people of paradise. The dream blurs the facts of how the Fall occurred. ("I only know that the cause of the Fall was I. Like a horrible trichina, like the germ of the plague infecting whole kingdoms, so did I infect with myself all that happy earth that knew no sin before me.")[28] But the cause can be found in the dreaming affections of the ridiculous man.

I walked among them, wringing my hands and weeping over them, but I loved them perhaps more than before when there was no sign of suffering in their faces and when they were innocent and—oh, so beautiful! I loved the earth they had polluted even more than when it had been a paradise, and only because sorrow and affliction, but only for myself, only for myself; for them I wept now, for I pitied them. I stretched out my hands to them accusing, cursing and despising myself. I told them that I alone was responsible for it all—I

alone; that it was I who had brought them corruption,
contamination, and lies! I implored them to crucify me, and I
taught them how to make the cross. I could not kill myself;
I had not the courage to do it; but I longed to receive
martyrdom in their hands. I thirsted for martyrdom,
I yearned for my blood to be shed to the last drop in torment
and suffering.[29]

The ridiculous man "fulfils" himself in the condition of
guilt, and there can be no greater guilt than guilt for the fall
of man. The figure of Christ in the ecstasy of martyrdom lurks
in this fantasy.

III

What is Dostoevsky's view of his immoralist hero? I have
already suggested a complicity between author and hero. But
the complicity is experimental, not final. Writers like
Shestov, who have interpreted Dostoevsky as a proto-
Nietzschean, have failed to make this important distinction.[30]*

---

* Nietzsche's praise of Dostoevsky is well known: "Dostoevsky
was the only psychologist from whom I had anything to learn;
he belongs to the happiest windfalls of my life, happier even than the
discovery of Stendhal" (*Twilight of the Idols,* p. 104). The word
"psychologist" conceals somewhat the spiritual character of
Nietzsche's affinity for Dostoevsky, a spiritual affinity
despite the obvious and profound disagreement about Christianity.
The heroes of Dostoevsky's novels have a proto-Nietzschean aspect,
for which Dostoevsky shows extraordinary sympathy at the
same time that he severely undermines their ideological claims from a
Christian point of view. The Nietzschean is the man unable to
summon faith in the Christian pieties who has nevertheless inherited
the intense spiritual feelings and yearnings of the Christian
tradition. His hatred of Christianity is a measure of its failure to
satisfy his needs. For him suffering is scarcely endurable (since he is
without the consolations of faith) and yet as necessary as
life itself. And so perversely he comes to delight in his suffering.
    This much may be conceded to the criticism of Dostoevsky's
Christian orthodoxy. On its positive ideological side, it is
unconvincing. Dostoevsky's insistence on the spiritual sanctity of the

To be sure, he had an unsurpassed (Christian) capacity for entering sympathetically into the consciousness of the immoralist hero. But the strength of his final view of immoralism is in his profound (and necessarily sympathetic) understanding of the immoralist hero.

The immoralist hero, in the Dostoevskian view, is ultimately incapable of sustaining his claims. This is the reason for Raskolnikov's self-revulsion. But the novel does not entirely illuminate why this should be so. In *The Devils,* the great "political" novel that follows *Crime and Punishment* and *The Idiot*, Dostoevsky exposes the source of the immoralist's incapacity.

The metaphysical drama of *The Devils* * is the effort of strong and impressive characters to create values from their own experience and energy. The two most important characters in the novel are Kirilov and Stavrogin.

Kirilov is obsessed with the idea of suicide—indeed, it is his sole object in life, because in a world in which God does

---

Russian people is mere insistence. Elsewhere (in *The Diary of a Writer*, for instance) he exalts the Russian Orthodox Church at the expense of Roman Catholicism, and this fanaticism is repeated in his fiction: *The Idiot, the Brothers Karamazov*. (Myshkin's attack on Roman Catholicism is absurdly inconsistent with his character.) The ideological side of Dostoevsky's commitment to Christianity (in its Russian Orthodox version) can be regarded only as a species of irrationality, like his anti-Semitism. Indeed, Dostoevsky's customary psychological acuity often fails in his perception of his Christian heroes. It is a commonplace of Dostoevsky criticism that Alyosha is the least impressive of the brothers Karamazov. In the characterization of Myshkin in *The Idiot,* Dostoevsky makes his most impressive and convincing effort to give the psychology of the Christian hero, and it is impressive precisely because it uncovers the corruptions in the Christian attitude and consequently does not issue in a sentimental affirmation. But the view that Dostoevsky is a proto-Nietzschean without knowing it suffers from the same fallacy which Blake and others commit in viewing Milton as unconsciously belonging to the devil's party. It deforms the work to fit a single tendency in the writer's imagination.

* Alternatively titled (in America) *The Possessed*.

not exist, it becomes impossible for man to live. Though he cannot summon faith in God, he knows the importance of God's existence: "All man did was to invent God so as to live without killing himself." [31] Kirilov's dilemma is that "God is necessary, and so must exist," though he knows that "He doesn't exist and can't exist," [32] He is one of those religious atheists tortured by a simultaneous belief in God and a "knowledge" of his nonexistence. The only escape for Kirilov is a monumental egoism, in which he plays God by taking his own life. Being the first one "to refuse to invent God," he is bound to assume the functions of God. Kirilov must take his own life, for suicide is the apotheosis of man's self-will: his moment of affinity with God.

Kirilov is an impressive and moving figure, but he is clearly suffering from a mania, and his philosophy can be taken seriously only as a symptom of a spiritual malaise. It is the character of the terrible and enigmatic Stavrogin that exposes fully the horror and vacuity of this monumental egoism. Stavrogin too takes his own life, but in contrast to Kirilov, without any philosophical justification. Throughout most of the novel, we see him, more accurately divine him, as a legendary figure like L——n, to whom he is compared and about whom it is said that

. . . he knowingly looked for danger all his life, that he revelled in the sensation of it and made it into a physical necessity; that as a young man he would fight a duel for no reason at all; that in Siberia he would go hunting bears armed only with a knife, that in the Siberian forests he liked to meet escaped bears. There can be no doubt that these legendary gentlemen were capable of experiencing, and that to the highest degree the sensation of fear, otherwise they would have led much quieter lives and the feeling of danger would not have become a physical necessity to them. What fascinated them so much was, of course, the conquest of fear. What appealed to them was the continual flush of victory, and the consciousness that no one in the world would conquer them. L——n had long before his exile to Siberia struggled with hunger and laboured hard to earn a bare subsistence rather than accept his rich father's demands, which he considered unjust. His conception of struggle was therefore many-sided; and he did not esteem his steadfastness and strength of character so highly only in bear-hunts and duels.[33]

Stavrogin differs from L——n in that he could perform all these feats "without any sense of enjoyment, but simply from unpleasant necessity, languidly, listlessly, and even with the feeling of boredom."[34] Stavrogin, unable to sustain this heroic self-sufficiency, deflates the demonic and impressive presence that he has created, confessing his abysmal vileness: "Even negation has not come from me." And: "I know that I ought to kill myself, to brush myself off the earth, like some loathsome insect."[35] This is not true self-description, to be sure. It is the violent exaggeration of self-hatred, reminiscent of Hamlet's "O, what a rogue and peasant slave am I!" Indeed, Stavrogin shows himself capable of the magnanimity that he said he did not possess by taking his own life.

Monumental egoism (often manifesting itself through immoralist acts) creates in most human organisms a bad conscience, which immoralism has theoretically denied. Stavrogin's revulsion is a mark of his humanity which avenges itself on his immoralist presumption. The repentant Stavrogin (of the "confession" chapter in the unexpurgated edition) is not inconsistent with the character that Dostoevsky has been presenting (as some critics feel). He is the exhausted immoralist, who is compelled by the necessity of his human nature to return to his abandoned humanity.

Raskolnikov's desire for guilt, I am suggesting, is like Stavrogin's pleasure in the sensation of danger: it is a form of moral sensuality. But the desire for guilt, like the desire for pure sensation, is not—indeed cannot be—an ultimate human desire even in a pathological organism. In mixing with the crowd at the end of the novel, Raskolnikov gives up the excruciating pleasures and arrogance of his agonizing solitude: it is a gesture equivalent to Stavrogin's repentance.

The pathology of the Dostoevskian hero has its origins in the felt disappearance of God. This is the great theme of Dostoevsky's last novel, *The Brothers Karamazov*. The murder of Fyodor Karamazov by Smerdyakov, his bastard son, is traced to Ivan's argument as reported by the seminarian Rakitin: "If there's no immortality of the soul [that is, if God doesn't exist], then there's no virtue and everything is lawful." [36] Whether or not God exists for him, Ivan (like Raskolnikov and Stavrogin) cannot endure the practical consequences of his doctrine and suffers a nervous breakdown. It would almost seem that the drama of the novel subverts Dostoevsky's own understanding of the moral situation: for Dostoevsky apparently accepts Ivan's conclusion that "everything is possible" as a valid inference from a false premise, "that God does not exist." Indeed, the existence of God (in the light of the nihilist conclusion) becomes a necessity. *"Si n'existait pas Dieu, il faudrait l'inventer."* [37] Ivan's rationalistic "perversity" resembles Dostoevsky's own declaration that if he had to choose between Christ and truth, he would choose Christ. The sentiment of guilt survives "the death of God." The moral idea that man has inherited may in fact be a real alternative to the sense of vertigo which man suffers in a godless world. *

But Ivan's syllogism is not the spiritual center of the novel. God or Christ for Dostoevsky is more than the governor of the moral life. In Ivan's dream of the Grand Inquisitor, Dostoevsky in effect recasts the antagonists of Raskolnikov's *guerre éternelle*: the transgressor who bears the principle of absolute freedom is Christ, and the upholder of the moral law is the "satanic" Grand Inquisitor. Most interpretations of the Grand Inquisitor accept too readily the view that he is

---

* This is a version of the utilitarian argument which one finds, for instance, in George Eliot, who opts for duty in the failure of God and immortality. It need hardly be said that Dostoevsky would eschew all argument for the moral life from the utilitarian premise that self-interest is best served by the enlightened modification of man's fundamental egoism.

being repudiated. The support for the view comes from the reader's knowledge of Dostoevsky's passionate belief in Christ. But the view curiously disregards the unquestionable power of the Grand Inquisitor's speech in contrast to the rather equivocal response of Christ. Even if we were sure that Christ's kiss was the kiss of forgiveness and not of acquiescence (as Lawrence thinks),[38] why should that kiss weigh so heavily against the Grand Inquisitor's persuasiveness? It is true (as Lawrence, a defender of the Grand Inquisitor, has also pointed out) that the Grand Inquisitor is made to wear the guise of Satan,[39] that his vision of life is dismal, and that he is a projection of Ivan's tragic consciousness, which the novel does not "affirm." But it is precisely the dilemma of *The Brothers Karamazov*, indeed of Dostoevsky's imagination, that the vision and argument of the Grand Inquisitor have so much force. The underground man's dream of freedom and spiritual vitality can have its fulfilment only in Christ: in the transgression of love rather than of power. In this world, Christ must be sent away, for, as the Grand Inquisitor explains, such freedom is an unendurable burden for most men.

5

Nietzsche and
the Aristocracy of Passion

The view of Nietzsche that prevails among literary intel-
lectuals in America and England is that of the "good
European" (one of Nietzsche's favorite self-descriptions).
Nietzsche's concept of the will to power, which at one time
put him, falsely, into a connection with naziism, is now related
to traditional philosophic virtues: intelligence, reason, self-
possession. Indeed, Walter Kaufmann in his influential book
on Nietzsche virtually identifies the will to power with the
rationality of man.*[1] Kaufmann's book was written under
the postwar compulsion to destroy the false legend that
Nietzsche was a protonazi, a legend given currency by even
so distinguished a historian as Crane Brinton.[2] Kaufmann
argues his case with considerable ingenuity and immense

---

* A brilliant and more persuasive earlier version of the view of
  Nietzsche as the good European can be found in the chapter
  "Nietzsche *contra* Wagner" in Jacques Barzun's *Darwin, Marx
  and Wagner*, pp. 325–34.

scholarship, and he deserves respect. But it is still true that anyone who has read a good deal of Nietzsche and is responsive to his spirit and tone feels that the view of Nietzsche as the good European, the immediate heir of Goethe, is a very partial view.

One of the compelling motives of what I would call the humanist interpretation of Nietzsche is the will to make him respectable. Kaufmann acknowledges the boldness of Nietzsche's rhetoric when he cites his loathing of "Tartufferie," the writer's philistine impulse to "stroke the hypersensitive ears of the bourgeois."[3] To be sure, Nietzsche's love of the bold phrase is sometimes an autonomous force in his work, and the scholar's attempt to recall the phrase to its context and to qualify and correct its excesses is necessary and valuable. But Kaufmann does more than merely correct the occasionally excessive statement: he revises the very intention of Nietzsche's thought.

One instance will suffice: like Plato, Aristotle, and Kant (Kaufmann tells us), Nietzsche believed that the aim of life is self-overcoming or self-perfection. Nietzsche shares with all philosophers a "generic conception of morality."[4] What this comparison blurs are the radically different conceptions of self-perfection. In Plato and Aristotle, man perfects himself within the *polis*. Thus Socrates' isolation from the community was an accident of the corruption of Athens, not a generic condition of the relation between self-perfection and the communal idea.* For Nietzsche, the pursuit of self-

---

* I am passing over too quickly a difficult and tangled issue. It is possible to argue—indeed it has been argued—that *The Republic* demonstrates the impossibility of ever achieving a reconciliation between the true (uncompromised) philosopher and the state. Socrates is aware of how difficult such a reconciliation, more accurately transformation, would be: this is the burden of the allegory of the cave. But he is unwilling to concede the impossibility of such a transformation, a concession which would have nipped the dialogue in the bud. Socrates admits the possibility that the philosopher king may never arrive, but this admission does not undercut the dream of the marriage of philosophy and political power.

perfection is inevitably a lonely one—the state is either indifferent or hostile. The hostility of the state is not simply a matter of stupidity or misunderstanding. Nietzsche is keenly aware of how inimical philosophy, as he understands it, is to the interests of the state.

> If there should come one who really proposes to cut everything to the quick, the state included, with the knife of truth, the state, that affirms its existence above all, is justified in banishing him as an enemy, just as it bans a religion that exalts itself to be its judge. The man who consents to be a state philosopher, must also consent to be regarded as renouncing the search for truth—the state.[5]

And again:

> The state has never any concern with truth, but only with the truth useful to it, or rather, with anything that is useful to it, be it truth, half-truth or error. A coalition between state and philosophy has only meaning when the latter can promise to be unconditionally useful to the state, to put its wellbeing higher than the state.[6]

These are passages from Nietzsche's early work, when he was still under the spell of Schopenhauer and before he had formulated the immoralist doctrines of his later work. But in writing these passages, Nietzsche anticipates the dangerous intellectual adventure on which he was soon to embark, an adventure which would, for instance, result in the following statement:

> To talk of intrinsic right and intrinsic wrong is absolutely nonsensical; intrinsically an injury, an oppression, an exploitation, an annihilation can be nothing wrong, inasmuch as life is *essentially* (that is, in its cardinal functions) something which functions by injuring, oppressing, exploiting and annihilating, and is absolutely inconceivable without such a character.[7] *

---

* The only state that might countenance such a conception is a fascistic state that could justify its own tyranny in these terms.

Nietzsche knows how dangerous such a doctrine is, and his qualifications suggest all those qualities of intelligence and sanity with which his humanist apologists credit him. For instance, at the conclusion of *The Genealogy of Morals* Nietzsche makes the following grudging case for values all too human: "I believe that everything which we Europeans of to-day are in the habit of admiring as the values of all these respected things called 'humanity,' 'mankind,' 'sympathy,' pity,' may be of some value as the debilitation and moderating of certain powerful and dangerous primitive impulses."[8] But Nietzsche goes on to state that "all these things are nothing else than the belittlement of the entire type of 'man,' his mediocrisation, if in such a desperate situation I may make use of such a desperate expression."

Nietzsche viewed himself and his work as dangerous, and it is no discredit to his achievement to read him as he himself wanted to be read—with a full sense of the danger in his work.

II

In 1845 Max Stirner, a student of Hegel, published a book, *The Ego and His Own,* which in a crude way anticipates Nietzsche's immoralism. In Stirner's view, the history both of thought and of institutions is a history of the domination of the *I*. Hegel, of course, had already spoken of the alienation of the self to the nonhuman. The novelty of Stirner's view is that he perceives the domination of self in philosophies and institutions ostensibly dedicated to the fostering of the individual: in particular, modern humanism and the modern state. According to Stirner, the idea of Man under the modern dispensation has replaced the idea of God, and the particularity, the uniqueness of the individual is now denied in favor of the essence Man, which each person must realize. Stirner concludes from his historical observations that the general strategy of all forms of domination is to justify the particular by a general idea.

Stirner proposed what he considered to be the first authentic philosophy of the ego. The individual self, requiring no external sanctions, *is* its own justification. The concluding statement of Stirner's book is that the *particular* (the individual ego) is based on *nothing*. Literally: "I have set my affair on nothing." The goal of self-perfection, which the whole philosophical tradition has upheld, represents an insidious attempt to dominate the ego. Stirner, in contrast, affirms the actual "perfection" of the ego. Though Stirner performs as dialectician in refuting the heritage of Western philosophy, he can present the ego only as the result of immediate intuition. The image of the true ego is that of a passional *body* that *devours* and *destroys* in order to *enjoy* life. "If I concern myself for myself, the unique one, then my concern rests on its transitory, mortal creator, who consumes himself. . . ." [9] The *I*, in Stirner's view, is a consumer, an appropriator of people and things for the satisfaction of desires. Stirner's affirmation of the devouring ego suggests the faith of the classical economists in extreme economic individualism. Stirner's doctrine is the consumer counterpart of the doctrine of productive economic individualism. *

Stirner's thought (particularly on its positive side) is primitive. He never once conceives the ego as something complex, to be analyzed and understood. What of the ego that does not know what it wants? If the ego has been tyrannized

---

* "The sole thing which he has to his credit is against his will and without his knowledge: he is the expression of the German petit bourgeois of today, whose aspiration is to become bourgeois. It was completely logical that, narrow-minded, timid, and prejudiced as these bourgeois are, 'the individual' should swagger into the world as their philosophical representative, equally gaudy, bragging, and impertinent. It is quite in agreement with the circumstances of the bourgeoisie that they want nothing to do with their theoretical braggart, nor he with them, that they are in mutual disagreement and that he must preach his own peculiar egoism: now perhaps Sancho will see the umbilical cord which connects *his* 'union' with the Customs Union." (Engels' view of Stirner quoted in Karl Lowith, *From Hegel to Nietzsche*, p. 248.)

for so long, is it not possible that its very constitution has been affected, if not re-created, by the various forms of domination? Perhaps the ego itself must be qualified by terms such as Christian or rational: is there an unqualified ego?

> Whether what I think and do is Christian, what do I care?
> Whether it is humane, liberal, whether inhuman, illiberal,
> inhuman [*sic*], what do I care about that? If only, it
> accomplishes what I want, if only I satisfy myself in it, then
> overlay it with predicates as you will; it is all alike to me.[10]

Stirner fails to perceive that the "I want" may be conditioned by the complex culture (e.g., Christian culture) that has shaped the ego. Stirner cannot free the ego of its cultural determinants simply by refusing to recognize their existence.

It need hardly be said that Nietzsche (who substantiates the cultural content of the ego and who staunchly champions the goal of self-perfection) is incomparably the greater thinker. But like Stirner, Nietzsche locates value in the passional body. He is the great philosopher of consciousness as a consumer: as we shall see, this is a large part of the explanation of his immoralism.

III

"It is obvious that everywhere the designations of moral value were at first applied to *men,* and were only derivatively and at a later period applied to *actions.* . . . The noble type of man regards *himself* as a determiner of values; he does not require to be approved of; he passes judgment. 'What is injurious to me is injurious in itself.' "[11]

This is not merely historical description. Nietzsche endorses this antinomian morality: the belief that value lies not in the act, but in the graced condition of the doer, so that any action he performs is immediately justified by virtue of the grace that resides in him. Nietzsche himself is conscious of this appropriation of the religious idea of grace: a quality which is unearned, a *given* in certain (not all) human souls.

It is not the works, but the *belief* which is here decisive and
determines the order of rank—to employ once more an old
religious formula with a newer and deeper meaning—it is
some fundamental certainty which a noble soul has about
itself, something which is not to be sought, is not to be found,
and perhaps also, is not to be lost—*The noble soul has
reverence for itself*.[12]

Unlike the Christian view, Nietzsche's view does not presuppose a God, a supreme being who bestows grace out of a
gratuitous love of his creatures. For Nietzsche grace is a
given, without a giver, so that the possession of it is unconditioned by gratitude or humility. The noble soul is in a state
of grace, the slave—or, in a democratic society, the member
of the herd—is ungraced, and between them is an unbridge-
able gulf.

The assigning of value to oneself does in itself confer that
value. As Nietzsche points out, it is one of the characteristics
of the democratic social order that the assigning of value,
which had originally been the prerogative of the aristocrat,
becomes a universal activity: "the originally noble and rare
impulse to 'think well' of themselves will now be more and
more encouraged and extended."[13] But the slave habit
persists in the desire of each man to have everybody's good
opinion of him.

Nietzsche rejects the egoism of the slave, an egoism that
proceeds from weakness.

The Christian gloominess of La Rochefoucauld, who saw
egoism in everything and imagined he had therefore *reduced*
the worth of things and virtues! In opposition to him, I first
of all tried to show that nothing else could exist save egoism,—
that in those men whose ego is weak and thin, the power of
love also grows weak,—that the greatest lovers are such owing
to the strength of their ego,—that love is an expression of
egoism.[14]

The egoism that Nietzsche affirms is based on "knightly-
aristocratic values," on the "cult of the physical, on a flower-
ing, rich and even effervescing healthiness, that goes

considerably beyond what is necessary for maintaining life, on war, adventure, the chase, the dance, the tourney, on everything, in fact, which is contained in strong, free and joyous action."[15] By asserting that the origin of value is in men, not in their actions, Nietzsche not only introduces into moral discourse a radical relativism of values (the egocentric world of Nietzsche has as many centers of value as there are extraordinary human beings), but he also transfers value from activity to passion. The value of the action is in the joyous vitality of the actor. It is not *what* a man accomplishes or does or creates that finally interests Nietzsche, but the *feeling* of power that attends the accomplishment. Unlike Plato and Aristotle, for instance, who are concerned with the teleological realizations of consciousness when it is creatively or rationally disposed, Nietzsche is preoccupied with the passional states of consciousness when the self is active. The political implication of Nietzsche's view is not naziism (which is concerned with political organization) but aristocratic anarchism, an elite testifying in its life to its capacity for power, largely indifferent to the social interest and justifying the indifference by the doctrine that neither life nor culture is served by the inhibition of the will to power and that the attempt to do so is an absurdity.

To require of strength that it should not express itself as strength, that it should not be a wish to overpower, a wish to overthrow, a wish to become master, a thirst for enemies and antagonisms and triumphs, is just as absurd as to require of weakness that it should express itself as strength.[16]

The distinction between passion and activity has its *historical* counterpart in the difference between the "knightly-aristocratic" mode of valuation and the bourgeois mode. In the theories of Adam Smith and Ricardo, value is created by labor; in feudal theory, by conquest and occupation. The *raison d'être* of the aristocrat is his enjoyment of the power he possesses, which is historically founded on possession, conquest, gift, and the privileges of the eldest son. The *raison d'être* of the bourgeois (and the proletarian) is the capacity to create value through labor.[17] In the Nietzschean view, the charge of parasitism against the aristocrat is an expression of the envy and resentment of the bourgeois, who must justify himself through labor, since he lacks that "which is not to be sought . . . not to be found . . . not to be lost,"[18] the quality Nietzsche attributes to the noble soul. From the Nietzschean point of view, the charge of parasitism is absurd, because the aristocrat is high on the ascending scale of life. It is the bourgeois who is life-destroying, for whom work is a strenuous and perpetual drain on the sources of vitality.

In a series of aphorisms in *Human, All Too Human*, Nietzsche charges active people with laziness. They are "deficient in the higher activity. . . . The active roll as the stone rolls, according to the stupidity of mechanics."[19] This criticism of activity recalls Carlyle's indictment of mechanical activity and his praise of the *dynamic* higher activity of individual life. But unlike Carlyle, Nietzsche chooses to write "in favour of the idle," those for whom activity takes a contemplative form. He warns, of course, that in speaking of idleness and idlers, he is not alluding to the "sluggards." But he is resisting that modern spiritual restlessness which prevents a man "from drawing water out of his own well," a restlessness that Carlyle, with his puritan insistence on activity and his exaggerated mistrust of idleness, could not avoid.

Nietzsche's conception of power is psychological. In his vocabulary psychology has an ambivalent meaning: when freed of moral prejudices, it is the method for discovering the virtue of each man. "All psychology has run aground on moral prejudices and timidities, it has not dared to launch out into the depths."[20] It is also a weapon in "the strife of all egos to discover that thought which will remain poised above men like a star—the ego is a *primum mobile*."[21] In opposing psychology and morality, Nietzsche implies the standard of a new "morality": the full expression of the energy or power of each individual.

The *moral* view of man is false, because it rests on a false idea about the nature of man. The moral idea presupposes that man has an essence which he is obliged to realize. In Nietzsche's view, man is distinguished from other animals by the fact that he is as yet *unclassified,* that is, that there is no generic essence that defines the whole class.[22] The moral idea is a traitor to the self, because it prematurely and falsely characterizes the energies and dispositions of men. The most obvious indication of its falsity is its generalizing character—as if one can say of all men, of Man, that it is their or his nature to be rational or passionate or moral or whatever the generic term may be. Nietzsche does not deny that the various categorical imperatives that have dominated the thought of Western history are true for certain men, but he insists on a multiplicity of moralities, which would express the various energies of human life.

I recognize virtue in that: (1) it does not insist upon being recognized; (2) it does not presuppose the existence of virtue everywhere, but precisely something else; (3) it does *not suffer* from the absence of virtue, but regards it rather as a relation of perspective which throws virtue into relief: it does not proclaim itself; (4) it makes no propaganda; (5) it allows no one to pose as judge because it is always a *personal* virtue; (6) it does precisely what is generally forbidden: virtue as I understand it is the actual *vetitum* within all gregarious legislation; (7) in short, I recognize virtue in that it is in the Renaissance style—virtù—free of all moralic acid.[23]

All the moralists that Nietzsche cherishes have one thing in common: a fierce militant individuality, which is indifferent to its social consequences. He goes against the traditional concern of ethical philosophy with the social implications of behavior. Nietzsche tests his "doctrine" with the aggressive emotions.

The aim of malice is *not* the suffering of others in itself, but our own enjoyment; for instance, as the feeling of revenge, or stronger nervous excitement. All teasing, even, shows the pleasure it gives to exercise our power on others and bring it to an enjoyable feeling of preponderance. Is it *immoral* to taste pleasure at the expense of another's pain? Is malicious joy (Schadenfreude: joy at the misfortune of others) devilish, as Schopenhauer says? We give ourselves pleasure in nature by breaking off twigs, loosening stones, fighting with wild animals, and do this in order thereby to become conscious of our strength. Is the knowledge, therefore, that another suffers through us, the same thing concerning which we otherwise feel irresponsible, supposed to make us immoral? But if we did not know this we would not thereby have the enjoyment of our own superiority, which can only *manifest* itself by the suffering of others, for instance, in teasing. All pleasure *per se* is neither good nor evil; whence should come the decision that in order to have pleasure ourselves we may not cause displeasure to others?[24]

Here the moral issue is the "purity" of intention. This is the significance of the rhetorical questions that Nietzsche asks. What does it matter if harm is done, so long as the intention was not to give pain, but to discharge one's vitality, to express joy? Indeed, it might be a condition of vitality to give pain. "Insects sting, not from malice, but because they too want to live . . . they desire our blood, not our pain." [25] Nietzsche's "celebration" of war is really an assertion of the legitimacy of the aggressive element in life. He might have agreed with William James that what is needed is a moral equivalent of war; but lacking the equivalent, there was no alternative for him but to prize the arts of war.

War Indispensable—It is nothing but fanaticism and beautiful soulism to expect very much (or even, much only) from humanity when it has forgotten how to wage war. For the present we know of no other means whereby the rough energy of the camp, the deep impersonal hatred, the cold-bloodedness of murder with a good conscience, the general ardour of the system in the destruction of the enemy . . . can be forcibly and certainly communicated to enervated nations as is done by every great war.[26]

In Nietzsche, the renunciation of aggression is equivalent

to a renunciation of life. And the desire to live (or to die) is a matter of fatality, not choice. Nietzsche's case rests on his realism: "the murderous innocence" (to use Yeats's phrase) of much of life. In our daily actions, we give pain to others as a matter of course, without necessarily intending to do so. But we distort the meaning of these actions when we assume responsibility for them and convert them into "bad conscience." Nietzsche wants this process halted. "We no longer wish causes to be sinners and effects to be executioners." [27] He rejects the idea of free will as a major and disastrous error in the history of Western thought. By denying that the will has alternatives, that is, options to act differently from the way it actually exercises itself, Nietzsche disallows the claim of Christian morality, the claim that man is to blame for his actions and must suffer guilt for the sins he has committed. "We immoralists are trying with all our power to eliminate the concepts of guilt and punishment . . . we recognize no more radical opponents than the theologians . . . 'a moral order of things' pollutes the innocence of becoming." [28] Nietzsche's denial of free will proceeds from his perception of man as a quantum or disposition of energy, which acts in spite of, though paradoxically through, his will and to which he has no choice but to submit. The doctrine of eternal recurrence is a metaphor for Nietzsche's belief in the fatality of energy. This "unfreedom" characterizes the strong and weak equally, though for the strong the tyranny of energy and the condition of passion—that is, of suffering passively the energy that flows through the strong man's veins—is a source of delight; the weak man can only lament his weakness. Freed of guilt, the strong man can enjoy or suffer his energy in all innocence.

"The innocence of becoming" is a sophisticated version of Rousseau's state of nature.* Devoted to the moral idea,

---

* Nietzsche's view of Rousseau is scornful: "Rousseau, this first modern man, idealist and *canaille* in one person: who was in need of moral 'dignity' in order even to endure the sight of his own person" (*Beyond Good and Evil,* p. 216).

Rousseau in his view of nature is never free of moral sentimentality. According to Rousseau, the natural man is fundamentally "good." But the logic of Rousseau's conception is that the state of nature is premoral and innocent. The natural man in his pristine condition acts instinctively, prior to reason or a sense of duty. Indeed, Rousseau's insistence on his innocence, as we have seen, it not so much a denial of the actions of which he was accused as it is a genuine conviction of "the innocence of becoming." "This is my nature. I cannot be other than myself," Rousseau seems to be saying.

Much of the confusion about Rousseau's ethical philosophy derives from his conflicting loyalties to the moral idea and to the premoral (or should we say immoral) state of nature. Nietzsche's doctrine does not suffer from this confusion because he recognizes fully the immoralism of natural energies. He repudiates as fraudulent nature in its stoic or romantic incarnations.

> You desire to *live* "according to nature"? Oh, you noble stoics, what fraud of words! Imagine to yourselves a being like nature, boundlessly extravagant, boundlessly indifferent, without purpose or considerations, without pity or justice, at once fruitful and barren and uncertain: imagine to yourself *indifference* as power—how *could* you live in accordance with such indifference? To live—is not that just endeavoring to be otherwise than this nature? Is not living, valuing, preferring, being unjust, being limited, endeavoring to be different. And granted that your imperative, "Living according to nature" means actually the same as "living according to life" —how could you do differently? . . . In your pride, you wish to dictate your morals and ideals to nature, to nature herself, and to incorporate them therein.[29]

In contrast, Nietzsche's "morality" is an appropriate and reverent response to immoralism.

The immoralist accepts the fact that he can be no more than himself. He is above resentment or indignation, for though he acknowledges the injustice of the universe, he accepts the injustice as an inevitable fact of life.* Guilt, repentance, remorse (the emotions of the ethical life) are gratuitous emotions. The self-dissatisfaction of the immoralist is an expression of his desire to overcome the all too human emotions of the ethical life. Self-perfection is self-overcoming, and self-overcoming is the graceful accommodation to one's fate.

Nietzsche's insight into the self-destructiveness of guilt is one of the great achievements of modern thought. And we follow with admiration his attempt to replace guilt with self-responsibility, for without self-responsibility the unleashed energies of man would become bestial. In his *efforts,* Nietzsche exemplifies both elements of Goethe's remark: "Every emancipation of the spirit is pernicious unless there is a corresponding growth in control." [30]

And yet the achievement does not measure up to the Goethean standard, for the *control* that Nietzsche envisages is inadequate to his explosive imagination of human possibility. Nietzsche's preoccupation with the passions contributed to the atmosphere of subjectivism that he himself so severely criticized.

---

* Nietzsche is not insensitive to the claims of social justice, as this doctrine might seem to imply, but his aristocratic bias, combined with extraordinary psychological insight, enables him to cast light on the dubious and "unjust" motives of the claimants for social justice. The insight, however, does not mitigate his belief in social justice. "When the Socialists point out that the division of property at the present day is the consequence of countless deeds of injustice and violence, and, in *summa,* repudiate obligation to anything with so unrighteous a basis, they can only perceive something isolated. The entire past of ancient civilization is built up on violence, slavery, deception and error; we, however, cannot annul ourselves, the heirs of all these conditions, nay, the concrescences of all this past, and are not entitled to demand the withdrawal of a single fragment thereof. The unjust disposition lurks also in the souls of non-possessors, they are not better than the possessors and have no moral prerogative; for at one time or another their ancestors have been possessors. Not forcible new distributions, but gradual transformations of opinion are necessary; justice in all matters must become greater, the instinct of violence weaker." (*Human, All Too Human,* 1: 327, 452.)

Those men who have moments of sublime ecstasy, and who, on ordinary occasions, on account of the contrast and excessive wearing away of their nervous forces, usually feel miserable and desolate, come to consider such moments as the true manifestation of their real selves, of their "ego," and their misery and dejection, on the other hand, as the *effect of the "non-ego."* This is why they think of their environment, the age in which they live, and the whole world in which they have their being, with feelings of vindictiveness. This intoxication appears to them as their true life, their actual ego; and everywhere else they see only those who strive to oppose and prevent this intoxication, whether of an intellectual, moral, religious, or artistic nature.

Humanity owes no small part of its evils to those fantastic enthusiasts; for they are the insatiable sowers of the weed of discontent with one's self and one's neighbor, of contempt for the world and the age, and, above all, of world lassitude. An entire hell of criminals could not, perhaps, bring about such unfortunate and far-reaching consequences, such heavy and disquieting effects that corrupt earth and sky, as are brought about by that "noble" little community of unbridled, fantastic, half-mad people—of geniuses, too—who cannot control themselves, or experience any inward joy, until they have lost themselves completely.[31]

Nietzsche's anti-Protestantism can be viewed as another version of Protestantism. Ironically, he is vulnerable on the very same ground on which he attacks Christianity. It is Protestantism in its radical forms that intensifies guilt without offering adequate countermeasures of relief. The irony of Nietzsche's attack upon Protestantism is that his doctrine of heroic individualism creates a comparable burden for the individual psyche, relieved only by a precarious will to suffer one's destiny without guilt.* Indeed, Nietzsche was compelled to invent the superman to endure this heavy burden.

---

* "The problem was not suffering itself, but lack of an answer to the crying question, *To what purpose do we suffer?* Man, the bravest animal and the one most inured to suffering, does *not* repudiate suffering in

The potential tragedy of the Nietzschean (already fore-shadowed in the Dostoevskian hero) lies in his terrible isolation. Nietzschean egoism intensifies the suffering by inflating the importance and capacities of the self, by denying the self the consolations of religion or community and expecting it to yield those consolations by its own energy.

Nietzsche, with his characteristic perspicacity, is aware of the dangers. Thus he appreciates the force of the Christian critique of egoism.

> Christianity also has made a great contribution to enlightenment, and has taught moral scepticism in a very impressive and effective manner—accusing and embittering, but with untiring patience and subtlety; it annihilated in every individual the belief in his virtues. . . . When trained in this Christian school of scepticism, we now read the moral books of the ancients, for example those of Seneca and Epictetus, we feel a pleasurable superiority and are full of secret insight and penetration—and we know better what virtue is.[32]

"Do not will anything beyond your power."[33] And again: "Be not virtuous beyond your powers! And see nothing from yourselves opposed to probability."[34] This is the warning voice of Zarathustra, directed to "the higher men," those who pursue the ascetic ideal. "He whose fathers were inclined for women, and for strong wine and flesh of wildboar swine; what would it be if he demanded chastity of himself?" But we can direct this warning as well to the Dionysian egoist, who tries to surpass his power.

---

itself: he *wills* it, he even seeks it out provided that he is shown a meaning for it, a *purpose* of suffering. *Not* suffering, but the senselessness of suffering was the curse which till then lay spread over humanity—*and the ascetic ideal gave it meaning*! It was up till then the only meaning; but any meaning is better than no meaning; the ascetic ideal was in that connection the *faute de mieux par excellence* that existed at that time. It is that ideal suffering *found an explanation*: the tremendous gap seemed filled; the door to all suicidal nihilism has closed. It is one of the ironies of Nietzsche's achievement that he himself was to help open the door to modern nihilism." (*The Genealogy of Morals,* p. 210.)

Searching for an Archimedian point of leverage out in space so that he can raise the world to his own level, and missing that point, the Dionysian egoist may begin to feel vertiginous, desperate, and miserably alone. He wants a connection with others, so in words and actions he tries to find his way back to a common ground with others—and that ground is the old values. For this reason, the transvaluation of values is always impure, contaminated by the old values. In order to retain his connection with the outside world, he may be perverse and diabolical; by behaving contrary to the law, he will implicitly recognize the existence and power of the law. The mortal temptation of the immoralist is to slide into a kind of Baudelairean impotence, in which he begins to enjoy the aromas of the flowers of evil.

IV

Power (or the feeling of power) is in a sense beyond criticism in Nietzsche's thought. Being an ultimate value, power cannot be referred to values beyond itself. But Nietzsche reserves the right to unmask false power or impotence that masks itself as power. Thus he scorns the shrill power rhetoric of Carlyle, which he sees as a symptom of weakness. He also distinguishes among forms of power, preferring, for instance, the power of art to crude political power.

The Dionysian artist has the highest place in Nietzsche's pantheon of heroes. He not only suffers from "overflowing vitality," but possesses the marvelous secret of mastering his suffering through art. The artist is an aristocrat, a true immoralist in the Nietzschean sense.

Nietzsche's most substantial work on art is the brilliant and early book *The Birth of Tragedy*, written during the height of his admiration for Schopenhauer. The book is a celebration of the life-enhancing power of art, though the celebration is qualified by the Schopenhauerian influence, which expresses itself in the wisdom of Silenus: that life is too terrible to be borne. As everyone knows, Nietzsche in that book conceives of the birth and subsequent history of tragic art in terms of an antagonistic collaboration between the gods Dionysus and Apollo. The permutations and combinations of that collaboration are complicated and somewhat blurred in the exposition. It is clear, however, that Nietzsche's idea of the highest kind of tragic art (exemplified by Aeschylus and Sophocles) is a harmony, a moment when the antagonism between the gods is suspended, and Apollo, with his power of individuation, clarity, and control, brings us as close as possible, without overwhelming us, to the terrible, fierce, and chaotic mysteries of Dionysus. Art at once confronts and evades the passional mysteries. ("Art is with us in order that we may not perish through truth.")[35]

The Birth of Tragedy is characteristically more concerned with the creative energy of the artist than with the work of art itself. It is the creative will rather than the specific deeds that issue from the will that interests Nietzsche. Art is an activity in which the artist dramatizes himself. Thus he sees the very essence of tragic drama not in its action, but in the *grand pathetic scene*. Indeed, he complains of the general confusion between drama and action in the history of aesthetic thought from Aristotle onward. Nietzsche, the philologist, reminds us that the Doric word *spav* "has nothing to do with action."[36]

The fact that Nietzsche seems to prefer the "classical" artist to the romantic-subjective artist (Goethe, Stendhal, Heine, even Bizet to Wagner and Rousseau, to cite instances) should not distract us from the truth of Nietzsche's aesthetic. What he admires in the work of these "classical" artists is not impersonality (the capacity to lose oneself in one's work), but rather the personal capacity of the artist that radiates from the work: his intelligence, his ability to possess his passions without diminishing them.

Nietzsche's utopia is an anticommunity of artists, each creating his own world of beauty and power, which he governs with absolute authority. "Hundreds of profound lonelinesses together form the city of Venice: this is its charm, a picture for the men of the future." [37]

6

Walt Whitman: Democracy and the Self

A Brief Preface on the Poet as Hero

Of the writers discussed in the previous chapters, only Dostoevsky kept his religious faith intact—though even he was menaced with temptations inconceivable to earlier religious writers.* In Nietzsche's view, the dominant fact of the nineteenth century was "the death of God." No longer able to summon faith in the Christian pieties, the most sensitive and imaginative men of the nineteenth century nevertheless inherited the intense spiritual feelings and yearnings of the Christian tradition. Men sought, in Carlyle's

---

* Dostoevsky himself knew this and he refers to the temptations that he imagines with pride. Thus in a private notebook he writes: "Ivan is deep, he is not one of your present-day atheists whose unbelief demonstrates no more than the narrowness of their point of view and the obtuseness of their small minds. . . . They never dreamed of so powerful a negation of God . . . have never seen atheistical expressions of such power." (Quoted in Philip Rahv, "The Legend of the Grand Inquisitor," in *Partisan Review*, May–June, 1954, p. 252.)

quaint phrase, "new clothes" for the spiritual life. Before Nietzsche, the English and German poets (like Hölderlin, Keats, Shelley) had attributed to the poetic imagination a power or grace that had formerly been reserved for a transcendent God. It is art that redeems us from the suffering and chaos of life. To be sure, the idea of the divine inspiration of the poet had been in the Western tradition for thousands of years, but not until Romanticism had the artist achieved the kind of dignity appropriate to his supposed power.

Yeats's statement about Blake puts very well the romantic claim for the poet:

> He announced the religion of art . . . in his time, educated
> people believed that they amused themselves with books of
> imagination, but that they "made their souls" by
> listening to sermons and by doing or by not doing certain
> things . . . In our time we are agreed that we "make our souls"
> out of great poets.[1]

Yeats is here summing up and endorsing a sentiment shared by Blake, Hölderlin, Wordsworth, Keats, Shelley, and Yeats himself; one can go on naming many of the major poets of the nineteenth century. This view is inadequately rendered by the term aestheticism, because the term conceals the strenuous moral and spiritual character of art: "the maker of souls."* Nietzsche passes beyond the philosophy of *The Birth of Tragedy,* but he never really abandons his "aestheticism." The superman is intelligible and convincing only as a supreme artist. The will to power as a *positive* doctrine is productive primarily in the realm of art. (As a "method" for psychological discoveries, it is of course invaluable.) The arrogation of godhead by the poet (and this is the ultimate reach of the romantic claim) is presumptuous. That poetry has a decisive influence on the lives of some of its readers is undeniable: that it "makes the souls" of its readers is questionable, for two reasons: the spiritual imperfections of poet and poem

---

* What it has in common with the aestheticisms of Pater and Wilde,
  for instance, is the supreme value which it places on art.

and the frailty of poetry (indeed literature generally) as a spiritual agent against the mighty distractions of the world. Such a view may be no more than a necessary myth for the poet, an emotional scaffolding, so to speak, that sustains the poet in his activity. As a description of the activity, it is somewhat pretentious.

There is a modified view of the artist-hero, which accounts for the spiritual weakness and for all that the poet has to contend with. He is an exemplary figure, a hero and therefore not a god—for his situation is struggle and aspiration. If he makes the souls of others, he can do so only by making his own soul. This is Nietzsche's view of the artist, and the view of Rilke:

Not for all time will the artist live side by side with ordinary men. As soon as the artist—the more flexible and deeper type among them—becomes rich and virile, as soon as he *lives* what now he merely *dreams*, man will degenerate and gradually die out. The artist is eternity protruding into time.[2]

Rilke here assumes that the artist is the sole repository of value, though as yet (in his alienated condition living "side by side with ordinary men") only potential value. His dreams must become actual, one is tempted to say political, before the necessary egoism of his activity is fully justified. *

Rilke's idiom is Nietzschean, particularly in the phrase "man will degenerate and gradually die out." It is difficult to know how literally one is to take this vision. Nietzsche was anti-Darwinian: he did not believe in progress (see his doctrine of eternal recurrence), nor did he imagine in Darwinian terms the evolution of man into a higher species. The statement should perhaps be taken as a metaphor for Nietzsche's and Rilke's aristocratic view of the problem. For Rilke and Nietzsche, the estrangement of the artist from ordinary humanity can be solved only through the complete

---

* I am reminded of the statement of Sergei Eisenstein, an unlikely figure with whom to compare Rilke, that the task of Soviet art is to banish art, i.e., to convert the dream into reality.

triumph of the artist. The actual conditions of such a triumph are (perhaps necessarily) vague.

Every responsive reader of Nietzsche, Rilke, and the English Romantic poets can testify to the exhilaration that he experiences in the poet's claim to heroism and grace and his imperious rejection of the squalor of ordinary life. It is an exhilaration, to be sure, constantly baffled by one's daily life. The bafflement is enough to create the suspicion that the artist-hero, however beautiful and powerful he may be as a poet, has little efficacy as a "legislator of mankind." Baudelaire defines the situation perfectly in "The Albatross":

The Poet resembles the prince of the clouds
Who laughs at hunters and haunts the storms;
Exiled to the ground amid the jeering pack,
His giant wings will not let him walk.[3]

Indeed, for this very reason a poet like Rilke is futuristic or utopian: he presents as immediate experience an unfulfilled hope—or fear.

II

The uniqueness of Whitman is that he accepts—or seems to accept—the given world as realized dream: an appropriate arena for the "richness" and "virility" (to use Rilke's words) of his being. There is in Whitman's poetry no enervating solitude, no enfeebling division between the self and the world. He is "fond of persons and places," "a boy of Mannahatta," who withdraws from the crowd only "to muse and meditate," but soon finds himself chanting among the chants of crowds of other Americans.

Chants of the prairies,
Chants of the long-running Mississippi,
Chants of Ohio, Indiana, Illinois, Wisconsin, Iowa, and
    Minnesota
Inland Chants—chants of Kansas,
Chants of teeming and turbulent cities—chants of Kentucky
    and Tennessee

Chants of dim-lit mines—chants of mountain-tops,
Chants of sailors—chants of the Eastern Sea and the Western Sea
Chants of the Mannahatta, the place of my dearest love, the
    place surrounded by hurried and sparkling currents,
Chants inclusive—wide reverberating chants,
Chants of the Many In One.[4]

This is the way Whitman projects himself at the beginning of
Leaves of Grass (in the first series of poems in the edition of
1860), and he will continue to "chant" throughout the rest of
the book.* Expansive, sensual, commanding, strident,
comic, unembarrassed, the *I* of *Song of Myself*, the most
ambitious and the most important poem in the collection, is
confident of his spontaneous community with others. That
community is the major assumption of the poem, an assumption that the reader must share if the poem is not to be read
as a silly exercise in self-inflation. "What I assume you shall
assume,/For every atom belonging to me as good belongs to
you."[5] Whitman is not the first to have heroized the poet; nor
is he the first to have depended on the community of poetry,
which all men are supposed to share, as a guarantee of the
reader's interest in the poet's career. Wordsworth's *Prelude*
is the archetype, and the democratic doctrine implicit in
Wordsworth's choice of an autobiographical subject for an
epic is expressed in the Preface to *Lyrical Ballads*:

What is a Poet? To whom does he address himself? And what
language is to be expected from him?—He is a man
speaking to men: a man, it is true, endowed with more
lively sensibility, more enthusiasm and tenderness, who has a
greater knowledge of human nature, and a more comprehensive
soul, than are supposed to be common among mankind;
a man pleased with his own passions and volitions, and who
rejoices more than other men in the spirit of life that is in

---

* There is a good deal of controversy about which one of the
nine editions is the best version. Without entering the controversy
myself, I have chosen the 1892 (deathbed) edition as good for my
purposes and have referred to the third edition (of 1860), a favorite of
some, when necessary.

him. . . . The poet singing a song in which all human beings
join with him, rejoices in the presence of truth as an invisible
friend . . . The sum of what was said is, that the poet is
chiefly distinguished from other men by a greater
power in expressing such thought and feelings as are produced
in him in that manner. But these passions and thoughts
and feelings are the general passions and thoughts and
feelings of men.[6]

There is, however, a significant difference between *The
Prelude* and *Song of Myself*. The *I* of *The Prelude* is a discrete
self, like the self of autobiography. Wordsworth narrates the
life of the poet, presents the external events of that life in an
orderly, chronological manner. To be sure, it is the "inner
landscape" of the poet's life that Wordsworth wants to
illuminate, but he avails himself of the autobiographer's habit
of narrative and scenic presentation. For all the egoism of *The
Prelude,* the poem *seems* almost modest by comparison with
Song of Myself. *The Prelude* is about a discrete, finite self. The
I of *Song of Myself* is at once naked, plastic, unbounded, without
a discrete past, assuming multiple forms, dissolving into
formlessness, presenting itself in its contradictoriness ("Do I
contradict myself? well I contradict myself") as a "knit of
identity," "a knot of contrariety," a mysterious weave of
diverse, untraceable strands.

There is a skeptical view of the Whitmanian *I* among some
of Whitman's more intelligent critics that reflects a basic
hostility to the enterprise. Leslie Fiedler, for instance, has
ridiculed the personae of the poetry—*Song of Myself* in
particular—as rhetorical exercises in self-evasion.[7] Underneath the patriotic booster, the all-conquering lover and
celebrator, Fiedler finds—or believes he finds—the man
Whitman: furtive, impotent, nervous. It is difficult to resist
the suspicion of philistinism in Fiedler's view: the imagination when it tries for grand epic transformations of the self is
never to be trusted, for there is always the prosaic reality of
furtive, impotent man, and prosaic reality, of course, is
truth. Even if this were so, it is hard to understand why

Fiedler should remain an admirer of Whitman as a poet, as he does, for surely the furtive, impotent Whitman is not an interesting fact of the poetry. Richard Chase, in a more persuasive study, values the comic performance: the melanges of the sublime and the ridiculous in self-dramatization and rhetoric.[8] Much in the poetry supports this view, but such a reading seems to me a form of evasion, a sort of embarrassment (informed by the hard ironic atmosphere of modern literature) in the presence of Whitman's poetry.

A more academic view of Whitman's poetry is determined by a bias about the orderliness and rational organization of poetry. Though more sophisticated versions of the view necessarily admit the element of illogicality and irrationality in poetry, the academic critics stress order and structure.[9] We can avoid the difficult and complex question of the justice of the view in relation to poetry as a whole and still maintain that the attempt to find "structure" in *Song of Myself* is a vain attempt.

The movement of *Song of Myself* is too free and fluid to be contained by anything so rigid and Procrustean as "structure." The "structure" of the poem is determined by the waywardness (sometimes of a surrealistic order) of the protean *I* that will "loaf and invite [his] soul" and follow its every impulse. Section 6 offers a vivid example of Whitman's *significant* waywardness.

A child said *What is the grass?* fetching it to me with full hands;
How could I answer the child? I do not know what it is
    any more than he.

I guess it must be the flag of my disposition, out of hopeful
    green stuff woven.

Or I guess it is the handkerchief of the Lord,
A scented gift and remembrancer designedly dropt,
Bearing the owner's name someway in the corners, that we
    may see and remark, and say *Whose?*

Or I guess the grass is itself a child, the produced babe of the
    vegetation.

Or I guess it is a uniform hieroglyphic,
And it means, Sprouting alike in broad zones and narrow zones,
Growing among black folks as among white,
Kanuck, Tuckahoe, Congressman, Cuff, I give them the same,
I receive them the same.

And now it seems to me the beautiful uncut hair of graves.

Tenderly will I use you curling grass,
It may be you transpire from the breasts of young men,
It may be if I had known them I would have loved them,
It may be you are from old people, or from offspring taken
     soon out of their mothers' laps,
And here you are the mothers' laps.

This grass is very dark to be from the white heads of old
     mothers,
Darker than the colorless beards of old men,
Dark to come from under the faint red roofs of mouths.

O I perceive after all so many uttering tongues,
And I perceive they do not come from the roofs of mouths
     for nothing.

I wish I could translate the hints about the dead young men
     and women,
And the hints about old men and mothers, and the offspring
     taken soon out of their laps.

What do you think has become of the young and old men?
And what do you think has become of the women and
     children?

They are alive and well somewhere,
The smallest sprout shows there is really no death,
And if ever there was it led forward life, and does not wait at
     the end to arrest it,
And ceas'd the moment life appear'd.

All goes onward and outward, nothing collapses,
And to die is different from what any one supposed, and
     luckier.

   "What is the grass?": Whitman attempts to answer the

question through a series of discrete metaphors: "the flag of
my disposition," "the handkerchief of the Lord," "a child,"
"a uniform hieroglyphic," a plant again "sprouting," and
the extraordinary, vaguely lurid image "the beautiful uncut
hair of graves." What do the images have in common?
The grass is a symbol of an ineffable mystery, and like all
true symbols of a mystery, part revelation, part cipher:
flag, handkerchief (of the Lord), *hieroglyphic.* The mystery, we
know, is involved with the most elemental processes of life,
growth, and death: the *child,* the *sprouting plant,* and the
ambiguous *uncut hair of graves.* The discreteness of the imagery
shows itself, for instance, in the sudden transition between
"the produced babe of the vegetation" and "the uniform
hieroglyphic."

The waywardness is perhaps best illustrated by the
"beautiful uncut hair of graves" and its subsequent mutation.
It is a striking and, as I have already remarked, a somewhat
lurid image. The key word is "hair," which gives to the
"scene" an almost surreal quality. And the incongruous
surreal quality of the image is confirmed by the way it is
subsequently perceived. It becomes the "curling hair" of the
breasts of lovers. One imagines the *I* of the poem contemplating the grass and the grass undergoing metamorphoses
in his imagination. It has been the "flag of [his] disposition,"
"the babe," "the uniform hieroglyphic" (all opaque images,
elusive and inaccessible), and now suddenly a penetrable
image, "the uncut hair of graves." We imagine him lying on
the grass, his imagination erotically stirred: he becomes the
lover of the grass, curling it as he would the hair of the breasts
of lovers; indeed, the grass *is* the hair of lovers.

The question *What is the grass?* becomes for Whitman an
erotic occasion. He can know the answer to the question not
through his mind (that is, through discursive answers to the
questions he raises), but through his bodily or sensuous
imagination. What he experiences in the grass is its vitality
(the love embrace *here at least* is not necrophilia), and this
experience of the constant vitality of the grass through all its

changes makes it possible for him to contemplate death with equanimity: "The smallest sprout shows there is really no death." (Elsewhere: "And as to you Life I reckon you are the leavings of many deaths,/[No doubt I have died myself ten thousand times before.]")[10] This is "the eternity of the phenomenon"[11] of which Nietzsche speaks. Death comes to individuals: it is the termination of the curve of an individual life. But if one can imagine cosmic energy repeatedly individuating and dissolving itself, then one can conceive death as ephemeral, not eternal, the means by which cosmic energy transmutes itself and creates the multiple forms of existence. But this is a discursive and abstract way of stating what is Whitman's *erotic* intuition of the enduring vitality of the phenomenal world.

Before Lawrence, Whitman celebrated what Lawrence called "the greater life of the body."

I sing the body electric,
The armies of those I love engirth me and I engirth them,
They will not let me off till I go with them, respond to them,
And discorrupt them, and charge them full with the charge of the soul.

Was it doubted that those who corrupt their own bodies conceal themselves?
And if those who defile the living are as bad as they who defile the dead?
And if the body does not do fully as much as the soul?
And if the body were not the soul, what is the soul?[12]

The verse here has a doctrinal ring. Elsewhere the mysteries of the body enter into and create an excitement in the poetry.

Houses and rooms are full of perfumes, the shelves are crowded with perfumes,
I breathe the fragrance myself and know it and like it,
The distillation would intoxicate me also, but I shall not let it.

The atmosphere is not a perfume, it has no taste of the distillation, it is odorless,

It is for my mouth forever, I am in love with it,
I will go to the bank by the wood and become undisguised
  and naked,
I am mad for it to be in contact with me.[13]

And again:

I am not an earth nor an adjunct of an earth,
I am the mate and companion of people, all just as
  immortal and fathomless as myself,
(They do not know how immortal, but I know.)
Every kind for itself and its own, for me mine male and female,
For me those that have been boys and that love women,
For me the man that is proud and feels how it stings to be
  slighted,
For me the sweet-heart and the old maid, for me mothers and
  the mothers of mothers,
For me lips that have smiled, eyes that have shed tears,
For me children and the begetters of children.

Undrape! you are not guilty to me, nor stale nor discarded,
I see through the broadcloth and gingham whether or no,
And am around, tenacious, acquisitive, tireless, and cannot be
  shaken away.[14]

Sex is one of the main *implicit* metaphors for the poetic
imagination. When the imagination "contemplates" or
"experiences" an object or a person or an atmosphere, it is
in *contact* with it, it is capable of *entering* into it or being
penetrated by it.

Richard Chase sees the diffuse sexuality of the poetry as
symptomatic of a failure in the poet.[15] In life sexual diffuseness
may be a sign of illness or deficiency, but in the imagination
this diffuseness becomes a power to charge erotically the
whole landscape of the poems. The main movement of
Whitman's poetry is toward fusion—between body and soul,
self and other—finally toward a vision of the unity of the
whole cosmos. It is in the sexual act that all the separate
things of the universe combine and billow out into a vast and
all-inclusive unity.

I mind how once we lay, such a transparent summer morning,
How you settled your head athwart my hips and gently turn'd
      over upon me,
And parted the shirt from my bosom-bone, and plunged your
      tongue to my bare-stript heart,
And reach'd till you felt my beard, and reach'd till you held my
      feet.

Swiftly arose and spread around me the peace and knowledge
      that pass all the argument of the earth,
And I know that the hand of God is the promise of my own,
And I know that the spirit of God is the brother of my own,
And that all the men ever born are also my brothers, and the
      women my sisters and lovers,
And that a kelson of the creation is love,
And limitless are leaves stiff or drooping in the fields,
And brown ants in the little wells beneath them,
And mossy scabs of the worm fence, heap'd stones, elder,
      mullein and poke-weed.[16]

This impulse toward fusion generates in Whitman a care-
lessness about himself: a fearlessness about spending himself,
because he feels assured of "vast returns." He makes himself
available to all and one: "What is commonest, cheapest,
nearest, easiest, is Me."[17] The poetic analogue for this
indiscriminate availability to experience is the catalogue.
The Whitmanian ego is a grab bag of every sort of experience.
After the long catalogue in section 15, Whitman declares:

And these tend inward to me, and I tend outward to them,
And such as it is to be of these more or less I am,
And of these one and all I weave the song of myself.[18]

In a famous passage at the beginning of section 19 Whitman
suggests that his indiscriminateness is a form of justice.

This is the meal equally set, this the meat for natural hunger,
It is for the wicked just the same as the righteous, I make
      appointments with all,
I will not have a single person slighted or left away,

The kept-woman, sponger, thief, are hereby invited,
The heavy-lipp'd slave is invited, the venerealee is invited;
There shall be no difference between them and the rest.[19]

It was Christ who, in one version of his love, made no discriminations, loved the high and the low, the good and the evil—perhaps the low and the evil even more, because they provided occasions for dramatizing the power of his love. It would be wrong, however, to find in Whitman's use of the Christ image a Christian significance. He is not imitating Christ's love, even when he recalls it. In Whitman's desires for and contacts with other selves, there is no selflessness, no suspension of the *me* so that the other might live, might be redeemed—which is what would be involved in a true *imitatio*. The effect of Whitman's embraces might be to invest the *other* with imaginative value: the kept-woman, sponger, thief, heavy-lipp'd slave. Whitman elsewhere affirms the restorative power of his imagination: "I moisten the roots of all that has grown."[20] But the motive of Whitman's embraces is self-gratification. He is forever "searching for an outlet": in another poem, he speaks of the pent-up rivers of himself, which he wants to discharge. He will adopt the mode of self-abnegation, but even there the egoistic center of sensual desire is strong.

There is, to be sure, great danger to the self in its protean impulse to touch and assume the shape of everything it encounters. The danger was first pointed out by Lawrence in his famous chapter on Whitman in *Studies in Classic American Literature*; in Whitman's "amorous ache" for everything and everyone, Lawrence saw the death wish, the drive for self-annihilation. The love of death is unquestionably very strong in Whitman. Two of his greatest poems, "Out of the Cradle Endlessly Rocking" and "When Lilacs Last in the Dooryard Bloom'd" are love songs to death. In the first of the poems, Whitman's embrace of lovely and soothing death, his insistence on its deliciousness, has a morbid and decadent suggestiveness. But the embrace does not necessarily reflect the desire for self-annihilation. It is not extinction that

Whitman courts, but sensual gratification at the outermost limits of experience: the moment of ecstasy when the dikes that contain the pent-up rivers of the self burst. Whitman's poems remain suspended, so to speak, at that moment. The clue to the poet's destiny in "Out of the Cradle" is in the "delicious word death," but the self does not dissolve in a *liebestod*. On the contrary, the experience has been an initiation into the rites of poetry: the poet remembers the event as a time when he discovered himself and his vocation.

A word then, (for I will conquer it,)
The word final, superior to all,
Subtle, sent-up—what is it?—I listen;
Are you whispering it, and have been all the time, you sea-waves?
Is that it from your liquid rims and wet sands?

Whereto answering, the sea,
Delaying not, hurrying not,
Whisper'd me through the night, and very plainly before
      daybreak,
Lisp'd to me the low and delicious word death,
And again death, death, death, death,
Hissing melodious, neither like the bird nor like my arous'd
      child's heart,
But edging near as privately for me rustling at my feet,
Creeping thence steadily up to my ears and laving me softly all
      over,
Death, death, death, death, death.

Which I do not forget,
But fuse the song of my dusky demon and brother,
That he sang to me in the moonlight on Paumanok's gray beach,
With the thousand responsive songs at random,

My own songs awaked from that hour,
And with them the key, the word up from the waves,
The word of the sweetest song and all songs,
That strong and delicious word which, creeping to my feet,
(Or like some old crone rocking the cradle,
      swathed in sweet garments, bending aside,)
The sea whisper'd me.[21]

III

We are at the difficult point of trying to understand Whitman's conception of the self. Against the danger of disintegration, Whitman affirms the discrete unitary *I*.

Apart from the pulling and hauling stands what I am,
Stands amused, complacent, compassionating, idle, unitary.[22]

The same sentiment of possessing the *me* as against the other is in the reserve of the line: "My final merit I refuse you." [23] But elsewhere, Whitman has conceived the self quite differently.

Out of the dimness opposite equals advance, always substance
        and increase, always sex,
Always a knit of identity, always distinction, always a breed
        of life.[24]

I have already referred to the passage in which Whitman speaks of weaving a "song of myself" out of all the experiences he had just catalogued.

Here is one of Whitman's most egregious "contradictions": not simply a matter of thought or logic, for which poets are always excused, but more seriously a matter of metaphor. For in one version, the self has a homogeneous center or core underneath its diversity, its susceptibility to disintegration (from the pulling and the hauling); in another version, the self is a diversity or a knit or weave of diverse, opposing strands. The contradiction, of course, is at the very heart of Whitman's poetic enterprise: it is adumbrated in the first of the Inscriptions:

One's-Self I sing, a simple separate person,
Yet utter the word Democratic, the word En-Masse.[25]

How is the paradox or contradiction resolved? We have already discussed the protean sensuality of Whitman's poetic imagination: its capacity for instantaneous expansion, contraction, and self-transformation as it moves through a field of people and events. This extraordinary capacity is a source of enormous confidence (note the way he is willing to spend himself, as he says), for it means that he can elude the kind of confinement in a single role that will judge him, reduce him, condemn him. Lawrence speaks of the Whitmanian self as "tricksy-tricksy"; Chase calls him evasive; and Fiedler sees the evasiveness as a flight from the reality of impotence. Only Chase grants that the evasiveness might be a power, the power of the comedian to impersonate a variety of roles. The power to impersonate, to transform oneself, is the capacity of the *I* to escape reduction.

The distinctively American or democratic aspect of Whitman's role-playing can be illustrated by comparison with a role-playing European poet, Baudelaire. In a poem in which Baudelaire impersonates Beauty, he speaks of her insolent poses, borrowed from the proudest of statues: this is a fine image of Baudelaire's aesthetic dandyism. In his famous address to his reader, Baudelaire exclaims the word that is the clue to *his* poetic destiny, "ennui". His poetry (the insolent poses borrowed from the proudest of statues) may be seen as an attempt to avoid "the reeling vertiginous"[26] disequilibrium that ennui produces. He would like not to be at the mercy of life, nature, the world, and so he contrives through the poetic imagination places of power and refuge.

Then I'll dream horizons the blue of heaven controls,
Of gardens, fountains weeping in alabaster bowls,
Of kisses, of birds singing morning and eve,
And of all that's most childlike the Idyll has to give.
The tumult at my window vainly raging grotesque
Shall not cause me to lift my forehead from my desk;

And when Winter comes with monotonous snowfalls
I shall close all around me shutters and lattices
To build into the night my fairy palaces.
For I shall be absorbed in that exquisitely still
Delight of evoking the Spring with my will,
Of wresting a sun from my own heart and in calm
Drawing from my burning thoughts an atmosphere of balm.[27]

Out of his discontent with "everyone and with himself," Baudelaire longs for the only redemption that he knows: "to produce a few lovely verses that will prove to me that I am not the least of men, that I am not inferior to those I scorn."[28] But the aesthetic idyl is merely a glimpse of paradise; the misery, the ennui return constantly to plague him. Moreover, the aesthetic power is a kind of lie: it is productive of Baudelaire's habit of creating false impressions about himself. He laments: "to have boasted (why?) about several sordid acts I have never committed, and to have denied like a coward a few other misdeeds committed with joy."[29] And yet perversely he celebrates the lie:

Shall not the semblance alone suffice for me
To rejoice my heart, since Verity I foreswore?
What matters stupidity or indifference?
Hail, mask, dear counterfeit! I bow, adore![30]

Of course, the spiritual reality of Baudelaire's life is nevertheless communicated by the poetry: the act of self-falsification or evasion (as in "Landscape") is itself dramatized.

Baudelaire experiences himself as a prisoner or victim of whom he is at the same time jailer and victimizer.

I am the wound and the knife!
I am the blow and the cheek!
I am the limbs and the wheel,
And condemned and executioner!

I am the vampire of my heart:
One of the lost forever,
Condemned to eternal laughter
And who can never smile again.[31]

"Wound and knife," "blow and cheek," "limbs and wheel," "condemned and executioner": these are images of a major portion of modern European literature and that portion of American literature that is European. The self creates roles to gain freedom and power in an oppressive world only to discover that the role is another kind of prison. Even as a poet who has the creative power to climb the skies, Baudelaire finds that when he inevitably returns to earth he is jeered like the albatross whose giant wings will not let him walk.

How different (and how American) Whitman is! The thousand roles that he assumes are a kind of spiritual acrobatics, in which he can display himself fully. But none of the postures or roles confine him: he enjoys and eludes them at will. So he need not worry about his sluttishness, his indiscriminateness. Unlike Baudelaire, who must accept condemnation and turn it into a perverse pleasure, Whitman eludes all judgment. He can afford to let go, to undress, to appear stark naked, because even the nakedness is not the final *me*. With his plastic chameleon-like power (connected with his sensuality), he can become everything and everyone, including himself. He does not need the protective self-irony of a man who is in danger of being reduced, had, conquered. ("Encompass worlds, but never try to encompass me.")[32]

Whitman is, so to speak, the poet of "social mobility." In a traditional European society, in which the self is often predestined (before birth) to its station in life, a rebellious refusal to make the accommodation, to seek other modes of being, has a revolutionary or immoralist impact. Moreover, the constraints of European life (its social stratification, the burden of all kinds of tradition) may provoke a violent, even apocalyptic reaction. Baudelaire, Rimbaud, Nietzsche, Rilke experience the actual world as a violent assault upon their consciousness, and their own violence is a measure of it. Whitman, on the other hand, seems to inhabit a space so expansive and accommodating that his most violent verbal gestures become almost vaporous.

Let murderers, thieves, bigots, fools, unclean persons, offer
    new propositions! . . .
Let faces and theories be turn'd inside out! Let meanings be
    freely criminal, as well as results! . . .
Let churches accommodate serpents, vermin, and the corpses of
    those who have died of the most filthy of diseases![33]

The exhortations are unmeant: they are a sort of mindless flexing of the spirit, a demonstration of how free and easy the Whitmanian *I* is. Earlier in this series of exhortations, Whitman had "pronounced openly" for "a new distributions of roles."[34] He is harmlessly, playfully trying on the immoralist role.*

In one of his late poems, Whitman speaks of "the terrible doubt of appearances."[35] Behind these appearances death (unindividuated life) lurks. The relation between appearances and death is analogous to the relation between the role and the unitary *I*. Whitman has a keen sense of the contingency of life in all its forms, but behind them he sees with visionary penetration the "eternal float"[36] of cosmic community (life-in-death), so that he can dissolve and disintegrate without fear, with an almost voluptuous assurance of what awaits him.

IV

One of the main ideas of *Leaves of Grass* is that there is an indissoluble connection between sexual freedom and democracy. In his reply to Emerson's praise of the first edition of *Leaves of Grass* (a reply which became part of the appendix of the 1856 edition), Whitman writes:

Of women just as much as men, it is the interest that there should not be infidelity about sex, but perfect faith. Women in these states approach the day of that organic equality with men, without which, I see men cannot have organic equality among themselves . . . I say that the body of a man or woman, the main matter, is so far quite unexpressed in poems, but that the body is to be expressed, and sex is. Of bards for these states, if it come to a question, it is whether they shall be the bards of the fashionable delusion

---

* Significantly, these exhortations (in the edition of 1860) were eliminated from subsequent editions.

of the inherent nastiness of sex, and of the feeble and
querulous modesty of deprivation. This is important in
poems, because the whole of the other expressions of a nation
are but flanges out of its great poems.[37]

Without the free expression of sexuality, women cannot
achieve equality with men, and without that, equality and
organic equality among men is impossible. This is the simple
"logic" of Whitman's sexual ideology.

Nietzsche, who celebrated the bodily instincts, arrived at
different (that is to say, aristocratic) conclusions. If, as
Nietzsche believed, vitality (including sexual vitality) is
unevenly distributed throughout mankind and the distribu-
tion is a *given* (anterior to both will and consciousness),
then aristocratic conclusions necessarily follow. One can
express only what is there: and to insist on vitality where the
instincts are missing is as grotesque a blasphemy against life
as to thwart them where they are to be found. (Thus Nietzsche
values the organic ascetic—though he castigates Christianity
for what it did to Pascal, for instance, a man of extraordinary
natural vitality.) Whitman, on the other hand, with his
visionary-prophetic faith in the potential capacities of all
men, refuses to make "metaphysical" inferences from the
actual contemporary condition of men. Who knows what
the vitality of an impotent and repressed man might be if
he were liberated from the "fashionable delusion of the
inherent nastiness of sex, and of the feeble and querulous
modesty of deprivation"?

Some of the sexual attitudes in Whitman's poetry are
exceedingly odd, attitudes which even suggest an antisexual
strain. For instance:

Let us all, without missing one, be exposed in public, naked,
   monthly, at the peril of our lives! let our bodies be
   freely handled and examined by whoever chooses![38]

The "candor" here is a form of bravado that has little to do
with the passional mysteries—or sexual pleasure.

But there is a sensuality in the poetry which is strong and

politically significant. It charges, so to speak, the space between the observing poet and the observed.

I knew a man, a common farmer, the father of five sons,
And in them the fathers of sons, and in them the fathers of sons.

This man was of wonderful vigor, calmness, beauty of person,
The shape of his head, the pale yellow and white of his hair and
 beard, the immeasurable meaning of his black eyes, the
 richness and breadth of his manners,
These I used to go and visit him to see, he was wise also,
He was six feet tall, he was over eighty years old,
 his sons were massive, clean, bearded, tan-faced, handsome,
They and his daughters loved him, all who saw him loved him,
They did not love him by allowance, they loved him with
 personal love;
He drank water only, the blood show'd like scarlet through the
 clear-brown skin of his face,
He was a frequent gunner and fisher, he sail'd his boat himself,
 he had a fine one presented to him by a ship-joiner, he had
 fowling pieces presented to him by men that loved him;
When he went with his five sons and many grand-sons to hunt
 or fish, you could pick him out as the most beautiful and
 vigorous of the gang,
You would wish long and long to be with, you would wish to
 sit by him in the boat that you and he might touch
 each other.[39]

Whitman's poetry represents the spiritual enfranchisement of the masses. * American democracy had placed the broad masses of people in the foreground of the stage of history. America was *their* destiny, not the destiny of a particular class or great man. (Whitman constantly reminds his readers that the President, the government, architecture, music, etc., are for

---

* Whitman's subject is "the broadest average of humanity and its
 identities in the now ripening Nineteenth Century, and especially
 in each of their countless examples and practical occupations in
 the United States today." ("A Backward Glance o'er Travel'd
 Roads," in *Leaves of Grass and Selected Prose,* ed. John
 Kouwenhoven, p. 547.)

them.) He attempts to translate this political reality or opportunity into a spiritual fact. In the catalogue, Whitman, like the master of ceremonies of modern democracy, calls each man forward to take a bow. Occasionally he pauses for a more lingering regard, as in the case of the old farmer and his five sons. At such moments he dramatizes the grace of the poetic act: its power to charge or rather discover the life of a person or an event. In wanting to touch the man, Whitman indicates a recognition of his beauty and dignity. The sensuality is part of the symbolic or ritual character of the event. Whitman's democratic tact is original. In Wordsworth's poetry there are also recognitions of the value and dignity of humble people: the Cumberland beggar and the leech-gather, however, remain rustics. Moreover, their value is in the occasion they provide for the poet to discover the significance of his creativity. In Whitman's poetry the *I* and the other person meet on equal ground. They touch each other into life.

There is an ambiguity in the Whitmanian recognition. It presupposes at once the value of what is being recognized and touched and its lack of realization before it has been celebrated by poetry. This ambiguity results in a curious feeling that Whitman is presenting in the present tense a future condition. What he celebrates is not yet achieved, is in the state of becoming, but its realization can be anticipated by the poetic act. Whitman projects a marriage between poetry and democracy. Democracy creates the conditions of a new poetry, greater than Shakespeare and the prophets, and poetry re-creates democracy, becomes its spirit and soul.

Whitman's celebrations are not descriptive actions—at least, not in intention. They are creative realizations of the object or event. *The grass* before the poetic event is different from what it is after the event. The presumption is that poetry—and Whitman anticipates future generations of poets —can realize the potential spiritual life of America and, since America is ultimately a symbol, the life of mankind. Only an American poet could be "guilty" of this presumption: for it assumes a view of personality as unfixed, in the process of becoming, and a vast innocent faith in the plasticity of human life. In a European poet (Lawrence or Rilke, for example), so much vitality and intensity would have the effect of depreciating the value of the surrounding life. The tragedy of Nietzsche, Rilke, and Lawrence lies in the contrast between so much isolated intensity and the "abyss" of normal life. But Whitman, with his democratic congeniality and polymorphous sexuality, is able to flood his environment with his own vitality, is able to see the world as a projection of his own expansive egoism.

Democratic Vistas (1871) shows Whitman's faith being tested. The poet who has been celebrating city and farm, worker, President, athlete, suddenly testifies to his awareness of the corruption of American life. The antinomian indifference to good and evil in the poetry proves to be a kind of exercise, for in *Democratic Vistas* Whitman writes in the spirit of the Victorian moralist. The occasion, of course, is what has come to be called the Gilded Age—the period in American history when the dream had been cheapened, turned into a materialistic nightmare. The dehumanizing effect of industrialism was beginning to reveal itself, and Whitman (in the tradition of Carlyle and Ruskin) makes his indictment.

I say that our New World democracy, however great a success in uplifting the masses out of their sloughs, in materialistic development, products, and in a certain highly-deceptive superficial popular intellectuality is, so far, an almost complete failure in its social aspects, and in really grand religious, moral, literary, and esthetic results.[40]

And in a footnote he pays tribute to Carlyle:

"Shooting Niagara"—I was at first roused to much anger—
and abuse by this essay from Mr. Carlyle, so insulting to the
theory of America—but happening to think afterwards how
I had more than once been in the like mood, during which
his essay was evidently cast, and seen persons and things in
the same light, (indeed some might say there are signs of the
same feeling in these vistas)—I have since read it again,
not only as a study expressing as it does certain judgments

from the highest feudal point of view, but have read it with
respect as coming from an earnest soul, and contributing
certain sharp-cutting metallic grains, which, if not gold or
silver, may be good hard, honest iron.[41]

Whitman concedes, indeed argues, that every great civilization needs a strong material base, but there must be no confusion between ends and means, a confusion that is occurring
in America. Yet for all his strictures on contemporary
American life, he holds onto the democratic idea as fiercely
as ever. He attacks the inferiority complex of American
writers vis à vis Europe (itself a symptom of the corruption).
The current phase through which America is passing has only
fortified his confidence that American writers must not imitate
the cultural forms of Europe—that way lies sterility—but
create poetry out of the native vigor and idiom of American
democracy. Whitman's poetry belongs to the heroic period
(in spirit if not in time) of American democracy, when it
seemed possible, indeed probable, that a whole people would
achieve a dignity formerly reserved for an aristocratic elite.
Whitman saw the dangers to the new democracy with
uncommon clarity, but he was too absorbed in the heroic
dream to be seriously unsettled by what he saw.

I have begged the question by speaking of Whitman's
awareness of the dangers *to* democracy. It is possible to
argue that there are dangers *in* democracy to which Whitman
is insensitive. In *Democracy in America* De Tocqueville argued
that there is an inherent tendency in democracy to level
distinctions—that equality is the operative value in the
democratic trinity of liberty, fraternity, equality. In this view,
democracy is mistrustful of distinction of all sorts, indeed
harbors deep and dangerous resentments against everyone
and everything that is not mediocre. There has been enough
evidence for this in American life, particularly in the American
attitude toward artistic and intellectual achievement. It
remains to be shown, of course, that what De Tocqueville
described is a law of democratic life, not merely an empirical
fact of a phase of democracy. It may even be that the leveling

tendency in industrialism, which is the historical twin of democracy, has been the chief culprit. The degradation of the worker to his productive function (his value is defined by his productive function), the fact that money becomes the very atmosphere in which people live—may be the true source of the mediocritizing of life. In other words, it may be argued against the aristocratic view that when democracy emancipates itself from the conditions of its early industrial life, Whitman's heroic vision will become a real possibility.

Contemporary literary attitudes toward democracy have been seriously affected by the aristocratic views of writers like De Tocqueville and Nietzsche. Even those who share Mill's vision of democracy as the best of all possible worlds from a political point of view share it with a certain reluctance—indeed, satisfy their aristocratic dispositions by creating cultural hierarchies. The democratic *sentiment* exists in a vulgarized form only in crowds, political movements, and bands of enthusiasts.* The fraternity between man and man that an aristocratically disposed artist like Lawrence praised as Whitman's great imaginative achievement is an unrealized dream.

V

It may be necessary ultimately to dispense with the word egoism in speaking of Whitman.† He does not value himself at the expense of others. His poems are paeans to "adhesiveness,"[42] a rather unfortunate but important word (another "clue") in Whitman's later poems: the fantasy is of a world thickly crowded with companions, whose touch is a guarantee

---

* The "hippie" movement of the present day is an experiment in Whitman's sensuous-democratic mode. So far it shows little, if any, creative result.

† Whitman's egoism is, to use Rousseau's distinction, *amour de soi* rather than *amour propre*.

of his own and their reality ("That the soul of the man I speak for rejoices in comrades").[43] The unitary *I* is what is left over from the knit of identity, the weave of other persons and events that compose the song of myself—the *I* that can enjoy what it takes into itself. Whitman in one sense represents the transcendence of egoism. He knows, as other great egoists before him knew, that when the *I* separates itself sharply from the surrounding life, it risks all sorts of disease: vertigo, sterility, inhumanity. For this reason, the great egoists (like Nietzsche and Lawrence) reserve some of their strongest loathing for the ego. Whitman feels no aversion to egoism, because he is nonchalantly at ease in the company of others: he is thus able to achieve an identification of egoism and community. (Thus there is no place in *Song of Myself* for the personal discrete Walt Whitman and his particular history, a fact which, as I have already remarked, distinguishes Whitman's epic poem from *The Prelude*. What a silly irrelevance the personal Walt would be on the cosmic stage he creates!)

In his essay on Whitman, Lawrence distinguishes between two Whitmans, the great and the false poets. The great poet, in Lawrence's view, is the poet of sympathy or comradeship between man and man (the poet of the *Calamus* poems); the false poet is the poet of an impossible universal love, of the "amorous ache" for everything and everyone. Whatever value Lawrence's distinction has on moral grounds, it represents, it seems to me, a misreading of Whitman's poetry: for in the *Calamus* poems Whitman exhibits the same tendency toward universal love that he shows in the poems of amorous aching. He does not want the profound solitude and isolation of a particular friendship: he seeks rather the bracing spirit of multitudes of comrades, who will surround, touch, and enhance him.

That shadow my likeness that goes to and fro seeking a
    livelihood, chattering, chaffering,
How often I find myself standing and looking at it where it flits,
How often I question and doubt whether that is really me;

But among my lovers and caroling these songs,
O I never doubt whether that is really me.[44]

Lawrence, of course, may still be right when he says that universal love is a hoax, but if he is, he must indict the whole poet. Lawrence's view proceeds from a psychological realism that prejudges a human possibility, odd as this may seem in the light of his own utopian imagination. Whitman is imagining—or trying to imagine—a world in which the sentiment of universal comradeship is possible: the fact that Lawrence responds to the *Calamus* poems might indicate the possible validity of this imagination.

How successful is Whitman's enterprise? Whitman certainly knew how precarious the enterprise was, how much it depended on the willingness of the reader to share the assumption of an unbounded vitality. (" . . . what I assume you shall assume,/For every atom belonging to me as good belongs to you.") The gulf between the despisers and the enthusiasts of Whitman cannot be bridged, it seems to me, by rational discourse, that is, by an appeal to the canons of poetry or to the standard of moral or psychological realism. "Objective" demonstrations fail inevitably, because a reader who does not share or who is unwilling to suspend his disbelief in the assumptions of Whitman's poetry will encounter the large gesture, the uninhibited energy, the extravagant imagery with cynicism. Unquestionably, a lot of the bad poetry in *Leaves of Grass* results from this attitude toward life: it is at once too relaxed and too willful to submit itself to aesthetic discipline. But the bad poetry is the price for one of the most daring and important "experiments" in the history of literature. Like Nietzsche, Whitman tries out a new mode of being in his imagination. "Behind all else that can be said, I consider "Leaves of Grass" and its theory experimental—as, in the deepest sense, I consider an American republic itself, with its theory. (I think I have at least enough philosophy not to be too absolutely certain of anything, or any results.) In the second place, the volume is a *sortie*—whether to prove triumphant and conquer its field of aim and escape and construction, nothing less than a hundred years from now can fully answer." [45] *Leaves of Grass* is the spiritual-physical incarnation of the democratic possibility.

7

Lawrence and Christ

In recent years Lawrence has been made to serve causes not of his own choosing, notably the moral tradition of the English novel and more recently Christianity. The impetus for the remaking of Lawrence was initially provided by T. S. Eliot's attack on Lawrence in *After Strange Gods,* in which Eliot found the son of a Midlands coal miner heretical and sinister, the inevitable result of a deficiency in the kind of tradition that a good education gives.[1] F. R. Leavis, coming to Lawrence's defense, argued insistently (sometimes impressively, often extravagantly) for Lawrence's place in "the great tradition" of the English novel.[2] Or in another view, he is the last great writer who embodies the attack on industrialism which began in England with Wordsworth and became so pervasive a theme in Victorian literature that Pater, surveying the whole of poetry, could define "all great poetry" as "a continual protest" against "the predominance of machinery."[3] There are real provocations for seeing

Lawrence as traditional and moral. If one reads *The Rainbow* for its depiction of English country life, one is impressed with Lawrence's resemblance to the George Eliot of *Adam Bede*. The essay "Democracy," read without reference to his other works, yields a social and morally earnest Lawrence not unlike the Carlyle of "Signs of the Times." These views, however, have the unfortunate effect of domesticating Lawrence by neutralizing his subversiveness.

A particularly interesting instance of this is a recent tendency in the criticism of Lawrence to stress his kinship with Christianity. There is, to be sure, some evidence for this view. Toward the end of his career Lawrence evinced an admiration for the pagan element in the Catholic church and was even hopeful about the regeneration of Christianity as an active religious force. Moreover, Lawrence's attraction to the figure of Jesus was deep and abiding, and *The Man Who Died,* despite the elements of parody and satire that it contains, is a significant and, in certain ways, reverent re-creation of the Christ story. Lawrence's affection for the idea of the Resurrection alone would seem to provide a ground for asserting his kinship with Christianity. One critic suggests that Lawrence may have been working all along toward a Christian view of things and calls Lawrence "almost a Christian."[4]

All this, of course, is to ignore the fact that the essential animus of his work is averse to Christianity. If he celebrates the Resurrection, he reminds us in *Apocalypse* that resurrections are prominent in pre-Christian religions. Indeed, Christianity involves the transcendence of the idea of resurrection. Man is to rise to a place in the eternal scheme of things, never to rise again. For Lawrence the rhythm of death and rebirth is an eternal rhythm which can never be transcended so long as there is life. Lawrence, consequently, loathed the idea of immortality. Even more crucial to Lawrence's view of Christianity is his peculiar appropriation of the idea of the Holy Ghost. The Holy Ghost, according to Lawrence, is that capacity within man which "can scent the new tracks of the Great God across the Cosmos or Creation."

It is not the way or the word; it is rather the eternal capacity in man to discover the way and the word at every moment of his quest. Lawrence writes: " . . . never did God or Jesus say there was only one way of salvation, for ever and ever. On the contrary, Jesus plainly indicated the changing of the way."[5] Lawrence appropriates the idea of the Holy Ghost precisely to free himself from a commitment to Christianity. He separates Christ from Christianity, and it is this separation that has given him the freedom to pursue God in his own way. Nietzsche (in *Thus Spake Zarathustra*) provides us with a motto for Lawrence's version of the Christ story in *The Man Who Died*.

> Verily, too early died that Hebrew whom the preachers of slow death honour. . . . Had he but remained in the wilderness, and far from the good and just! Then, perhaps, would he have learned to live, and love the earth—and laughter also!
> Believe it, my brethren! He died too early; he himself would have disavowed his doctrine had he attained to my age! Noble enough was he to disavow![6]

The Man Who Died begins on an ironic note. Lawrence's Christ is miraculously recalled to life by a "loud and splitting" cock crow. Pained and disillusioned, he discovers that the world he tried to deny for the illusory glory of eternal life has its own undying glory. "The world, the same as ever, the natural world, thronging with greenness, a nightingale singing winsomely, wistfully, coaxingly calling from the bushes beside a runnel of water, in the world, the natural world of morning and evening, forever undying, from which he had died."[7]

With his keen religious intuition, Lawrence has perceived the religious heresy of the Christian impulse toward self-transcendence. By trying to exceed the reach of his hands and feet in order to achieve communion with God, man is separated from God and diminished in the separation. The nausea, emptiness, and disillusion that the man suffers are the punishments that Lawrence imagines for the sacrilege. Lawrence is presenting in a new way the old paradox of the Christian critique of the Renaissance conception of man: that the centering of the universe around man results in a diminution of his stature. As Lawrence exploits the paradox, however, man in his full splendor and potency is conceived according to the Renaissance model. For Lawrence, as for every religious writer, the imagination of divinity and the imagination of the self are inextricably bound together. As the imagination of divinity fails, so does the imagination of the self. Lawrence's loathing of modern literature derives in part from a feeling that it offers us the spectacle of small selves in a godless universe, attempting to achieve significance through a psychological magnification of their most trivial feeling. ("... it is self-consciousness, picked into such fine bits that the bits are most of them invisible, and you have to go by the smell. Through thousands and thousands of pages Mr. Joyce and Mrs. Richardson tear themselves to pieces, strip their emotions to the finest threads.")[8]

The effect of Lawrence's contempt for what he called "the idiotic foot-rule" that "man is the measure of the universe" * is often a kind of misanthropy. In *The Man Who Died* the repudiation of Christ's mission to convert men to the God of Love ("to lay the compulsion of love on all men") is accompanied by an intense hatred of the City of Man.

So he went his way, and was alone. But the way of the world was past belief, as he saw the strange entanglement of passions and circumstance and compulsion everywhere,

---

* In a letter (June 6, 1925) to Trigant Burrow, Lawrence writes the following: "People are too dead and too conceited. *Man is the measure of the universe.* Let him be it: idiotic foot-rule which even then is *nothing.* In my opinion, one can never *know:* and never-never *understand.* One can but swim like a trout in a quick stream...." (*The Letters of D. H. Lawrence,* p. 635.) This is a very compressed statement of Lawrence's view of the humanist presumption. The fatality of consciousness is that it separates man from the world, compels him to regard himself, and makes the moment of self-regard the meaning of the world.

but always the dread insomnia of compulsion. It was fear,
the ultimate fear of death, that made men mad. So always he
must move on, for if he stayed, his neighbors wound the
strangling of their fear and bullying around him. There was
nothing he could touch, for all, in a mad assertion of ego,
wanted to put a compulsion on him, and violate his
intrinsic solitude. It was the mania of cities and societies
and hosts, to lay a compulsion upon a man, upon all men.
For men and women alike are mad with the egoistic fear of
their own nothingness.[9]

We are reminded in the above passage of Lawrence's
kinship with other misanthropes:— Swift and Nietzsche, for
example. The misanthropy is connected with Lawrence's
attraction to the "inhuman" and the "impersonal": Lawrence's characters seek to transcend the human world of
circumstance and compulsion in order to enter the other
world of cosmic energy, what Lawrence calls (in *The Man
Who Died*) "the greater life of the body." At the end of
Apocalypse Lawrence unmistakably indicates the cosmic
character of the greater life of the body.

We ought to dance with rapture that we should be alive and
in the flesh, and part of the living, incarnate cosmos. I am part
of the sun as my eye is part of me. That I am part of the sea.
My soul knows that I am part of the human race, my soul is an
organic part of the great human soul, as my spirit is part
of my nation. In my own very self, I am part of my family.
There is nothing of me that is alone and absolute except my
mind, and we shall find that the mind has no existence by
itself, it is only the glitter of the sun on the surface
of the waters.[10]

In order to see what is involved in moving from the little
world to the greater world of the body we should turn to
Women in Love, his richest if not his most successful novel, in
which we are given a striking demonstration of his imagination of transcendence.

As critics have pointed out, the relationship between
Birkin and Ursula is intended to represent the expansion and

realization of vitalities in them, while the relationship between Gudrun and Gerald develops, in contrast, toward catastrophe and death. The love of Birkin and Ursula, however, is successful *only* by contrast with the disastrous connection between Gerald and Gudrun, for if we ignore the counterpointing of the two relationships and consider simply the evolution of Birkin in the novel, then the fulfilment of his relationship with Ursula seems a rather dubious affair.

The source of the trouble is Birkin's problematical character. He is the hero of the novel, but not unequivocally its protagonist, as he is often taken to be. His contradictions are simply too egregious: he is something of a windbag, a man of abstractions who hates abstractions, a believer in the sacrosanct integrity of each individual who is nevertheless a moral bully (he bullies Gerald and Ursula in particular); he wants to be alone, yet he is cursed with the *Salvator Mundi* touch. His sexuality is complicated. His desire to break free from Hermione cannot be explained exclusively as a recoil from a predatory female. To be sure, Hermione in her awful willfulness is an enemy of life and spontaneity, and Birkin's flight from her is the necessary act of self-preservation. But Birkin's suspicion of Hermione remains a constant posture, which determines his relations with Ursula. His recoil from Ursula is a response to the "eternal feminine": this is graphically illustrated by the episode (in the chapter "Moony") in which Birkin tries to destroy the reflection of the moon upon the water. The image, of course, is indestructible. When Birkin's anger exhausts itself, he becomes more receptive to Ursula—though the erotic emotion is surprisingly thin and fragile. Predictably, the battle between them is soon resumed.

If we consider the consummation of their love or the "love ethic" to which it is attached, we can perhaps begin to appreciate the extent of Birkin's recoil from the act of love. The merging of identities—what the Elizabethans called "the little death"—is passionately repudiated by Birkin. Instead the act of love becomes a male-female polarity—or, in one of Lawrence's metaphors, "a star equilibrium"—in which the separate identities of the lovers are maintained even at the moment of consummation. To be sure, Birkin's "argument" against love has a certain cogency. He is setting himself against the romantic conception of love as a *Liebestod*. Lawrence evidently wants Birkin's argument vindicated, when he has Ursula, who insists that Birkin is her whole life, reject love as an ideal. Ursula makes the rejection in an argument with Gudrun toward the end of the novel: "Love is too human and little. I believe in something inhuman of which love is only a part. I believe that what we must fulfill comes out of the unknown to us, and it is something infinitely more than love. It isn't so merely human."[11] Given Ursula's statement that Birkin is enough for her—"I don't want anybody else but you"[12]—Ursula's little speech to Gudrun seems like a justification of Birkin's life, not her own. It is as if Lawrence wanted a confirming statement from Ursula to vindicate Birkin's actions to the reader.

The suspicious critic, oriented to psychoanalysis, sees in this rejection of love and of woman a concealment of a "fear in Birkin perhaps as deep as, or deeper than, his longing for Ursula."[13] The critic has only to invoke in support of this view Birkin's strange relationship with Gerald, particularly as it is expressed in the homoerotic wrestling episode and the peculiar note of discontent on which the novel ends, in which Birkin expresses his desire for "eternal union with a man."[14] Birkin, from this point of view, suffers from a homosexual fear of women.

That there is something in this view can be denied only by those whose commitment to Laurentian values is fanatical. But the homosexual impulse in Birkin is inadequate to explain the *experience* that is gained by a rejection of a love all "too human and little"—that experience of the "unknown" of which the passionate embraces of Birkin and Ursula do give us a glimpse and of which there is an intimation in Birkin's speculations about the elegant sculptured figure from West Africa.[15] (Birkin earlier characterized the African "process" as a "further sensual experience—something deeper, darker, than ordinary life can give.")[16] He rejects the African way because it involves dreadful mysteries beyond the phallic cult. He asks himself, "How far in their inverted culture, had these West Africans gone beyond phallic knowledge?"[17] And in imagining the distance—"the goodness, the holiness, the desire for creation must have lapsed"[18]—Birkin recoils in fear.

The mysteries from which he recoils are doubtless Dionysian mysteries, in which man is "led back to the very heart of nature." In *The Birth of Tragedy* Nietzsche understood this experience as a moment when "the state and society, and, in general, the gaps between man and man give way to an overwhelming feeling of oneness which leads back to the very heart of nature."[19] Elsewhere he characterizes the Dionysian festival as a time when "all of Nature's excess in joy, sorrow and knowledge became audible, even in piercing shrieks."[20] Lawrence's instinct warned him that the consequence of an unmediated return to nature may be, in Nietzsche's words, an "abyss of annihilation."[21] ("The Woman Who Rode Away," for instance, can be read as a kind of cautionary tale about the risks of the Dionysian.) But despite the fear of being devoured by the experience, Lawrence's heroes constantly court it. We find the fascination with the Dionysian in the following passage from "The Woman Who Rode Away."

Only the eyes of the oldest were not anxious. Black and fixed, and as if sightless they watched the sun, seeing beyond the sun. And in their black, empty concentration there was power, power intensely abstract and remote, but deep, deep to the heart of the earth, and the heart of the sun. In absolute motionlessness he watched till the red sun should send his ray through the column of ice. Then the old man should strike, and strike home, accomplish the sacrifice and achieve the power.[22]

In Lawrence's "Study of Thomas Hardy" there is a remarkably vivid description of this state of being.

... I wish we were all like kindled bonfires on the edge
of space, marking out the advance-posts. What is the aim of
self-preservation, but to carry us right to the firing line;
there what *is* is in contact with what is not. If many lives be
lost by the way, it cannot be helped, nor if much suffering is
entailed. I do not go out to war in the intention of avoiding
all danger or discomfort: I go to fight for myself. Every step I
move forward into being brings a newer, juster proportion
into the world, gives me less need of storehouse and barn,
allows me to leave all and to take what I want by the way,
sure it will always be there; allows me in the end to fly
the flag of myself, at the extreme tip of life.[23]

What Lawrence and his heroes desire—and it is implicit
in the passages quoted above and in numerous descriptions
of the sexual act at the moment of consummation (e.g.,
"he felt as if he were seated in immemorial potency")[24]—is
to be, as it were, the point at which all the energies of the
universe converge, and to experience them incarnate in their
beings as sheer *power*. This experience, from which Birkin
recoiled in his speculations about the inverted culture of the
"African way," holds the secret of power that the Laurentian
hero desires to possess.

But Birkin is a compelling figure not simply for what he
wants, but for what he is or has. Despite his pallor and illness
(marks of a sick spirituality in the Nietzschean sense), Birkin
has *vitality*. It shows itself principally in his volatility, his
inconsistency, his restiveness. He is restive, volatile, but not
frivolous.

Why bother! Why strive for a coherent, satisfied life?
Why not drift on in a series of accidents—like a picaresque
novel? Why not? Why bother about human relationships?
Why take them seriously'—male or female? Why form
any serious connections at all? Why not be casual, drifting
along, taking all for what it was worth?
And yet, still, he was damned and doomed to the old effort
at serious living.[25]

In his search for life or power, Birkin follows the various

promptings of energy or impulse within him. Birkin is alive by virtue of his mobility and changeableness.

One of the most striking instances of Birkin's changeableness is in the chapter "Excurse." Birkin drives Ursula through the countryside, and during the ride, without apparent provocation or transition, runs the whole gamut of emotions: coldness, irritation, exasperation, tenderness, anger, passion.[26] It is as if Birkin is in the grip of a demon which constantly disequilibrates him and tells him in effect that he is unrealized, that if he remains faithful to his demon by allowing free expression to his emotions, he may achieve reality.

Among the main efforts of *Women in Love* is Birkin's attempt to achieve verbal consciousness of his experiences, which, as Lawrence says in his foreword to the novel, is a great part of life. Since Birkin is not a fully realized character, since his soul has more than one motion and the motions are sometimes contradictory, one cannot expect a completely articulate or systematic verbal consciousness. Thus Birkin's ideas are not necessarily final truths, but rather attempts to discover and formulate the deepest motions of his soul. They have dramatic significance in revealing a character, and even in their occasional fatuity they reflect Birkin's *heroic* quality: his passionate desire for growth and change. In this respect he contrasts sharply with a fixed character like Hermione or Gerald. It is, I think, somewhat misleading to see Birkin as a "free" character (the view of Mark Schorer and others),[27] for Birkin's demon gives a compulsive quality to his behavior. But Birkin's compulsiveness or "unfreedom" is not necessarily an evil—indeed, it may be no more than a mark of his participation in the human condition. As Nietzsche has taught, a man can only express the energy within him, and the difference between man and man may lie not so much in his "freedom" as in the quality of his energy and his faithfulness to its promptings.

This is what Lawrence means when, in his famous letter to Edward Garnett (June 5, 1914), he explains the intentions of *The Rainbow*:

. . . what is interesting in the laugh of the woman is the
same as the binding of the molecules of steel or their
action in heat: it is the inhuman will, call it physiology, or like
Marinetti—physiology of matter, that fascinates me. I don't
so much care about what the woman feels—in the
ordinary usage of the word. That presumes an ego to feel with.
I only care about what the woman is—inhumanly,
physiologically, materially—according to the use of the
word. . . . You mustn't look in my novel for the old stable *ego*
of the character. There is another *ego,* according to whose
action the individual is unrecognizable, and passes through, as
it were allotropic states which needs a deeper sense than
any we've been used to exercise, to discover are states of
the same radically unchanged element.[28]

The other ego to which Lawrence refers is *creative,* and in
saying so we associate Lawrence with the romantic exaltation
of art and the imagination, despite the fact that Lawrence
repeatedly attacked aestheticism in the name of Life. Though
they do not have the professional credentials, Lawrence's
heroes (like himself) are artists. Their spiritual adventures are
adventures in the poetic-visionary imagination, and for this
reason they sometimes seem incongruous in the social
context of a novel.

In *Christ and Nietzsche* G. Wilson Knight remarks that the
self, in becoming one with the cosmos, achieves a hermaphroditic unity in which it engages in a kind of sexual intercourse
with itself. Knight, following Nietzsche, suggests an analogue
for this state of being in the creative act itself. What is
involved is a passive (feminine) receptivity to the inspirational
Dionysian flow into consciousness and an active (masculine)
exertion of the Apollonian will to make order, significance,
and beauty.[29]

If this idea of Lawrence's achievement is true, then the
view that Lawrence is "almost a Christian" becomes bizarre.
Indeed, only an insensitivity to Lawrence's imagination of
transcendence could produce the statement of one critic that
the difference between the Laurentian idea and the Christian

"is not ineradicable. Whether man receives the sacred flow of life which God has given him, and remains thankful for that, or whether man transcends his finite self, to participate in the God-stuff, the ultimate effect is the same."[30] It is precisely Lawrence's point that this difference makes all the difference in the universe. "To pretend that all is one stream is to cause chaos and nullity. To pretend to express one stream in terms of another, so as to identify the two, is false and sentimental."[31] The idea of the immanence of deity in the body (in the individual body as well as the body of the universe) is a powerful idea, and it keeps its power only if its meaning is not reduced to an idea which is really its opposite. To blur the distinction is to domesticate the tiger. Power, the body, the imagination: these are "cognate" words in the Laurentian vocabulary, and the dominant traditions of Christianity are antagonistic to the values they express.

The action of *The Man Who Died* is the painful recovery of the god in the body, which culminates in the man's passionate embrace of the priestess of Isis. The fierce and raging physical life that had earlier seemed resistant and defiant now responds to their passion. "All changed the blossom of the universe changed its petals and swung round to look another way. The spring was fulfilled, a contact was established, the man and the woman were fulfilled of one another."[32] Significantly, the priestess of Isis is abandoned at the end of the tale, having fulfilled her role as the conduit to the mysteries of "the greater life of the body."

If Lawrence is averse to Christianity, there remains nonetheless his deep attraction to the figure of Christ. Lawrence's Christ retains the chastity, the purity of soul that marks the Christ of the Gospels. Before his embrace of the priestess of Isis there had been a long and difficult "rebirth," in which the man had learned "the irrevocable *noli me tangere* which separates the reborn from the vulgar."[33] Like the heroes of Lawrence's other novels, the man who dies must resist the lure of false self-diminishing connections; in reliving his old experiences with "humanity," with Madeleine, with Judas, he undergoes a kind of purification. But the purification refers not to any justification in the presence of God, but to the strengthening of creative-visionary power.

It is impossible not to read *The Man Who Died* as an allegory on Lawrence himself. The man's speech to Madeleine, for instance, unmistakably registers a personal note: "But my mission is over, and my teaching is finished and death has saved me from my own salvation. Oh Madeleine, I want to take my single way in life, which is my portion. My public life is over, the life of my self-importance."[34] One has in mind the frail red-bearded writer with the messianic vision. Lawrence here rejects not only Christ's particular mission, but also the self-created legend that had its absurd apotheosis in the notorious "last supper" at the Café Royale. If he assumed the messianic role, he soon learned its bitter fruits. There were plenty of Judases within his own circle, and like the man of the Christ story, Lawrence learned how much he himself was responsible for the betrayals he had suffered. In his letters we are given anticipations of his abdication of the messianic role, admissions that his own doctrine of spontaneity and individual being was compromised by the categorical imperatives that he was constantly issuing. In a letter to Lady Cynthia Asquith (November 15, 1916) Lawrence admits his own impulse to lay compulsions upon other people—to dictate *his* spontaneous feelings to others.

And never again will I say, generally, "the war"; only "the war to me." For to every man the war is himself, and I cannot dictate what the war is or should be to any other being than myself. Therefore I am sorry for all my generalities, which must be falsities to another man, almost insults. Even Rupert Brooke's sonnets which I repudiate for myself, I know how true it is for him, for them.[35]

The presumption that Lawrence disavows in himself is the attempt to make political and communal that which is by its very nature an individual and private condition. And so he urges others to that condition of solitude in which a man can obey his deepest creative impulse. He writes to Catherine

Carswell (November 7, 1916): "Shelter yourself above all from the world, save yourself, screen and hide yourself, so subtly in retreat, where no one knows you . . . hiding like a bird, and living busily the other creative life, like a bird building a nest."[36] Like Christ (and here we can see again the attraction that Christ had for him), Lawrence chose the single way. In Karl Jaspers' characterization of Kierkegaard and Nietzsche we may get a glimpse of the significance of Lawrence's aloneness.

. . . With them, a new form of reality appears in history. They are, so to speak, representative destinies, sacrifices whose way out of the world leads to experiences for others. They are by the total staking of their whole natures like modern martyrs, which, however, they precisely denied being. Through their character as exceptions, they solved their problem.

Both are irreplaceable, as having dared to be shipwrecked. We orient ourselves by them. Through them we have intimations of something we could never have perceived without such sacrifices, of something that seems essential which even today we cannot adequately grasp. It is as if the Truth itself spoke, bringing an unrest into the depths of our consciousness of being.[37]

The creative spirits of whom Jaspers speaks must enact their destiny, no matter what the risks may be, and that destiny is to remain faithful to a vision which may defy what Lawrence called "the little fold of law and order." The greatest of these characters was Christ himself (Jaspers' insistence on the uniqueness of the modern "martyrs" notwithstanding). If Christ comes to fulfil the law (whatever it may be), he also comes to destroy the version of the law that prevails in the world. Blake, for instance, makes this the central fact of Jesus' career when he invokes him as an ally in his war against life-killing rules that govern the human spirit: "I tell you, no virtue can exist without breaking these ten commandments. Jesus was all virtue, and acted from impulse, not from rules."[38] Dostoevsky's Christ brings the gift of complete spiritual freedom, because the Church that bears his Name has taken it away from mankind in exchange for mystery, miracle, and authority. The opposition between Christ and law in its worldly embodiment is the opposition between creative spirit and dead matter, between freedom and coercion, between spontaneity and compulsion. If it is the nature of the world to turn energy into matter, power into weakness, the spirit into the word, then Christ exists as the permanent possibility of the renewal of energy, power, and spirit. Though he has no permanent abode in the world, there is always the possibility of his return.

From this point of view even Nietzsche, the great "Anti-Christ" of modern culture, is, as G. Wilson Knight has pointed out, "analogous to Christ himself in [Christ's] challenge against the rigidity of Judaic Law."[39] Knight has persuasively argued for the Dionysian or power content of Christ's doctrine as opposed to the traditional Christian views of Christ's doctrine. Thus he distinguishes between the inclusive "super-sexuality" of Christ and "the ghostly, bloodless, nasalised and utterly unsexual . . . tone of our Church tradition."[40] Jesus' dread of the crowd, his impulse to solitude, and the pain and joy of the Crucifixion and Resurrection are regarded by Knight as the Dionysian involvement with the cosmos that carries the self beyond the "normal" sensual experience of the world into a hermaphroditic oneness of the self with the universe, of the self with the self.

Lawrence's version of the Christ story, in which the man separates himself from the vulgar after he descends from the cross, is a repudiation of something central in the Christian ethos. Lawrence has seen through the willed and enervating democratic character of Christianity and rejected it for a fierce aristocratic aloneness. Whatever ultimate significance the life of Jesus had, Christianity for writers like Blake, Nietzsche, and Lawrence had come to be an enemy of life, and the attempts of commentators and critics to reconcile them to Christianity on some higher ground have the effect of depriving them of the weapon that Jesus himself was permitted: the sword. Lawrence came with the sword. His message was not peace and reconciliation, but destruction and re-creation. The gentle Jesus, who embodied the hopes and aspirations of the meek and poor (the Jesus of Christianity), is an alien spirit to Lawrence.

In an introduction that Lawrence wrote to Dostoevsky's version of the Christ story, the unchristian and aristocratic power bias of Lawrence's imagination is revealed in an extraordinary way. In summarizing the argument of the Grand Inquisitor, Lawrence makes his characteristic effort to rescue the tale from the artist. According to Lawrence, Christ's kiss, paralleled in the Karamazov story by the kiss that Ivan receives from Alyosha, is a kiss of acquiescence in the rightness of the Grand Inquisitor's argument. "Ivan had made a rediscovery of a truth that had been lost since the eighteenth century."[41] The truth, which puts the lie to the Enlightenment belief in the perfectibility of all men, is that the burden of freedom can be endured only by the gifted, unhappy few who must assume the burden for all mankind. Lawrence very shrewdly observes that the Grand Inquisitor's argument is close to the Christian idea of a single man, supremely endowed, assuming the burden for all mankind. But we are kept from seeing the resemblance by the dramatic situation, the "cynical Satanical"[42] pose that the Grand Inquisitor is made to affect. He is supposedly in league with the Devil, and the fact that "the wise [humane] old man"[43] has put on the garb of the terrible Inquisitor of the auto-da-fé distracts us from the wisdom and the humanity of his argument.

Lawrence turns the Grand Inquisitor's argument into a justification of his mistrust of what Nietzsche called "the herd," and of the necessity of protecting the freedom and power of the few from the presumption that all men are capable of creative freedom. "So let the specially gifted few make the decision between good and evil and establish the life values against the money values. And let the many accept the decision, with gratitude, and bow down to the few, in the hierarchy."[44]

It is, of course, a curious fact that Lawrence sides with the Grand Inquisitor against Christ. Throughout Lawrence's work there is a fear that the doctrine of spontaneity and freedom will be perverted by those for whom freedom is an excuse for self-indulgence and the coercion of others. Lawrence's willingness to send Dostoevsky's Christ away is a salutary warning to his readers of the danger that his own work embodies. His misanthropy, paradoxically, keeps him from wanting his doctrine to become the property of all men. Lawrence's "political period," immediately preceding *The Man Who Died,* was very instructive in this respect. The hero of *Kangaroo,* for instance, learns that he must repudiate political connections that will violate his singleness. There is a qualifying humility in Lawrence (a consequence of his religious character, perhaps) which keeps him from sharing Blake's and Nietzsche's belief in the power of men (even the best of them) to transcend themselves infinitely. Lawrence mistrusted what Mark Schorer has called (writing of Blake) the politics of vision. His respect for human limitations counteracted somewhat the anarchic Dionysian tendency of his imagination. His work at moments seems a balance of opposing tendencies, and this balance gives the impression of health and normality, which critics like F. R. Leavis make so much of. Even in Lawrence's fierce repudiations and self-affirmations, the imagination of distinction, relation, balance, and hierarchic order often appears. Nevertheless, Lawrence is essentially like Blake and Nietzsche in his praise of the untapped powers of man and his hatred of the rules and forms that curb those powers.

Like Blake and Nietzsche before him, Lawrence has managed to see and judge the quality of life (its norms and perversities) from a vantage point outside of civilization— a vantage point, one might add, not without its share of perversities. Denis de Rougemont remarks in *Love in the Western World*: "To plunge down below our moral rules is . . . not to abolish their restraints, but merely to indulge in more than animal insanity. The mistake lies in supposing that 'the real thing,' the longing for which has now become an obsession is there to be found."[45] As a caveat against the glorification of instinct, this statement is valuable, but as a theoretical statement about human possibility it seems to me presumptuous and unacceptable. To regard the moral rules as absolutes against which there is no radical appeal is both to indulge in the humanistic presumption that this is the best of all possible worlds and to invalidate *a priori* any radical criticism of the norms of a civilization. It is to reject as valueless the visionary genius.

Lawrence's mistake (sporadic, not constant) was to confuse the visionary and the ethical. His vision of life should not be taken as a guide to conduct, the hortatory, preacherish manner of much of his work notwithstanding. The urging to follow one's "deepest impulse" is either nonsensical or dangerous, for given the nature of man, impulsiveness would sooner issue in horror than in vitality. Only those in a state of grace can be trusted when they follow their deepest impulses. And these aristocrats of the spirit (artists, heroes, saints) need no exhortation, for they must follow these impulses by virtue of what they are. When Lawrence converts his vision into doctrine and turns prophecy into moral prescription, he is confused about his achievement. The demonic element in art, urging the poet on to unknown and perhaps unrealizable futures, makes the visionary poet an alien to the moral life. To confuse the visionary and the ethical is to hold out a promise to the *demos* (everyone can have a vision if he would only care), a temptation that even the visionary artist finds hard to resist in a democratic society. Lawrence did not see the opposition between the visionary and the ethical with the clarity with which Nietzsche saw it.

In "Richard Wagner in Bayreuth," Nietzsche makes a strong case for the autonomy of art. Contrasting the tragic idea with the pedagogic view of tragedy, he asserts that

. . . art is . . . no teacher or educator of practical conduct:

the artist is never in this sense an instructor or adviser,
the things after which a tragic hero strives are not
necessarily worth striving after. As in a dream so in art, the
valuation of things only holds good while we are under its
spell. What we, for the time being, regard as so worthy of
effort, and what makes us sympathize with the tragic hero
when he prefers death to renouncing the object of his desire,
this can seldom retain the same value and energy when
transferred to everyday life: that is why art is the business
of the man who is recreating himself.[46]

The prominence of the demonic in art from romanticism
to the present fortifies this antididactic view of art. For the
artist who is bent on "recreating himself" must be able to
experiment on himself—to experiment and fail. The experiments and conclusions do not necessarily become the kind of
wisdom that one communicates pedagogically to a whole
community. But in a genuine artist-hero these experiments
create an atmosphere in which the whole community may
unconsciously begin to live. And this is true equally for poets
of democratic and aristocratic sentiments. The aristocratic
poet conceives his community as an elite of sensitive spirits
constitutionally capable of being nourished by his vision.
The democratic poet, on the other hand, believes that the
vision can become the soul of the whole community. But in
the present situation, the aristocratic visionary artist and the
democratic visionary artist both share a prophetic antagonism
to the community, an antagonism of self-dramatization as
well as doctrine.

The power of the visionary artist is in his autonomy, in his
exclusive love of the mysterious and the inchoate, in what
Lawrence called his otherness. In his immediate life, he does
not have the spirit of community. He may regret this, long
for it, and dream of a splendid community of men and women,
but he himself is doomed to a terrible and exalted solitude.
And because of this, the visionary artist has within him an
extraordinary power of judgment. He keeps us from the
hubris of complacency and self-congratulation and from a

facile faith in humanity and civilization. He is a dangerous fellow because of his world-smashing impulse, and in an age which has come to be in many ways a horrible parody of the Dionysian element that inspires the artist, it is hard not to be mistrustful of him. But to write him off as a dangerous fellow is to do a disservice not only to "life" but to the human community as well—indeed, it is to make intolerable the very idea of human life. For he not only provides an image of *individual* life, the ego in its unconditioned unfolding, but he also suggests through that image the possibility of new communities of men. In Lawrence's version of James Fenimore Cooper's "dream beyond democracy" we have precisely this imagination of a new community of men.

What did Cooper dream beyond democracy? Why, in his immortal friendship of Chingachgook and Natty Bumppo he dreamed the nucleus of a new relationship. A stark, stripped human relationship of two men, deeper than the deeps of sex. Deeper than property, deeper than fatherhood, deeper than love. So deep that it is loveless. The stark, loveless, wordless unison of two men who have come to the bottom of themselves. This the new nucleus of a new society, the clue to a new epoch. It asks for a great and cruel sloughing first of all. Then it finds a great release into a new world, a new moral, a new landscape.[47]

In *Fantasia of the Unconscious* Lawrence rejects the Freudian idea that the sexual impulse is the deepest impulse in man and consequently the essential "motivity" of the unconscious. The impulse of "higher importance, and greater dynamic power" is "the desire of the human male to build a world . . . to build up out of his own self and his own belief and his own effort something wonderful."[48] Lawrence asserts that the "religious or creative motive" is "the first motive for all human activity."[49] The unconscious is the divine presence in man, from which all genuine civilization draws its energy. Civilization and culture, which have always been conceived to exist under the aegis of Apollo, the god that brings order to the wild Dionysian energies at large in the world, are conceived by Lawrence as products of those energies themselves. Lawrence conceived of culture in its ideal form as a fulfilment of the passional-visionary self, whereas Freud has the view that there exists a generic tragic opposition between the passional self and culture. "Even the Panama Canal would never have been built *simply* to let ships through. It is the pure disinterested craving of the human male to make something wonderful out of his own head and his own self, and his own soul's faith and delight, which starts everything going."⁵⁰ The opposition between Apollo and Dionysus is then a perverse contrivance of civilization in its present form, and the violence and destructiveness of the passional life is a function of the opposition between the gods, not a generic truth about the passional life itself. The destructiveness of the passional life is really its resentment at the repression from which it has suffered.

Though he may be able to resolve the dualism in argument, Lawrence's imaginative work reveals the opposition between the visionary and the ethical at every moment. "Never trust the artist, trust the tale." Lawrence's argument in *Fantasia of the Unconscious* often reads like the casuistry against which he directed his fire when he discovered it in other writers. But it is a casuistry with which we must sympathize, for it reflects the anxious atmosphere in which he worked: the need to connect with others, to participate in the human communion, was in keen struggle with the need to keep faithful to a vision that was anarchically individual, explosive, and subversive. His impulse to argue for the vision represents an effort to join, in Malraux's phrase, his "madness to the universe." We respect the vision, but we cannot embrace it as doctrine. Between Lawrence and every serious reader of him there must be, I believe, a permanent tension: a sense of provocation and danger.

Lawrence is like Blake and Nietzsche, an artist beyond good and evil who compels our admiration and mistrust. Like Christ, Lawrence enters the human community a stranger and an enemy, possessed by a vision so subversive and dangerous that he can be endured only if he modifies it in communicating it—or if he is misunderstood. Lawrence does modify his vision and he has been, understandably, misunderstood: that is, made to serve the gods of a humanistic civilization. This too has been the fate of Blake and Nietzsche.

8

Joyce and the Career of the Artist-Hero

I

"My intention was to write a chapter of the moral history of my country and I chose Dublin for the scene because that city seemed to me the centre of paralysis."[1] Joyce is here speaking of *Dubliners,* but the statement applies to his subsequent work as well. What it leaves out is the other term of the Joycean dialectic: the role of the artist and art in the moral history of his country. The drama of the *Portrait* is the attempt of the artist to wrest images of beauty out of the squalor, to transcend the "paralysis" of Dublin life, and *Ulysses* gives us the aesthetic artist in decline, overwhelmed by the city and his own ineffectuality. There is no artist in *Dubliners.* Gabriel Conroy, the hero of the most ambitious of the stories, "The Dead," has something of the artist's sensibility, but it is the absence of artistic power in him that makes for his tragedy. He is a writer of articles, a sensitive, a man with a vision of Dublin's "paralysis," but without the ultimate grace of art and passion; in the figure of Michael

Furey, who exists in the memory of Gabriel's wife, we are given a fleeting glimpse of the heroic poet-lover.

Yet it would be false to say that the theme of the artist and art is missing from *Dubliners*. Its very absence from the action or subject matter of the stories is felt by virtue of its presence in the form and technique of the stories. We feel the action of art in the stories as a sort of compensation for its absence in the lives of the characters.

In *Stephen Hero*, an early draft of the *Portrait*, the hero speaks of his desire to write a book of epiphanies: *Dubliners* is that book. If *Dubliners* is a record of a series of defeats and failures (none of the characters is able to rise above the squalor of Dublin life), the book itself is the triumphant action of an artist who has perceived in the trivial and vulgar events of the lives of *Dubliners* moments of significance, even moments of "delicate and evanescent" beauty.[2] The epiphany is the point of light toward the end of the story at which all the details and events converge into significance: the religious word suggests that the moment of significance is a moment of spiritual revelation, a manifesting or bodying forth of the real life of a character or a situation

"Evelina," one of the simplest of the stories, offers a fine illustration of the epiphanal technique. The story begins with Evelina sitting next to the window of her house, immobile, thinking about her past. She is about to run off with a romantic sailor, Frank, to start a new life in Buenos Aires. The decision to leave with Frank is the occasion for reverie; in the reverie the meaning of her life is summed up (for us, not for Evelina)—her attachment to the familiar objects of her home, the security of shelter, food, and job. "Life is hard, but now that she is about to leave, not undesirable." Meanwhile time passes ("evening invades the street"); later on "evening [darkens] the street": the passing of time creates a sense of urgency about the decision to leave, the meaning of which remains in suspension until the end of the story. She has misinterpreted her attachment to the past as a need to escape from it. When at the end of the story she goes down to meet Frank, but can go no farther than the iron railings ("the seas of the world tumbled about her heart and she gripped with both hands at the iron railing"), we recall all the details of this self-defeating attachment to what she tried vainly to escape. The epiphany is anticipated by the clanging of a bell. In its starkness and simplicity, "Evelina" is a prototype of the Joycean story.

There is no apparent recourse against the paralytic power of Dublin. The hero of "Araby" is a romantic boy (like the young Stephen, perhaps) who imagines himself in the squalid world of Dublin as a knight, bearing a chalice through a throng of foes as a gift to a Dublin girl. The lyricism of the story (narrated by the young boy) cannot, however, survive the squalor. The boy goes to a bazaar, a place of enchantment, which turns out to be, despite his romanticizing, a commercial venture. The clanging turnstiles, the counting of money, the trivial conversation he overhears shock the boy into a vision of his vanity. "Gazing up into the darkness I saw myself as a creature driven and derided by vanity, and my eyes burned with anguish and anger." Like the "blind" street on which he lives, his dream of transfiguration has no issue in reality. In "The Dead," Gabriel Conroy has a vision of the paralysis of Dublin and finally of the whole world: the language and imagery are appropriately apocalyptic.

Other forms were near. His soul had approached that region where dwell the vast hosts of the dead. He was conscious of, but could not apprehend, their wayward and flickering existence. His own identity was fading out into a grey impalpable world: the solid world itself, which these dead had one time reared and lived in, was dissolving and dwindling. . . . His soul swooned slowly as he heard the snow falling faintly through the universe and faintly falling, like the descent of their last end, upon all the living and the dead.[3]

The stories are deliberately uneventful. The movement is one of perspective, a slow revelation of a situation that becomes fully intelligible with the sudden "spiritual" manifestation at the end. Every detail in a story, we soon come to feel, no matter how casual and insignificant it may appear at first, has a resonance, an implication which will become explicit in the epiphany: the snow on Gabriel's galoshes ("The Dead"), the "blindness" of North Richmond Street ("Araby"), the ginger beer and peas that Lenahan and Corley eat ("Two Gallants"). The fate of each character is determined, one feels, by the governing will of the artist. If in naturalistic fiction character is conceived as an inevitable victim of a socio-economic fate, in *Dubliners* Joyce controls his characters by a kind of symbolic fate. North Richmond Street is blind. The fate of the romantic boy of "Araby" is sealed. Whatever alternative possibilities we might envisage for him are suppressed by relentless adumbrations of the destiny Joyce has prepared for him. One of the main pleasures in reading the stories is in discovering Joyce's virtuosity in composing the detail into the inevitability of the epiphany.

What remains firm and impressive throughout the vision of paralysis and dissolution that *Dubliners* presents is the artistic will of Joyce. The stories have a classical severity, a precision of detail and image that Nietzsche would have called Apollonian. Lawrence could have placed Joyce as well as Mann in the tradition of Flaubert: the Joyce of *Dubliners* is content to make "the perfect statement in a world of corruption."[3] The cult of the artist is implicit in the fastidious precision and control of the stories. It is inevitable that when Joyce as a young writer thought of the possibility of heroism in such a world, he would contemplate the artist.

A Portrait of the Artist, it would seem, is the *locus classicus* among novels of artistic egoism. There are more ambitious and greater novels in the genre (*Dr. Faustus* and *Remembrance of Things Past,* to name the greatest instances), but the *Portrait* is distinguished by its peculiar obsessiveness with the theme of the artist as hero. The very title indicates its (virtually) allegoric intention. Its compulsion (one might call it a lyric argument) is almost scientific in that (unlike the other novels in the genre) it tries to "prove" the heroic status of the artist.

The focus of *Dr. Faustus* is the moral and political implications of art as demonic possession, and Proust's incomparable work *assumes* the heroic power of art, which it shows working through the agency of memory. But the *Portrait* is concerned purely with the status of the artist and art, and because it is a novel it succeeds, unlike the poems of artistic heroism, in giving a social and dramatic context to the theme.

The heroic status of Stephen has been widely challenged. Joyce himself seems to lend support to the challenges by not always preserving the right balance between irony and sympathy in his treatment of Stephen. Joyce struggled hard between *Stephen Hero* and the *Portrait* to gain a distance between himself and his hero that would make it possible to see his hero truly. Sometimes the irony is very severe. For example, toward the end of the novel Stephen seems to deflate utterly his aesthetic heroics by suggesting that they are simply the calculated expression of his egoism.

> Asked me, was I writing poems? About whom? I asked
> her. This confused her more and I felt sorry and mean.
> Turned off that valve at once and opened the spiritual-heroic
> refrigerator apparatus, invented *and* patented in all countries
> by Dante Alighieri. Talked rapidly of myself and my plans.
> In the midst of it unluckily I made a sudden gesture of a
> revolutionary nature. I must have looked like a fellow
> throwing a handful of peas into the air.[4]

But the novel concludes with Stephen's grandiose assertion that he "goes to encounter for the millionth time the reality of existence and forge within the smithy of my soul the uncreated conscience of my race." The assertion is unqualified by the concluding sentences and the novel ends on a note of affirmation and celebration.

Caroline Gordon has argued that Joyce did not succeed in making his case for the artist-hero: "the primal plot may operate in a work of art not only without the artist's conscious knowledge but almost against his will."[5] (Lawrence put this dictum less cumbersomely when he cautioned the reader:

"Never trust the artist, trust the tale.") The implication of the primal plot, in Caroline Gordon's view, is that the story is about the damnation of Stephen—so powerfully and movingly is the Catholic idea presented in the novel. It would be hard to deny that Stephen's religious communion during his period of faith is more richly presented than his aesthetic creed, which too often issues in purple passages in the manner of Pater or vaporous philosophizing about the nature of art. If Stephen's artistic aspirations simply had the vagueness of youthful energy, we would not wonder about Joyce's attitude toward him. For toward youthful energy, no matter how aimless its direction, one must be sympathetic. But Stephen's aspirations are in the already effete idiom of Pater's prose, and so we are made to suspect even the authenticity of his energy.

Miss Gordon's view suffers, however, from a serious disability: its failure to account for the abject squalor of the Irish Catholic scene—the school at Clongowes, the unsympathetic Jesuit teachers, the fanatical Dante. Miss Gordon's reading is prejudiced: she shows an unwillingness to make the necessary suspension of disbelief.* Stephen is unquestionably a sinner from the Catholic point of view and perhaps damned, but Joyce tries to transvalue the sin, to make it an aspect of something great and valuable in Stephen. Joyce tries and fails. Or perhaps the success of the novel is the honesty with which it presents the failure.

One gift of the artist is his possession of the fresh perceptiveness of the child. The notation of the first chapter is sensuous, immediate, childlike.

Once upon a time and a very good time it was there was a moocow coming down along the road and this moocow that was coming down along the road met a nicens little boy named baby tuckoo . . .

---

* An analogue would be denying Dante his vision of God because of our liberal sentimental abhorrence of the suffering of those in hell.

When you wet the bed first it is warm then it gets cold.
His mother put on the oilsheet. That had a queer smell.

Suck was a queer word . . . And when [the water] had all
gone down slowly the hole in the basin had made a sound
like that: suck. Only louder.

Was it right to kiss mother. . . . What did it mean, to kiss? . . .
His mother put her lips on his cheek; her lips were soft
and they wetted his cheek; and they made a tiny little noise:
kiss. Why did people do that with their two faces?

There was a noise of curtain rings running back along the
rods, of water being splashed in the basins: There was a noise of
rising and dressing and washing in the dormitory: a noise
of clapping of hands as the prefect went up and down
telling the fellows to look sharp. . . . The sunlight was
queer and cold.

. . . Wells' face was there. He looked at it and saw that Wells
was afraid. . . .

The face and voice went away. . . . It was not Wells' face;
it was the prefect's.[6]

The sense of queerness is a form of wonder, a feeling of
strangeness in the presence of pure sensation, of disembodied
voices and faces. The sensuous aspect of things is for Stephen
a touchstone for his judgments and convictions. His early
sensations at home and at the school are not immediately
significant, but they will be remembered in his later dis-
satisfactions and rebellions. When Stephen finally sees the
spiritual vacuity of the priest ("In his eyes burned no spark
of Ignatius' enthusiasm"),[7] he has achieved the consciousness
of the squalor he so sharply sensed in his childhood. During a
moment of religious devotion, he is characteristically beset
by these impressions. "Images of the outbursts of trivial anger
which he had often noticed among his masters, their twitching
mouths, close-shut lips and flushed cheeks recurred to his
memory, discouraging him, for all his practice of humility,
by the comparison."[8]

But Stephen's acute sensitivity is only one aspect of his

artistic nature. Out of the welter of sensuous experience, the artist will wrest an image of beauty—fix it, insulate it from the chaotic, disintegrating world. The principal image of that effort in the *Portrait* is the series of girls who pass impressively though somewhat vaguely through Stephen's consciousness and are stripped of all accidental accessories to their platonic beauty.

The aesthetic doctrine that Stephen develops toward the end of the novel is the intellectual formulation of the effort.[9] The two principal points in the doctrine are: (1) the distinction between kinesis and stasis and (2) the idea of impersonality. Feelings excited by proper art are static; by improper art, kinetic. Stephen displaces the religious idea of eternity and permanence to the realm of art. The artist discovers, so to speak, his eternal salvation in the aesthetic image and offers the possibility of salvation to his readers or spectators. The idea of the impersonality of the artist is consistent with the idea of art as stasis. By impersonality, Joyce means two different but not incompatible things: he means the absorption of the artist into the narrative—that is, the disappearance, so to speak, of the artist—and he also means the apotheosis of the artist into a kind of god.[10] As in the distinction between stasis and kinesis, Stephen tries to sever the connection between art and practical life. Art must remove us from the daily life of emotion, movement, desire. It is self-contained, undisturbed by the compromising currents of life.

But the drama of the novel does not support Stephen's effort. The images that Stephen pursues are curiously elusive and changeful. If he arrests them, it is only for the moment; they return quickly to common life.

Shrinking from that life he turned towards the wall, making a cowl of the blanket and staring at the great overblown scarlet flowers of the tattered wallpaper. He tried to warm his perishing joy in their scarlet glow, imagining a roseway from where he lay upwards to heaven all strewn with flowers.[11]

But Stephen cannot insulate his imagination from the

changing sensuous world. The desire to be "a priest of the eternal imagination, transmuting the daily bread of experience into the radiant body of everlasting life,"[12] is hubris. Changefulness is not only in the nature of the world: it is the condition of every soul, even the artist's soul. Thus the ecstasy in Stephen's soul is "routed" by "rude brutal anger" which "broke up violently her fair image and flung the fragments on all sides. On all sides distorted reflections of her image started from his memory: the flower girl in the ragged dress with damp coarse hair and a hoyden's face who had called herself his own girl. . . ."[13] The attempt at transcendence may be understood as a phase in the growth of the artist, not as the ultimate wisdom of the mature artist.

No artist believed more passionately in the power of art than Joyce, and yet his development shows an increasingly severe view of the artistic personality.

In *Ulysses*, Stephen goes into a sharp decline. He is no longer the hero, that place having been ostensibly usurped by Leopold Bloom, Everyman. Moreover, there is some question whether Stephen is a true artist. He has the artist's personality and sensibility, but he lacks discipline, the capacity for converting the gift into artifice.

It is as if the artistic personality has overtaken the artist in Stephen. Volatile, capricious, solipsistic, the artist's life is often chaotic and self-destructive. The volatility and capriciousness are connected with an article of his faith: he must have the courage and capacity to submit to demonic urges without ever being sure of their consequences. He encounters experience with a certain "openness," which often means a lack of resistance. He propitiates the gods only through his art—the "moment" of *disciplined* creation. Substitute "grace" for "art" and we see the antinomian element in the artist-hero: the art justifies the life. Nevertheless, the work of art is a deed. Without the work of art, the "justification" falls back on the personality: the antinomianism is complete.

Ulysses takes us to the end of the road of the artist-hero. The "hero" is really Joyce absenting himself from the work and dramatizing his own technique for heroically capturing the world, spatially and historically, between the covers of a book.

II

In *Ulysses* Joyce attempts to realize Mallarmé's ambition to put the whole world between the covers of a book and make subsequent literature unnecessary, by exhausting all the possibilities of representation and expression.*

Representation: *Ulysses* is the apotheosis of naturalism. In traditional naturalism the world is assumed to be commonly available and objectively intelligible. The model for naturalism is science, with its passion for facts and laws. The aim of naturalism is to communicate life in its immediacy and to understand it. Joyce cannot make the assumption that the objective world is intelligible. There is the Berkeleyan doubt about the objective reality of the world. In the Proteus chapter, Stephen, dramatizing the doubt, tests the doctrine of solipsism and discovers that there is a world beyond his imagination:

> Open your eyes now. I will. One moment. Has all vanished since? If I open and am for ever in the black adiaphane. Basta! I will see if I can see.
>
> See now. There all the time without you: and ever shall be, world without end.[14]

He had closed his eyes and opened them again to discover that the world had not disappeared. But the world is nevertheless present only through the senses, the particular consciousness of each person, and we never emerge (in *Ulysses*) from the subjectivity of the particular consciousness into the objective consciousness of realism.

The technique of stream of consciousness is a necessary

---

* Joyce's half-playful comment that the ideal reader should devote a lifetime to the study of his work has its point.

outcome of Joyce's belief in the inescapable subjectivity of consciousness. Traditional naturalism, from the Joycean point of view, presumes to a clarity that belies its intention of giving us a view of actual life. In the stream of consciousness, we get something like the inconsequence, irrelevance, and redundancy of life itself. Impressions, thoughts, half thoughts are presented on a straight line, so to speak. Repetitions of events and phrases may indicate the importance of a theme (e.g., allusions to Blazes Boylan and Bloom's Jewishness), but the variety of motifs * is so great that it sometimes requires an extraordinary sensitivity or perhaps an effort of scholarship simply to distinguish what is obsessive from what is an occasional recurrence. Indeed, the result of this presentation of apparently indiscriminate impressions is that readers usually testify to remarkably disparate experiences of the book. All that a reader can do is to abstract from the book a pattern or tendency or perhaps series of patterns or tendencies that interests him. A grasp of the total work, which is possible in reading most literature, is impossible with *Ulysses*. *Ulysses* baffles the reader's desire to dominate it, just as the inconsequence, chaos, and unintelligibility of life refuse to satisfy the will to order. The reader may reconstruct in his own mind a realistic novel out of his experience of *Ulysses,* just as we give meaning or significance to life by abstraction and interpretation, but he is abstracting from the book, not possessing it. Thus the relationship between Bloom and Stephen can be understood in a variety of ways, varying from the view that Stephen has found his spiritual father to the view that the "communion" between them (after Bloom rescues Stephen from the brothel) ends in failure. Each reader makes his own reconstruction of the events. There is no coherent comprehensive view to which he can refer his interpretation.

The aesthetic consequences of this "surrender" to the disorder of life subverts certain cherished aesthetic ideas.

---

* According to Richard Kain, verbal motifs associated with
  Leopold Bloom alone total 700 (*The Fabulous Voyager,* p. 277).

"Point of view" ceases to be relevant. Each reader develops his own view. Aesthetic form becomes problematical. Permissive in the extreme, the form or structure of *Ulysses* allows for redundancy, superfluity, irrelevance, debris—or at least the impression of them. The complaint that certain sections, like "Aeolus" (the collage of newspaper squibs) and "Oxen of the Sun" (the pastiches of English literary style), are not relevant to the "structure" of the work reflects an old-fashioned expectation of formal shapeliness. The "form" of *Ulysses* is so elastic that it can, like life, contain everything. It also follows that the book can go on and on indefinitely.

Expression: All novels, indeed all literature, must use language to represent reality, but naturalistic or realistic fiction in particular does not draw attention to its language. In realistic fiction, language is subordinate to the subject or action, to be valued primarily for its transparency. In *Ulysses*, on the other hand, language itself becomes the subject matter of the novel. Buck Mulligan (Stephen's friend) not only announces his name, he scans it metrically. "Malachi Mulligan, two dactyls. But it has a Hellenic ring, hasn't it? Tripping and sunny like the buck himself."[15] There is a double mediation of reality in *Ulysses*: reality is mediated through the senses and through language, which refracts the experience of the senses. Joyce's love of language has a certain autonomy, but the preoccupation with language in *Ulysses* is not simply a gratuitous outcome of this love, it belongs to the epistemology of the novel.

There is an affinity between Joyce's preoccupation with language and the apotheosis of naturalism which occurs in *Ulysses*. In the stream of consciousness, words are not restricted or controlled by formal grammatical considerations, for example, subject-predicate, sentence-paragraph. Words and phrases, when they are not simply opaque, are highly connotative. Unless the reader works against the connotativeness of *Ulysses* by analyzing and reconstituting the book in his mind—that is, turning it into a conventional novel—the possibilities of association are endless. It is almost as if Joyce were rendering or representing every conceivable way of saying something, just as he is representing total sensuous reality. If *Ulysses* exhausts, so to speak, all the possibilities of naturalism—is at once the *summa* and the cul-de-sac of naturalism (after this book every naturalistic effort seems trivial)—*Ulysses* also exhausts all the possibilities of saying anything in the available styles and modes of expression. Thus "Oxen of the Sun" (the episode of pastiches of English literature) is an emblem of Joyce's conscious summing up of the expressive power of language and literature. After *Ulysses* the only possibility is to invent a new language, as Joyce does in *Finnegans Wake*. Joyce speaks somewhere of traditional language as a prison. In *Finnegans Wake* he won his freedom.

A representation of the total reality of a character must give us not only his present but his past, and not only his personal past but his cultural past. The Homeric parallel and the other achievements of the cultural past (Vico, Dante, *Hamlet,* the poetry of Blake) complete the work of total artistic domination of reality. The presence of a character like Stephen with his vast erudition makes it possible for Joyce to render the cultural past as psychological event. One of the misleading things about Stuart Gilbert's study of *Ulysses* is that it strongly implies that *Ulysses* is allegorical, that is, that Joyce is presenting the cultural past outside the consciousness of his characters as a kind of commentary, satiric or otherwise, on the quality of their lives. There are unquestionably moments in *Ulysses* when allusions strain psychological credibility, but it is remarkable how successful Joyce is in preserving the psychological verisimilitude of the allusions to the cultural past, as in Stephen's reflections on *Hamlet*.

The paradox of *Ulysses* is that its "anti-art" presupposes the most inventive and scrupulous of artistic consciences. *Ulysses* simulates the illusion of chaos; it is not in itself chaos. The forms or techniques (stream of consciousness, pastiche, Homeric parallel) that permit the rich and chaotic density of life to enter into the book also order it. Even stream of consciousness has its principle of order. It brings together quickly items that belong together but which conventional habits of apprehension tend to keep apart. Stream of consciousness makes possible a simultaneous presentation of past and present. The conventional way of conceiving past and present as a continuum in time or as discrete periods of time conceals the psychological reality that the past is often significantly *present* in the mind. During his walk on the seashore, Stephen's mind moves without transition from Swinburne's conception of the sea as a mighty mother to reflections on naked Eve, the first mother, to original sin, his own birth, his sense of guilt about his mother.[16] The confusion is accompanied by a sense of illumination.

Ulysses is not an orgiastic surrender to the practical, sensuous kinetic world. Joyce rather uses the tactics of surrender to achieve an even more impressive victory. The victory is anticipated by Stephen's celebrated remark: "History is a nightmare from which I am trying to awake,"[17] though perhaps not in the sense that Stephen intended. By bringing symbolically under his control the total past of culture and individuals, Joyce has in a sense brought about the apocalypse of which his "artist-hero" dreamed. In *Ulysses* we emerge from the kinesis of history into a vision of total reality. The ideal reader, who possesses the comprehension of deity and therefore does not exist, is one who can behold this reality in a single instant: *Ulysses* as epiphany. The whole enterprise is a form of hubris (the apotheosis of artistic egoism), redeemed only by the comic awareness of the artist and the magnificence of his genius.

III

It is an injustice to say that *Ulysses* is simply a dramatization and celebration of the artistic act, for the book has an extraordinarily rich humanity that makes it a great novel. But one can already feel in *Ulysses* that Joyce has entered the cul-de-sac which he was to call for years *Work in Progress* and ultimately *Finnegans Wake*. Joyce's "technique" is exhaustive rather than re-creative. It is as if Joyce lays the ghost of "reality" in *Ulysses*, so that his art can become purely self-reflective: language commenting on language.

The attitude cannot be maintained. Reality avenges itself, reasserting its chaotic unmanageable quality, punishing art for its presumption in believing that even in its ultimate exercise it could bring everything under control.

The novels of Beckett represent precisely this recoil of reality from the attempt of art to dominate it. Beckett is a crucial instance, because he is Joyce's immediate successor. He does not *attack* the Joycean attitude, he declares and enacts its exhaustion.

"I speak of an art turning from it [*sic*] in disgust, weary
of its puny exploits, weary of pretending to be able, of doing a
little better the same old thing, of going a little further along a
dreary road."
The interviewer: "And preferring what?"
"The expression that there is nothing to express, nothing
with which to express, nothing from which to express,
together with the obligation to express."[18]

The landscape of the Beckett novel is the *I*. Unbounded, unlimited by others, by anything outside him, the Beckett character is in complete disintegration. Nothing in Beckett's art or "style" is permitted to check the process. Even the style is infected by the disorder.

But my ideas on this subject were always horribly
confused, for my knowledge of men was scant and the
meaning of being beyond me. Oh I've tried everything.
In the end it was magic that had the honour of my ruins,
and still today, when I walk there, I find its vestiges.
But mostly they are a place with neither plan nor bounds and of
which I understand nothing, not even of what it is made,
still less into what. And the thing in ruins. I don't know
what it is, what it was, nor whether it is not less a question

of ruins than the indestructible chaos of timeless things, if that is the right expression. It is in any case a place devoid of mystery, deserted by magic, because devoid of mystery.[19]

The barbarously awkward syntax, the discontinuity of thought, the inept use of pronouns testify to the weariness with art as well as with life.

What remains to Beckett is a paradoxical, though persistent, attachment to the self. "I can't go on, I'll go on."[20] One might think that the devotion to the self is vestigial and sentimental in the light of the complete demoralization of the Beckett character. Perhaps. But the self-devotion has the intensity of narcissism—a narcissism without self-love.

This paradoxical attachment to self is a "major premise" of the French new novel (of which Beckett is a master). On the one hand, the world of the new novel is constituted by the perceiving consciousness of the hero, suggesting the omnipresence of the ego.[21] The objective "air" of the new novel, its inveterate opposition to all romanticizing of people and objects, has misled readers into viewing the new novel as classical and objective. The new novel aims at total subjectivity. On the other hand, the new novelist insists on the *distance* between self and object. *Alienation* and *estrangement* are forms of appropriation of the environment, pathetic distortions of the relation between the object and the self. The observing self, in a novel by Robbe-Grillet, for instance, refuses to enter into a sentimental complicity with objects, as if the dignity of things would be compromised by their association with the human. Robbe-Grillet enjoins the novelist to cultivate the visual sense because it is the sense that least deforms the environment.

Irony, judgment, indignation—all the traditional humanistic forms of response are undermined by the view that a thing, no matter how banal, is simply itself. Whether the doctrine is subjectivist or objectivist, the new novel collaborates with what it presents in the sense that it offers neither judgment nor resistance: it is neither satiric nor parodic in its intentions,

for example. Suspicious of the corruptions of human judgment, it maintains its purity by rendering as faithfully as
possible the banality of things as grasped by consciousness.
(The banality of things is perhaps the best gloss on the statement that objects and characters are only what they are:
that they have neither depth nor transcendence.)

The observing self in the new novel is omnipresent and
passive: it becomes, so to speak, a landscape to be filled with
the debris of daily life. The exhaustion of the belief in the
resistant or redemptive power of art has led to this. Robbe-
Grillet speaks of the interrogative rather than the declarative
method of the novel: its openness to the surfaces and con-
fusions of a world no longer intelligible.* Yet his belief in
style and the extreme stylization and repetitiousness of the
new novel suggest that he has not freed himself from the
commitment to art—as Beckett seems to have done. If art is
insufficient to manage the chaotic element in life, the "surrender" to chaos or insignificance, to the quotidian banality of
things, may lead to the end of literature. Robbe-Grillet's
inconsistency is perhaps no more than the artist's instinct for
survival.

The new novelists cannot escape the fact that what they
present is interpretation, indeed, has all the impurities and
infirmities of a human understanding of experience. If in
Nietzschean fashion we question, for instance, Robbe-
Grillet's motives (Robbe-Grillet's aesthetic forbids this kind
of questioning: like an orthodox American new critic he
insists on the self-enclosed, intransitive quality of art), we
find a passion for novelty and a perverse affection for the
quotidian: as if the constant searching for something new and
the almost tumorous attention to the quotidian might yield
the transcendence with which the new novelists claim to have
nothing to do.

---

* The openness is largely illusory, for the belief that objects are only
what they are is really an "atheistic" refusal to admit the possibility
that they may have depth or transcendence.

But the poverty of the new novel suggests impasse rather than the opening up of new creative possibilities. Like contemporary films without subject, plot, or character, the new novel is imprisoned in the images perceived by the observing consciousness, images without resonance or transcendence, merely "aesthetic" and consequently uninteresting.

The new novelists are by their *performance* proving the opposite of what they intend to prove. The most interesting business of life and literature is the moral (in the most generous sense of the word) development of character—its capacity for human relationship, its vitality and capacity for growth and resistance, its ability to appropriate and use its environment—not the photographic or even "aesthetic" rendering of the surfaces of things. It is a commentary on our exhaustion that our literature has either lost interest or no longer seems capable of engaging in what traditionally has been its deepest concern.

Notes

Introduction.

1. Samuel Beckett, *Mulloy*, in *A Trilogy*, p. 49.
2. Samuel Beckett, *Malone Dies*, in *A Trilogy*, p. 266.
3. *Ibid.*, p. 306.
4. *Ibid., p.* 307.
5. Samuel Beckett, *The Unnameable*, in *A Trilogy*, p. 516.
6. *Ibid.*, p. 517.
7. Beckett, *Mulloy*, p. 88.
8. Beckett, *The Unnameable*, p. 552.
9. See Hugh Kenner, *Samuel Beckett: A Critical Study*, pp. 117–32.
10. Beckett, *The Unnameable*, p. 579.
11. Quoted in William Jackson Bate, *From Classic to Romantic*, p. 75.
12. D. H. Lawrence, "Study of Hardy," in *Phoenix: The Posthumous Papers of D. H. Lawrence*, pp. 409–10.
13. Friedrich Nietzsche, *Human, All Too Human*, 2: 199.
14. Quoted in John William Corrington, Review of *An American Dream*, p. 58.

15. Karl Jaspers, "Kierkegaard and Nietzsche" in *Existentialism: From Dostoevsky to Sartre,* ed. Walter Kaufmann, p. 174.

16. See Norman O. Brown, *Life against Death* and *Love's Body.*

17. Norman Mailer, "The White Negro," in *Advertisements for Myself on the Way Out,* p. 345.

18. Günter Grass, *The Tin Drum,* p. 197.

1

The Antinomianism Of Jean-Jacques Rousseau

1. Jean-Jacques Rousseau, *The Confessions of Jean-Jacques Rousseau,* 1: 1.

2. Quoted in Walter Jackson Bate, *From Classic to Romantic,* p. 21.

3. Rousseau, *Confessions,* 1: 1.

4. *Ibid.,* 1: 16.

5. Stendhal, *The Red and the Black,* 1: 251.

6. Rousseau, *Confessions,* 1: 76.

7. *Ibid.,* 1:, 77.

8. *Ibid.,* 2: 234.

9. *Ibid.,* 2: 261.

10. Jean Guehenno, *Jean-Jacques Rousseau,* 2: 115.

11. Rousseau, *The Social Contract and Discourses,* p. 203 n.

12. Rousseau, *Rousseau: Juge de Jean-Jacques,* p. 669.

13. Guehenno, *Jean-Jacques Rousseau,* 1: 375.

14. James Hogg, *The Private Memoirs and Confessions of a Justified Sinner.*

15. Anders Nygren, *Agape and Eros,* pp. 307–8.

16. Rousseau, *Emile,* p. 254.

17. Rousseau, *Confessions,* 1: 179.

18. Rousseau, *Reveries of a Solitary Walker,* p. 66.

19. *Ibid.,* p. 86.

20. Rousseau, *Rousseau: Juge de Jean-Jacques,* p. 769.

21. *Ibid.,* p. 823.

22. *Ibid.,* p. 774.

23. *Ibid.,* p. 824.

24. Rousseau, *A Discourse on the Origin of Inequality,* in *The Social Contract and Discourses,* p. 226.

25. See Rousseau, *Reveries,* p. 40.

26. Rousseau, *Confessions,* 2: 17.

27. *Ibid.,* 2: 18.

28. See D'Alembert's characterization of Rousseau in *Letters of Eminent Persons Addressed to David Hume,* ed. J. H. Burton, pp. 133–35.

29. Rousseau, *Confessions,* 2: 283. See also "Lettres à Malesherbes" in *Correspondance Générale de J.-J. Rousseau,* pp. 173, 240.

30. Rousseau, *Rousseau: Juge de Jean-Jacques,* p. 825.

31. Friedrich Nietzsche, *Anti Christ,* p. 237.

32. See Robert Derathé, *Rousseau et la Science Politique de Son Temps.*

33. See *ibid.,* pp. 151–71, 228, 365–79.

34. Rousseau, *Discourse on the Origin of Inequality,* pp. 224–25.

35. Rousseau, *Social Contract,* pp. 18–19.

36. See J. L. Talmon, *Utopianism and Politics,* pp. 9–10.

37. Rousseau, *Social Contract,* pp. 18–19.

38. See Ernest Cassirer, *The Question of Jean-Jacques Rousseau* and *Rousseau, Kant, Goethe: Two Essays.*

39. Guehenno, *Jean-Jacques Rousseau,* 2: 188.

40. John Dryden, Preface to *Troilus and Cressida,* 1: 215.

41. Rousseau, *Eloise,* 1: 4.

42. See Rousseau, *Letter to D'Alembert.*

2
The Aesthetic Morality of Stendhal

1. Stendhal, *On Love,* p. 24.

2. See Victor Brombert, *Stendhal et la Voie Oblique.*

3. See Jean-Jacques Rousseau, *Reveries of a Solitary Walker.*

4. Stendhal, *Memoirs of an Egotist,* p. 2.

5. Stendhal, *The Life of Henri Brulard,* p. 4.

6. *Ibid.,* p. 219.

7. *Ibid.,* p. 279.

8. *Ibid.,* p. 219.

9. See Robert Martin Adams, *Stendhal: Notes on a Novelist,* pp. 5–6; for another view of Stendhal's passion for pseudonymity, see the extremely interesting essay on the subject in Jean Starobinski, *L'Oeil Vivant,* pp. 194–244.

10. Stendhal, *The Red and the Black,* 2: 270.

11. Quoted in Alain Girard, *Le Journal Intime*, p. 304. (Translations from *Le Journal Intime* are my own.)

12. *Ibid.*, p. 512.

13. *Ibid.*, p. 479 (May 30, 1880).

14. Stendhal, *The Charterhouse of Parma*, 1: 142.

15. *Ibid.*, 1: pp. 145–46.

16. *Ibid.*, 1: 157.

17. Stendhal, *The Red and the Black*, 2: 348.

18. *Ibid.*, 1: 247.

19. Stendhal, *The Charterhouse of Parma*, 2: 194.

20. *Ibid.*, 2: 113.

21. Victor Brombert, ed., *Stendhal*, p. 96.

22. Stendhal, *Lucien Leuwen*, 2: 298.

23. *Ibid.*, 2: 295.

24. Stendhal, *The Charterhouse of Parma*, 1: 140.

25. *Ibid.*, 1: 156.

26. *Ibid.*, 1: 123.

27. *Ibid.*, 2: 185.

28. *Ibid.*, 2: 188.

29. *Ibid.*, 2: 159.

30. *Ibid.*, 1: 114.

31. *Ibid.*, 2: 245.

32. *Ibid.*, 1: 256.

33. *Ibid.*, 1: 163.

34. Stendhal, *Lucien Leuwen*, 2: 161.

35. Stendhal, *The Red and the Black*, p. 114.

36. See Stendhal, *The Charterhouse of Parma*, 1: 128 ff.

37. *Ibid.*, 2: 288.

38. Friedrich Nietzsche, *Human, All Too Human*, 1: 405.

39. Stendhal, *The Charterhouse of Parma*, 2: 281.

40. Stendhal, *Racine and Shakespeare*, p. 83.

41. Standhal, *Memoirs of an Egotist*, pp. 2–3.

42. Brombert, ed., *Stendhal*, p. 91.

43. Stendhal, *Life of Henri Brulard*, p. 95.

44. *Ibid.*, p. 157.

45. *Ibid.*, p. 56.

46. Stendhal, *On Love*, pp. 97–98.

47. Stendhal, *The Red and the Black*, p. 251.

48. *Ibid.*, p. 131.

49. Stendhal, *Racine and Shakespeare*, p. 67.

50.   *Ibid.,* p. 68.

51.   Adams, *Stendhal: Notes on a Novelist,* p. 78.

3

Goethe, Carlyle, and "The Sorrows of Werther"

1.   Samuel Taylor Coleridge, *Bibliographia Literaria,* p. 54.

2.   Quoted in William Jackson Bate, *From Classic to Romantic,* p. 75.

3.   See Irving Babbitt, *Rousseau and Romanticism.*

4.   Johann Wolfgang Goethe, *Conversations with Eckermann,* p. 286.

5.   E. M. Butler, *Byron and Goethe,* p. 26.

6.   Goethe, *Poetry and Truth,* p. 682.

7.   *Ibid.,* p. 683.

8.   *Ibid.,* p. 476.

9.   Goethe, *The Sorrows of Werther and Selected Writings,* p. 24.

10.   *Ibid.,* p. 27.

11.   *Ibid.,* pp. 45–46.

12.   *Ibid.,* p. 47.

13.   *Ibid.,* p. 84.

14.   *Ibid.,* p. 102.

15.   *Ibid.,* pp. 102–3.

16.   *Ibid.,* p. 103.

17.   *Ibid.,* p. 104.

18.   *Ibid.,* p. 77.

19.   *Ibid.,* p. 79.

20.   *Ibid.,* p. 80.

21.   *Ibid.,* p. 61.

22.   *Ibid.,* pp. 50–51.

23.   *Ibid.,* p. 108.

24.   *Ibid.,* p. 83.

25.   Quoted in George Henry Lewes, *Life of Goethe,* p. 403.

26.   Goethe, *Tasso,* p. 89.

27.   Goethe, *Conversations with Eckermann,* p. 88.

28.   See Eric Heller, *The Disinherited Mind,* pp. 33–55.

29.   Goethe, *Elective Affinities,* p. 276.

30.   *Ibid.,* Introduction, p. xvi.

31.   Quoted in Carl Vietor, *Goethe: The Thinker,* p. 112.

32.   *Ibid.,* p. 152.

33.   Thomas Carlyle, in *Sartor Resartus; On Heroes, Hero-Worship, and The Heroic in History,* p. 12.

34.   *Ibid.,* p. 5.

35.   *Ibid.,* p. 117.

36.   Caryle, *Critical and Miscellaneous Essays,* 1: 218.

37.   Carlyle, *Sartor Resartus,* p. 128.

38.   Carlyle, *Critical Essays,* 2: 73.

39.   *Carlyle, On Heroes, Hero Worship, and the Heroic in History,* in *Sartor Resartus; On Heroes, Hero-Worship, and the Heroic in History,* p. 414.

40.   Carlyle, *Sartor Resartus,* p. 144.

41.   *Ibid.,* p. 145.

42.   *Ibid.,* p. 143.

43.   *Ibid.,* p. 142.

44.   *Ibid.,* p. 145.

45.   *Ibid.,* p. 197.

46.   *Ibid.,* p. 194.

47.   *Ibid.,* pp. 148–49.

48.   See E. D. H. Johnson, *The Alien Vision of Victorian Poetry.*

49.   See Heller, *The Disinherited Mind,* pp. 3–29.

50.   Carlyle, "Shooting Niagara," in *Critical Essays,* 5: 24.

51.   Carlyle, *Past and Present,* p. 138.

52.   *Ibid.,* p. 184.

53.   *Ibid.,* p. 187.

54.   Carlyle, *On Heroes and Hero-Worship,* p. 412.

55.   *Ibid.,* pp. 320, 322.

56.   Carlyle, "Characteristics," in *Critical Essays,* 3: 12–13.

57.   John Stuart Mill, *The Philosophy of John Stuart Mill,* ed. Marshall Cohen, p. 260.

58.   Carlyle, *Critical Essays,* 1: 56.

59.   Matthew Arnold, "The Function of Criticism at the Present Time."

60.   See Thomas Mann, *Lotte in Weimar,* p. 341.

61.   *Ibid.,* pp. 122–23.

62.   See Arnold Hauser, *The Social History of Art,* 3:126.

4

Dostoevsky and the Hubris of the Immoralist

1.   Edward Wasiolek, *Dostoevsky: The Major Fiction,* p. 39.

2.   Philip Rahv, "The Legend of the Grand Inquisitor,"
      Partisan Review, May–June, 1954, p. 268.

3.   Fyodor Dostoevsky, *The Best Short Stories of Dostoevsky*,
      p. 240.

4.   *Ibid.*, pp. 109–10.

5.   *Ibid.*, p. 111.

6.   *Ibid.*, p. 112.

7.   *Ibid.*, p. 113.

8.   *Ibid.*, pp. 114–15.

9.   *Ibid.*, p. 122.

10.   *Ibid.*, p. 115.

11.   *Ibid.*, p. 131.

12.   Joseph Frank, "Nihilism and *Notes from the Under-
      ground*," *Sewanee Review*, Winter, 1961, p. 10.

13.   Max Scheler, *Ressentiment*.

14.   Dostoevsky, *The Insulted and the Injured*, p. 64.

15.   Quoted in Albert Camus, *The Rebel*, p. 15.

16.   Friedrich Nietzsche, *The Genealogy of Morals*, p. 88.

17.   Alluded to in Frank, "Nihilism and *Notes*," p. 20.

18.   Dostoevsky, *Notes from the Underground*, p. 162.

19.   *Ibid.*, p. 231.

20.   *Ibid.*, p. 238.

21.   *Ibid.*, p. 152.

22.   Dostoevsky, *Crime and Punishment*, p. 277.

23.   *Ibid.*, p. 291.

24.   *Ibid.*, pp. 529–30.

25.   Jean-Paul Sartre, *Baudelaire*, p. 99.

26.   Rahv, "Dostoevsky in *Crime and Punishment*," *Partisan
      Review*, Summer, 1960, p. 400.

27.   Dostoevsky, "The Dream of the Ridiculous Man," in
      Best Short Stories, p. 298.

28.   *Ibid.*, p. 316.

29.   *Ibid.*, p. 319.

30.   See Leon Shestov, *La Philosophie de la Tragédie:
      Dostoevsky et Nietzsche*.

31.   Dostoevsky, *The Devils*, p. 613.

32.   *Ibid.*, p. 611.

33.   *Ibid.*, p. 212.

34.   *Ibid.*, p. 213.

35.   *Ibid.*, p. 667.

36.   Dostoevsky, *The Brothers Karamazov*, p. 93.

37.   *Ibid.*, p. 278.
38.   D. H. Lawrence, "Introduction to the Grand Inquisitor," in *Phoenix: The Posthumous Papers of D. H. Lawrence*, p. 290.
39.   *Ibid.*, p. 283.

5

Nietzsche and the Aristocracy of Passion.

1.   See Walter Kaufmann, *Nietzsche: Philosopher, Psychologist, Anti-Christ.*
2.   See Crane Brinton, *Nietzsche.*
3.   Quoted in Kaufmann, Nietzsche, p. 216.
4.   See *ibid.*, pp. 183–86.
5.   Friedrich Nietzsche, "Schopenhauer as Educator," in *Thoughts out of Season*, 2: 187.
6.   *Ibid.*, p. 196.
7.   Nietzsche, *The Genealogy of Morals*, p. 88.
8.   *Ibid.*, p. 228.
9.   Max Stirner, *The Ego and His Own*, p. 387.
10.   *Ibid.*, p. 377.
11.   Nietzsche, *Beyond Good and Evil*, p. 228.
12.   *Ibid.*, p. 256.
13.   *Ibid.*, p. 233.
14.   Nietzsche, *The Will to Power*, 1: 291–92.
15.   Nietzsche, *The Genealogy of Morals*, p. 29.
16.   *Ibid.*, p. 45.
17.   See Max Scheler, *Ressentiment*, pp. 137–74.
18.   Nietzsche, *Beyond Good and Evil*, p. 256.
19.   Nietzsche, *Human, All Too Human*, 2: 259–61.
20.   Nietzsche, *Beyond Good and Evil*, p. 33.
21.   *Ibid.*, p. 267.
22.   See Karl Jaspers, *Nietzsche: An Introduction to the Understanding of His Philosophical Activity*, pp. 249–86.
23.   Nietzsche, *Will to Power*, 1: 258.
24.   Nietzsche, *Human, All Too Human*, 1: 102–3.
25.   *Ibid.*, 2: 82.
26.   *Ibid.*, 1: 349.
27.   Nietzsche, *The Dawn of Day*, p. 223.
28.   Nietzsche, *Twilight of the Idols*, p. 42.

29. Nietzsche, *Beyond Good and Evil*, p. 13.

30. Quoted in William Jackson Bate, *From Classic to Romantic*, p. 75.

31. Nietzsche, *Dawn of Day*, pp. 54–55.

32. Nietzsche, *Joyful Wisdom*, pp. 164–65.

33. Nietzsche, *Thus Spake Zarathustra*, p. 354.

34. *Ibid.*, p. 357.

35. Nietzsche, *Will to Power*, 2: 264.

36. Nietzsche, *The Case of Wagner*, p. 26 n.

37. Quoted in Jaspers, *Nietzsche*, p. 283.

6
Whitman: Democracy and the Self

1. William Butler Yeats, "William Blake and the Imagination," in *Essays and Introductions*, p. 111.

2. Quoted in Eric Heller, *The Disinherited Mind*, p. 121.

3. Charles Baudelaire, "The Albatross," trans. Kate Flores, in *An Anthology of French Poetry from Nerval to Valéry in English Translation*, ed. Angel Flores, p. 21, lines, 13–16.

4. Walt Whitman, "Starting from Paumanok," stanza 3, in *Leaves of Grass*, 1860 edition. The chants are abbreviated in later editions.

5. Whitman, *Song of Myself*, section 1, lines 2–3, in *Leaves of Grass*, 1892 edition.

6. William Wordsworth, preface to *Lyrical Ballads*, 1800 edition.

7. See Leslie Fiedler, "Images of Walt Whitman," in *Leaves of Grass: One Hundred Years After*, ed. Milton Hindus, pp. 55–73.

8. See Richard Chase, *Walt Whitman Reconsidered*, pp. 58–76.

9. See Carl F. Strauch, "The Structure of Walt Whitman's 'Song of Myself,'" the *English Journal*, College Edition, September, 1938, 27: 597–607; and James Miller, Jr., *A Critical Guide to Leaves of Grass*, pp. 6–35.

10. Whitman, *Song of Myself*, section 49, lines 9–10.

11. Friedrich Nietzsche, *The Birth of Tragedy*, p. 128.

12. Whitman, "I Sing the Body Electric," section 1 of "Children of Adam," in *Leaves of Grass*, 1892 edition.

13. Whitman, *Song of Myself*, section 2, lines 1–7.

14.   *Ibid.,* section 7, lines 6–17.

15.   See Chase, *Walt Whitman Reconsidered,* pp. 35–40.

16.   Whitman, *Song of Myself,* section 5, lines 6–17.

17.   *Ibid.,* section 14, line 15.

18.   *Ibid.,* section 15, concluding lines.

19.   *Ibid.,* section 19, lines 1–6.

20.   *Ibid.,* section 22, line 20.

21.   Whitman, "Out of the Cradle Endlessly Rocking," concluding lines, in "Sea-Drift," in *Leaves of Grass,* 1892 edition.

22.   Whitman, *Song of Myself,* section 4, lines 10–11.

23.   *Ibid.,* section 25, line 17.

24.   *Ibid.,* section 3, lines 9–10.

25.   Whitman, *Inscriptions,* lines 1–2, in *Leaves of Grass,* 1892 edition.

26.   Baudelaire, "The Gulf," line 12, trans. Kate Flores, in *Anthology of French Poetry,* pp. 55–56.

27.   Baudelaire, "Landscape," lines 14–26, in *ibid.,* p. 31.

28.   Baudelaire, "At One O'Clock In The Morning," in *ibid.,* p. 57.

29.   *Ibid.*

30.   Baudelaire, "The Love of Deceit," last stanza, in *ibid.,* p. 39.

31.   Baudelaire, "Heautontimorousmenous," last two stanzas, in *ibid.,* p. 30.

32.   Whitman, *Song of Myself,* section 25, line 18.

33.   Whitman, *Chants Democratic and Native American,* no. 5, lines 6–8, in *Leaves of Grass,* 1860 edition.

34.   *Ibid.,* line 4.

35.   See Whitman, "Of the Terrible Doubt of Appearances," in "Calamus," in *Leaves of Grass,* 1892 edition.

36.   Whitman, "Crossing Brooklyn Ferry," section 9, line 7, in *Leaves of Grass,* 1892 edition.

37.   Edmund Wilson, ed., *The Shock of Recognition,* p. 261.

38.   Whitman, *Chants Democratic,* no. 5, line 36.

39.   Whitman, "I Sing the Body Electric," section 3.

40.   Whitman, *Democratic Vistas* in *Leaves of Grass and Selected Prose,* p. 468.

41.   *Ibid.,* p. 472 n.

42.   Whitman, "Not Heaving from My Ribb'd Breast Only," line 16, in "Calamus."

43.   Whitman, "In Paths Untrodden," line 7, in *Calamus.*

44.   Whitman, "That Shadow My Likeness," in *Calamus*.

45.   Whitman, "A Backward Glance o'er Travel'd Roads,"
        in *Leaves of Grass and Selected Prose*, p. 256.

        7

        Lawrence and Christ

1.   See T. S. Eliot, *After Strange Gods: A Primer of Heresy*,
        p. 58.

2.   See F. R. Leavis, *D. H. Lawrence: Novelist*.

3.   Walter Pater, *Appreciations*, p. 61.

4.   Mark Spilka, *The Love Ethic of D. H. Lawrence*, p. 217.

5.   D. H. Lawrence, *Phoenix: The Posthumous Papers of
        D. H. Lawrence*, p. 729.

6.   Friedrich Nietzsche, *Thus Spake Zarathustra*, p. 84.

7.   Lawrence, *The Short Novels*, 2: 61. *The Man Who
        Died* was not Lawrence's title; in editions published
        during his lifetime the book had its true title, *The
        Escaped Cock*.

8.   Lawrence, *Phoenix*, p. 518.

9.   Lawrence, *The Man Who Died*, in *Short Novels*, 2: 22.

10.   Lawrence, *Apocalypse*, p. 200.

11.   Lawrence, *Women in Love*, p. 429.

12.   *Ibid.*, p. 472.

13.   Eliseo Vivas, *D. H. Lawrence: The Failure and the
        Triumph of Art*, pp. 255–72.

14.   Lawrence, *Women in Love*, p. 473.

15.   *Ibid.*, p. 245.

16.   *Ibid.*, p. 72.

17.   *Ibid.*, p. 246.

18.   *Ibid.*, p. 245.

19.   Nietzsche, *The Birth of Tragedy*, p. 60.

20.   *Ibid.*, p. 967.

21.   *Ibid.*, p. 965.

22.   Lawrence, "The Woman Who Rode Away", in *The
        Complete Short Stories*, 3: 581.

23.   Lawrence, "Study of Thomas Hardy", in *Phoenix*,
        pp. 409–10.

24.   Lawrence, *Women in Love*, p. 310.

25.   *Ibid.*, pp. 293–94.

26.   See *ibid.*, pp. 345–53.

27. See Mark Schorer, *"Women in Love"*, in *The Achievement of D. H. Lawrence,* ed. Frederick J. Hoffman and Harry T. Moore, p. 168.

28. Lawrence, *The Letters of D. H. Lawrence,* pp. 197–98.

29. See G. Wilson Knight, *Christ and Nietzsche: An Essay in Poetic Wisdom,* p. 151.

30. Spilka, *Love Ethic of D. H. Lawrence,* p. 217.

31. Lawrence, *Mornings in Mexico,* in *Mornings in Mexico and Etruscan Places,* p. 46.

32. Lawrence, *Man Who Died,* p. 44.

33. *Ibid.,* p. 31.

34. *Ibid.,* p. 13.

35. Lawrence, *Letters,* p. 379.

36. *Ibid.,* p. 375.

37. Karl Jaspers, "Kierkegaard and Nietzsche" in *Existentialism: From Dostoevsky to Sartre,* ed. Walter Kaufmann, p. 174.

38. William Blake, "A Memorable Fancy", in *The Marriage of Heaven and Hell,* in *The Portable Blake,* p. 258.

39. Knight, *Christ and Nietzsche,* p. 119.

40. *Ibid.,* p. 210.

41. Lawrence, Introduction to "The Grand Inquisitor", in *Phoenix,* p. 290.

42. *Ibid.,* p. 283.

43. *Ibid.,* p. 290.

44. *Ibid.*

45. Denis de Rougemont, *Love in the Western World,* p. 237.

46. Nietzsche, *Thoughts out of Season,* 1:129–30.

47. Lawrence, *Studies in Classic American Literature,* p. 63.

48. Lawrence, *Fantasia of the Unconscious,* in *Psychoanalysis and the Unconscious;* p. 60.

49. *Ibid.*

50. *Ibid.*

8
Joyce and the Career of the Artist-Hero

1. James Joyce, letter to Grant Richards, May 5, 1906, in *The Letters of James Joyce,* 2:134.

2. See Joyce, *Stephen Hero,* pp. 210 ff.

3. D. H. Lawrence, "German Books: Thomas Mann," in *Phoenix: The Posthumous Papers of D. H. Lawrence,* p. 312.

4. Joyce, *A Portrait of the Artist as a Young Man,* p. 252.

5. Caroline Gordon, "Some Readings and Misreadings," in *Joyce's Portrait: Criticism and Critiques,* ed. Thomas E. Connolly, pp. 136–56.

6. Joyce, *Portrait of the Artist,* pp. 7, 11, 15, 21, 22.

7. *Ibid.,* p. 186.

8. *Ibid.,* p. 151.

9. See *ibid.,* pp. 204 ff.

10. See *ibid.,* p. 215.

11. *Ibid.,* pp. 221–22.

12. *Ibid.,* p. 221.

13. *Ibid.,* p. 220.

14. Joyce, *Ulysses,* p. 38.

15. *Ibid.,* p. 6.

16. *Ibid.,* pp. 38–39.

17. *Ibid.,* p. 35.

18. Quoted in Hugh Kenner, *Samuel Beckett: A Critical Study,* p. 30.

19. Samuel Beckett, *Mulloy,* in *A Trilogy,* pp. 48–49.

20. Beckett, *The Unnameable,* in *A Trilogy,* p. 579.

21. See Alain Robbe-Grillet, *For a New Novel.*

Bibliography
of Books and Essays cited

Adams, Robert Martin. *Stendhal: Notes on a Novelist*. New York: Noonday Press, 1959.

Arnold, Matthew. "The Function of Criticism at the Present Time."

Babbitt, Irving. *Rousseau and Romanticism*. Boston: Houghton Mifflin Co., 1919.

Barzun, Jacques. *Darwin, Marx and Wagner*. Boston: Little, Brown & Co., 1941.

Bate, Walter Jackson. *From Classic to Romantic*. Cambridge, Mass.: Harvard University Press, 1946.

Beckett, Samuel. *A Trilogy (Mulloy, Malone Dies, The Unnameable)*. Paris: Olympia Press, 1959. Translated by the author (*Mulloy*) in collaboration with Patrick Bowles.

Blake, William. *The Marriage of Heaven and Hell*. In *The Portable Blake*. Edited by Alfred Kazin. New York: Viking Press, 1953.

Brinton, Crane. *Nietzsche*. Cambridge, Mass.: Harvard University Press, 1941.

Brombert, Victor. *Stendhal et la Voie Oblique*. Paris and New Haven, Conn.: 1954.

————, ed. *Stendhal*. Englewood Cliffs, N.J.: Prentice Hall, 1962.

Brown, Norman O. *Life Against Death*. Middletown, Conn.: Wesleyan University Press, 1959.

————. *Love's Body*. New York: Random House, 1966.

Burton, J. H., ed. *Letters of Eminent Persons Addressed to David Hume.* Edinburgh: 1849. Pp. 133–35.

Butler, E. M. *Byron and Goethe.* London: Bowes & Bowes, 1956.

Camus, Albert. *The Rebel.* Harmondsworth, Middlesex: Penguin Books, 1965.

Carlyle, Thomas. *Critical and Miscellaneous Essays.* 5 vols. London: Chapman & Hall, 1899.

———. *Past and Present.* Oxford: Clarendon Press, 1958.

———. *Sartor Resartus; On Heroes, Hero worship, and the Heroic in History.* Everyman Library. London: J. M. Dent & Sons, 1964.

Cassirer, Ernest. *The Question of Jean-Jacques Rousseau.* Translated and edited with an introduction and Additional Notes by Peter Gay. New York: Columbia University Press, 1954.

———. *Rousseau, Kant, Goethe: Two Essays.* Translated by James Gutmann, Paul Osker Kristeller, and John Herman Randall. Princeton, N.J.: Princeton University Press, 1945.

Chase, Richard. *Walt Whitman Reconsidered.* New York: William Sloan Associates, 1955.

Cohn, Norman. *The Pursuit of Millenium.* New York: Harper Torchbooks, 1961.

Coleridge, Samuel Taylor. *Biographia Literaria.* Everyman's Library. London: J. M. Dent & Sons, 1956.

Corrington, John William. Review of *An American Dream. Chicago Review* 18 (1965): 58–66.

Derathé, Robert. *Rousseau et la Science Politique de Son Temps,* Paris: Presses Universitaires de France, 1950.

De Rougemont, Denis. *Love in the Western World.* Translated by Montgomery Belgion. New York: Pantheon Books, 1956.

Diderot, Denis. *Rameau's Nephew.*

Dostoevsky, Fyodor. *The Best Short Stories of Dostoevsky.* Translated and edited by David Margashak. Modern Library. New York: Random House.

———. *The Brothers Karamazov.* Translated by Constance Garnett. Modern Library. New York: Random House, 1950.

———. *Crime and Punishment.* Translated by David Margashak. Penguin Classics. Harmondsworth, Middlesex: Penguin Books, 1965.

———. *The Devils.* Translated by David Margashak. Penguin Classics. Harmondsworth, Middlesex: Penguin Books. 1965.

———. *The Idiot.* Translated by Constance Garnett. New York: Macmillan Co., 1948.

———. *The Insulted and the Injured.* New York: Macmillan Co., 1915.

———. *Winter Notes on Summer Impressions.* Translated by Richard Lee Renfield with an Introduction by Saul Bellow. New York: Criterion Books, 1955.

Dryden, John. *Preface to Troilus and Cressida.* Edited by Ker, 1926.

Eliot, T. S. *After Strange Gods: A Primer of Heresy.* London: Faber & Faber, Ltd., 1934.

Flores, Angel, ed. *An Anthology of French Poetry from Nerval to Valery in English Translation*. New York: Anchor Books. Doubleday & Co., 1958.

Frank, Joseph. "Nihilism and *Notes from the Underground.*" *Sewanee Review* (Winter, 1961), 1–33.

Gilbert, Stuart. *James Joyce's Ulysses*. New York: Vintage Books, 1956.

Girard, Alain. *Le Journal Intime*. Paris: Presses Universitaires de France, 1963.

Goethe, Johann Wolfgang. *Conversations with Eckermann*. Everyman's Library. London: J. M. Dent & Sons, 1946.

―――. *Elective Affinities*. Translated by Elizabeth Mayer and Louise Bogan with an Introduction by Victor Lange. Chicago: Henry Regnery Co., 1963.

―――. *Poetry and Truth*. Translated by R. O. Moon. Washington: Public Affairs Press, 1949.

―――. *Tasso*. London: David Nutt, 1861.

―――. *The Sorrows of Werther and Selected Writings*. Translated by Catherine Hutter. New York: New American Library, 1962.

Gordon, Caroline. "Some Readings and Misreadings." In *Joyce's Portrait: Criticism and Critiques,* edited by Thomas E. Connolly. New York: Appleton-Century-Crofts, 1962. Originally printed in *Sewanee Review,* Summer, 1953.

Grass, Günter. *The Tin Drum*. New York: Pantheon Books, 1962.

Guehenno, Jean. *Jean-Jacques Rousseau*. 2 vols. Translated by John and Doreen Weightman. New York: Columbia University Press, 1966.

Hauser, Arnold. *The Social History of Art*. 3 vols. New York: Vintage Books. Vol. 3.

Heller, Eric. *The Disinherited Mind*. Harmondsworth, Middlesex: Penguin Books, 1961.

Hindus, Milton, ed. *Leaves of Grass: One Hundred Years After*. Stanford, Calif.: Stanford University Press, 1955.

Hoffman, Frederick J., and Moore, Harry T., eds. *The Achievement of D. H. Lawrence*. Norman, Okla.: University of Oklahoma Press, 1953.

Hogg, James. *The Private Memoirs and Confessions of a Justified Sinner*. With an Introduction by Andre Gide. London: The Cresset Press, 1947.

Jaspers, Karl. *Nietzsche: An Introduction to the Understanding of His Philosophical Activity*. Translated by Charles F. Wallraft and Frederick J. Schwitz. Tucson, Ariz.: University of Arizona Press, 1965.

―――. "Kierkegaard and Nietzsche," in Walter Kaufmann, ed. *Existentialism: From Dostoevsky to Sartre*. New York: Meridian Books, 1959.

Johnson, E. D. H. *The Alien Vision of Victorian Poetry*. Princeton, N. J.: Princeton University Press, 1950.

Joyce, James. *The Letters of James Joyce*. 3 vols. Edited by Stuart Gilbert (vol. 1) and Richard Ellman (vols. 2 and 3). New York: Viking Press, 1966.

―――. *Dubliners*.

―――. *A Portrait of the Artist as a Young Man*. Edited by Richard Ellman. Compass Books. New York: Viking Press, 1964.

―――. *Stephen Hero*. Edited by Theodore Spencer. New York: New

Directions, 1955.

———. *Ulysses*. Modern Library. New York: Random House, 1946.

Kain, Richard. *The Fabulous Voyager*. Chicago: University of Chicago Press, 1947.

Kaufmann, Walter. *Nietzsche: Philosopher, Psychologist, Anti-Christ*. Princeton, N. J.: Princeton University Press, 1950.

———, ed. *Existentialism: From Dostoevsky to Sartre*. New York: Meridian Books, 1959.

Kenner, Hugh. *Samuel Beckett: A Critical Study*. New York: Grove Press, 1961.

Knight, G. Wilson. *Christ and Nietzsche: An Essay in Poetic Wisdon*. London: Staple Press, 1948.

Lawrence, D. H. *Apocalypse*. New York: Viking Press, 1932.

———. *The Complete Short Stories*. 3 vols. London: William Heinemann, Ltd., 1957. Vol. 3.

———. *Fantasia of the of the Unconscious; Psychoanalysis and the Unconscious*. With an Introduction by Philip Rieff. Compass Books. New York: Viking Press, 1953.

———. *The Letters of D. H. Lawrence*. Edited and with an Introduction by Aldous Huxley. London: William Heinemann, Ltd., 1956.

———. *Mornings in Mexico and Etruscan Places*. London: William Heinemann, Ltd., 1956.

———. *Phoenix: The Posthumous Papers of D. H. Lawrence*. Edited by E. D. McDonald. New York: Viking Press, 1950.

———. *The Short Novels*. 2 vols. London: William Heinemann, Ltd., 1957. Vol. 2.

———. *Studies in Classic American Literature*. Anchor Books. New York: Doubleday & Co., 1953.

———. *Women in Love*. London: William Heinemann, Ltd., 1957.

Leavis, F. R. *D. H. Lawrence: Novelist*. New York: Alfred A. Knopf, 1956.

Levin, Harry. "Toward Stendhal." *Pharos*, no. 3 (Winter, 1945).

Lewes, George Henry. *Life of Goethe*. Everyman's Library. London: J. M. Dent & Sons.

Lowith, Karl. *From Hegel to Nietzsche*. New York: Holt, Rhinehart & Winston, 1964.

Mailer, Norman. *Advertisements for Myself on the Way Out*. New York: G. P. Putnam's Sons, 1959.

Mann, Thomas. *Lotte in Weimar*. London: Secker & Warburg, 1947.

Mill, John Stuart. *The Philosophy of John Stuart Mill*. Edited by Marshall Cohen. Modern Library. New York: Random House, 1960.

Miller, James, Jr. *A Critical Guide to Leaves of Grass*. Chicago: University of Chicago Press, 1957.

Nietzsche, Friedrich. *Anti-Christ*. Translated by A. M. Ludovici. Edinburgh and London: J. N. Foulis, 1911.

———. *Beyond Good and Evil*. Edinburgh and London: J. N. Foulis, 1909.

———. *The Birth of Tragedy*. Translated by William A. Hausmann. Edinburgh and London: J. N. Foulis, 1909.

————. *The Case of Wagner*. Translated by Anthony M. Ludovici. Edinburgh and London: J. N. Foulis, 1909.

————. *The Dawn of Day*. Translated by J. M. Kennedy. Edinburgh and London: J. N. Foulis, 1911.

————. *The Genealogy of Morals*. Translated by Horace B. Samuels. Edinburgh and London: J. N. Foulis, 1910.

————. *Human, All Too Human*. 2 vols. Translated by Paul V. Cohn (vol. 1) and Helen Zimmern (vol. 2). London and Edinburgh: J. N. Foulis, 1910.

————. *Joyful Wisdom*. Translated by Thomas Common. Edinburgh and London: J. N. Foulis, 1909.

————. *Thoughts out of Season*. 2 vols. Translated by Adrian Collins. Edinburgh and London: J. N. Foulis, 1909. Vol. 2.

————. *Thus Spake Zarathustra*. Translated by Thomas Common. Edinburgh and London: J. N. Foulis, 1909.

————. *Twilight of the Idols*. Translated by A. M. Ludovici. Edinburgh and London: J. N. Foulis, 1903.

————. *The Will to Power*. 2 vols. Translated by A. M. Ludovici. Edinburgh and London: J. N. Foulis, 1909–10.

Nygren, Anders. *Agape and Eros*. Translated by Philip S. Watson. Philadelphia: Westminster Press, 1953.

Pater, Walter. *Appreciations*. London: Macmillan & Co., Ltd., 1924.

Rahv, Philip. "Dostoevsky in *Crime and Punishment.*" *Partisan Review* 27 (Summer, 1960).

————. "The Legend of the Grand Inquisitor." *Partisan Review*, May–June, 1954.

Robbe-Grillet, Alain. *For a New Novel*. Translated by Richard Howard. New York: Grove Press, 1966.

Rousseau, Jean-Jacques. *The Confessions of Jean-Jacques Rousseau*. 2 vols. Everyman's Library. London: J. M. Dent & Sons, 1931.

————. *Correspondance Générale de J.-J. Rousseau*. Edited by Théophile Dufour. Paris: Librairie Armand Colin, 1924–34.

————. *Eloise (La Nouvelle Héloïse)*. 4 vols. London, 1776. Vol. 1.

————. *Emile*. Everyman's Library. London: J. M. Dent & Sons, 1961.

————. *Letter to D'Alembert*. Edited and with an introduction by Allan Bloom. Glencoe, Ill.: The Free Press, 1960.

————. *Reveries of a Solitary Walker*. London: George Routledge & Sons, 1927.

————. *Rousseau: Juge de Jean-Jacques*. Paris: Bibliothèque de la Pleiade, 1959.

————. *The Social Contract and Discourses*. Everyman's Library. London: J. M. Dent & Sons, 1941.

Sartre, Jean-Paul. *Baudelaire*. Paris: Editions Gallimard, 1963.

Scheler, Max. *Ressentiment*. Edited by Lewis A. Coser. Glencoe, Ill.: The Free Press of Glencoe, 1961. Originally published in German in 1912.

Schiller, Friedrich. "On Naïve and Sentimental Poetry." In *Essays Aesthetical and Philosophical*. London: George Bell & Sons, 1884.

Shestov, Leon. *La Philosophie de la Tragédie: Dostoevsky et Nietzsche.* Translated into French by B. de Schloezer. Edition de la Pleiade. Paris: J. Schiffrin, 1926. Originally published in Russian in 1903.

Spilka, Mark. *The Love Ethic of D. H. Lawrence.* Bloomington, Ind.: Indiana University Press, 1957.

Starobinski, Jean. *L'Oeil Vivant.* Paris: Editions Gallimard, 1961.

———. *Rousseau: La Transparence et L'Obstacle.* Paris: Plon, 1957.

Stendhal. *The Charterhouse of Parma.* 2 vols. Translated by C. K. Scott Moncrieff. New York: Liverwright Publishing Corp., 1944.

———. *The Life of Henri Brulard.* Translated by James Stewart and B. C. J. G. Knight. New York: The Noonday Press, 1958.

———. *On Love.* Anchor Books. New York: Doubleday & Co., 1957.

———. *Lucien Leuwen.* 2 vols. Translated by Louise Varese. New York: New Directions, 1950.

———. *Memoirs of an Egotist.* Translated by T. W. Earp. New York: The Noonday Press, 1958.

———. *Racine and Shakespeare.* Translated by Guy Daniels. New York: Crowell-Collier Publishing Co., 1960.

———. *The Red and the Black.* 2 vols. Translated by C. K. Scott Moncrieff. Modern Library. New York: Random House, 1926.

Stirner, Max. *The Ego and His Own.* Translated by Steven T. Byington. New York: Boris & Loverington, 1899.

Strauch, Carl F. "The Structure of Walt Whitman's 'Song of Myself.'" *English Journal,* College Edition (September, 1938), pp. 597–607.

Talmon, J. L. *Utopianism and Politics.* London: Conservative Political Center, 1967.

Vaughan, C. E. *The Political Writings of Jean-Jacques Rousseau.* 2 vols. Cambridge: Cambridge University Press, 1915. Vol. 1.

Vietor, Carl. *Goethe: The Thinker.* Cambridge, Mass.: Harvard University Press, 1950.

Vivas, Eliseo. *D. H. Lawrence: The Failure and the Triumph of Art.* Evanston, Ill.: Northwestern University Press, 1960.

Wasiolek, Edward. *Dostoevsky: The Major Fiction.* Cambridge, Mass.: M.I.T. Press, 1965.

Whitman, Walt. *Leaves of Grass.* Editions of 1860 and 1892.

———. *Leaves of Grass and Selected Prose.* Edited by John Kouwenhoven. Modern Library. New York: Random House, 1950.

Wilson, Edmund, ed. *The Shock of Recognition.* Garden City, N.Y.: Doubleday, Doran & Co., 1955.

Wordsworth, William. Preface to *Lyrical Ballads.* Edition of 1800.

Yeats, William Butler. *Essays and Introductions.* London: Macmillan & Co. Ltd., 1961.

Index

Note: Names of characters from various works appear in capitals.

Goodheart

Cult of the ego